The Adventures of Waiterman

LORD OF THE RESTAURANT JUNGLE

by Aironius French

© Copyright 2003 Aironius French. All rights reserved.

No part of this publication may be reproduced, stored in a retrieval system, or transmitted, in any form or by any means, electronic, mechanical, photocopying, recording, or otherwise, without the written prior permission of the author.

National Library of Canada Cataloguing in Publication Data

French, Aironius, 1968-
    The adventures of Waiterman, lord of the restaurant jungle / Aironius French;
    illustrated by Aaron Navrady.
ISBN 1-55395-842-X
    1. Restaurants--Employees--Humor. I. Title.
PN6231.R43F74 2003   331.7'93'0207   C2003-900961-0

TRAFFORD

This book was published *on-demand* in cooperation with Trafford Publishing.
On-demand publishing is a unique process and service of making a book available for retail sale to the public taking advantage of on-demand manufacturing and Internet marketing. **On-demand publishing** includes promotions, retail sales, manufacturing, order fulfilment, accounting and collecting royalties on behalf of the author.

Suite 6E, 2333 Government St., Victoria, B.C. V8T 4P4, CANADA
Phone   250-383-6864   Toll-free   1-888-232-4444 (Canada & US)
Fax   250-383-6804   E-mail   sales@trafford.com
Web site   www.trafford.com   TRAFFORD PUBLISHING IS A DIVISION OF TRAFFORD HOLDINGS LTD.
Trafford Catalogue #03-0205   www.trafford.com/robots/03-0205.html

10   9   8   7   6   5   4   3   2   1

"Our deepest fear is not that we are inadequate.
Our deepest fear is that we are powerful beyond measure."

- Nelson Mandela

"I don't do great things. I do little things with great passion."

- Mother Theresa

Dedicated to a Few Good Men:

Jack Dalton French 1929-1996

James Wilfred Mitchell 1948-2000

Lenard Gordon Anderson 1939-2001

Wilfred Rudolph Anderson 1927-2002

CONTENTS

ACKNOWLEDGEMENTS	xi
INTRODUCTION	xv
PART I: SURVEYING THE JUNGLE ...	1
Chapter 1: Primates and Symbionts	3
Chapter 2: Beasts of Burden	23
Chapter 3: Ruminants and Sloths	33
PART II: REARED IN THE JUNGLE ...	39
Chapter 4: The Vegetation	45
Chapter 5: Reaching the Canopy	89
Chapter 6: Exiled	109
PART III: A NEW TROOP ...	117
Chapter 7: Rules of Engagement	121
Chapter 8: The Rain Forest	135
Chapter 9: Swinging from the Vines	165
SOME SOBER LAST WORDS	201
GLOSSARY	207
APPENDIX	217

ACKNOWLEDGEMENTS

"Ideas are like rabbits. You get a couple and learn how to handle them, and pretty soon you have a dozen."

- John Steinbeck

Hey, I was the science geek of the group back in 1993. I was a newborn fawn when it came to penmanship and really wasn't worthy of the company I kept. Jeff had completed his English degree (with Dean's list, or distinction, or something superfluous after it) and was considering entering a Master's programme, after which he planned to reform the world with his scathing environmental essays. Randy had also championed our mother tongue and was leaning toward a career in journalism or publishing after attaining his Master's and Ph.D. I, in stark contrast, had chosen the more pragmatic path of science and was favoring a career in health care. But regardless of our disparate education, we all became confidants while working together in the restaurant jungle.

Jeff and Randy were rare gems, albeit unpolished at the time. They were intelligent, insightful, charismatic, athletic, and real macks with the ladies. Fast times were always had, but not so much drunken stupidity as philosophical profligacy. In short, we aspired to be modern-day Renaissance men: masculine, but poetically communicative at the same time (no, we were not gay). Typically, Jeff would get loaded on rye and Coke and quote some Dylan Thomas ("Do not go gentle into that good night. Rage, rage against the dying of the light"); whereas Randy would get looped on gin and tonic (preferably Tanqueray) and speculate about what life might have been like for Papa Hemingway in Havana during the '50s, while penning *The Old Man and the Sea*. I just tried to keep pace and not appear like a rube.

But during the summer of '93, we found our triumvirate disbanded. Jeff went to Budapest with his basketball-playing fiancé, Randy went to Vancouver with his psychology-spouting fiancé, and I went to Osaka to teach English, of all things, with absolutely no fiancé. It was during this momentous juncture that the three of us first put quill to parchment and took our friendships to a higher level. Of course Jeff and Randy were decent writers, often causing me to laugh out loud, so I was continually trying to counter their prowess. Before long, though, we developed a fairly entertaining style amongst ourselves (satirical and ostentatious, yet pedantic and self-deprecating), which carried on for a couple of years. A good example is a foreword to a letter written to Jeff in '95: "Carpe diem indeed Herr Jeffrey. Thank you for breaking the silence with such metaphorical majesty. Your dutiful praise of my pedestrian script was certainly well received, but in the most humble of ways as your latest etude clearly outlines the difference, if not defines the hierarchy, between a B.Sc. (Honors) and B.A. (English - Dean's list). I can only hope you continue to humor this pallid little spider." And humor me they did. So I am eternally thankful to Jeff and Randy for challenging me to write well and motivating me to attain levels that would have otherwise seemed unreachable for a science geek. I hope this book captures the essence of our adventures and makes the two of them laugh out loud.

    I must also thank an old friend, Christine, for admirably choosing an artistic path against all convention and inspiring me to explore the atrophied right side of my brain. I will never be the artist she has become, but I'm hoping to achieve some balance, and make much more money... (I'm joking). After all these years, her beautiful essence and passion still linger in my cortex. As well, I miss the cheeky little faces she drew in the letters she wrote to me while I was languishing in Japan.

    A book on the restaurant industry would have been impossible without the crystal-clear recollections of my best friend since high school, Matthew. Not a week passes without us both laughing at the craziness that went on, but also being bloody thankful we survived it relatively unscathed. Wisely, we both realize our adventures within the restaurant jungle immeasurably shaped our characters (for the better, we would like to think); so in the final analysis, neither of us would change a single drunken night or sobering morning after. Cheers Matt.

    Of course any good I accomplish is directly related to the strength, perseverance, and loving character that I have witnessed all my life from my Mom, especially during the ten years when it was just the two of us. We must have been poor, but she shielded me from its pernicious effects in such wonderful ways. She is a rare treasure, more so than she can possibly imagine.

In addition, my true love, Carole, deserves much credit for being as supportive as anyone could. Although the manuscript for this book was largely finished when we met, her trust that I can do the right thing is tremendously encouraging. By god, she is such a fabulous little frog and justifiably loved unconditionally. She is also the perfect companion for all my future adventures.

And to the rest of my family who, on most occasions, become dumfounded and are lost as to how to respond to my seemingly ludicrous ideas and actions that stretch their perception of what is conventional and rational: thank you for realizing I'm not an extraterrestrial with Attention Deficit Disorder. Especially cousin Jeffrey, who really thought I should write a book. Well, here it is, mister.

I would clearly be remiss if I didn't acknowledge the various friends, foes, colleagues, patients, and other writers who have provided me with a bounty of ideas, inspiration, motivation, insight, adjectives, synonyms, and over-poured cocktails. To Peter, Jared, Gail, the Moose, Gino, Mike and Alana, Irv, Cam, Andrea, Shane, Shawna, Princess Sarah, the seventh Earl of Greystoke, Phil, Stuart, Paula, Mrs. Bigglesworth, Sally, Kristen, Cheetah, Natasha and Derrick, the Gagnons, Sheila, Alysa, Glenn, the Johnstons, Marlene, Dave, Jan, Bubba B, Monica, the Pepins, Bill Bryson, P.J. O'Rourke, John Rolfe, Peter Troob, Edgar Rice Burroughs, Denis Miller, Anthony Bourdain, Mike Myers, and Ashleigh Banfield - kudos to each and every one of them.

Last, but not least, thanks to the many important people within the editing realm (mainly the ever-giving Randy) who helped me corral all my ideas that were propagating like rabbits. Without them, I'd probably be exporting rabbit stew to the Japanese. Domo arigato to all.

INTRODUCTION

"Be careful going in search of adventure; it's ridiculously easy to find."

- William Least Heat Moon

From an insider's perspective, there are few industries that can provide the bewildering array of adventures that are so common within the restaurant industry. In essence, most restaurants are like jungles full of wild beasts, poachers, and headhunters who all conspire to mix a wide range of young people in big black cauldrons and then season the broth with booze, money, stress, and opportunity. Could there be a more solvent environment (save the Congo for Tarzan and Jane) to mix adventure with peril? Perhaps the whole Hollywood scene could compare, but not many teenagers get to play the lead role in a major motion picture for their first job. A restaurant is a much more common place to start. That's how I began, and ended up spending twelve years (intermittently) at four different restaurants. That's quite a tour of duty. As such, I know how sharp the double-edged axe can be within the restaurant world: it can chop through all the barriers to a jolly good time, but it can also decapitate without any warning. I also know great adventures (with or without a head) spawn great stories, which is what this book is a vehicle for.

The following accounts, intermingled with social commentary and vitriolic rantings, are divided into three sections. In Part I, the jungle is surveyed, so to speak, as it is an overview of the various restaurant positions and the dynamics existing between them. Part II is an account of my early years within the restaurant jungle, beginning with the job of "salad boy" and ending with me being "exiled" as a nubile waiter. Part III chronicles the lion's share of my waitering adventures from 1987 to '95. It was during this latter period that **WAITERMAN** came into his own out of absolute necessity and acquired special survival skills after having been exposed to the various perils within the jungle.

Simply said, **WAITERMAN** was my infallible alter ego, my Lord of the Jungle if you will. Whether he was my brash Tarzan or my cultured Earl of Greystoke, though, depended on the situation. Regardless, as him, I witnessed or partook in all the adventures mentioned in this book, unless otherwise stated. I do not condone, or mean to glamorize, any unethical acts that were committed, but when one is in Rome, one must do as the hedonistic Romans once did. And believe me, we all did things that would have made Caligula gasp and blush. But for the record, let me state unequivocally that stealing is unethical, unprotected sex is irresponsible, puking in public is uncalled for, stereotyping is unfair, drinking and driving is plain stupid, and swearing is blasphemous. There, I now feel completely purged and ready to take tea with the Pope.

Throughout the book, I use terms that may be unfamiliar to the reader in an attempt to flesh out and texturize the restaurant jungle. Don't panic. These words appear in outlined font and are sardonically defined in the glossary for your enjoyment. Feel free to expand your vocabulary and impress the servers at your favorite restaurant. I also use terms that are defined in most unabridged dictionaries as "coarse slang." These words are commonly spoken within the restaurant jungle and must be included, but I hope I haven't been too colorfully gratuitous. My sincere apologies to Pat Buchanan and the various prudes if I have.

Within Parts II and III, I am cavalier enough to offer serving and managerial tips, which are conveniently summarized in the appendix. I hope these lists will provide some concise, practical advice to the masses on how to be better servers and managers. Frankly it may prove futile, but what the hell. Efforts were also made to conceal the identities of the young, the innocent, and the feeble. I had no direct agenda to embarrass or unduly criticize any particular individual and have it widely known, but I did not sugar coat the truth in an effort to be overly benevolent either. Consequently, I relied on nicknames or fictional names to depict the main characters and I hope this was enough to maintain some mystery of identity. I also harbor no grudge, not even against the vilest of characters whom I encountered, but karma has a funny way of biting some offenders on the ass. The names "Trader's Inn" and "Duke's Place" are also fictional, but represent actual restaurants that continue to exist (and create stories, no doubt). As a result, all of the stories in this book are factual, sometimes altered in terms of people and places, but not embellished one iota. There was simply no need to embellish as truth is, indeed, stranger than fiction. Without further ado then, it is with great pleasure that I welcome you into the bizarre habitat known as the restaurant jungle. This satirical "eco-tour" will either be considered tres avant-garde, or forte fromage. If the latter, have a fondue.

PART I

SURVEYING THE JUNGLE

"The universe is not only queerer than we suppose,
but queerer than we can suppose."

- J.B.S. Haldane

Not surprisingly, most people's standards for a good meal are rather mundane and uncritical. If their food is the appropriate temperature, timely, modestly priced, and pushing the edges of their plates they are satisfied. These types of people do not eat out very often, nor are they too adventurous in their choices of restaurants. They take satisfaction in not having to wash dishes after their meal and often mention this to their cohorts with delight. They have disdain for their server because, although their temporary servant, they might well have higher incomes. They bitch about things that are entirely obvious in order to justify the six percent gratuity they invariably leave regardless of any controllable outcome. A $5 sirloin steak (cooked medium well or beyond) lacking flavor and tenderness in a Greek restaurant specializing in pizza, but run by an elderly Chinese couple? Well no bloody wonder Einstein.

A much smaller group of people, often referred to as "diners" (historically due to their extensive use of the once exclusive Diner's Card), are different animals altogether. Eating out is about the overall experience: the ambiance, the hope of being recognized by the owner, the ratio of cabernets to merlots, the imported chef whose bio appeared in the "Cuisine Section" of the Sunday paper, the controversial juxtaposition of the fusion entrees, etc. These people simply know more about food and beverage, but it does not seem to satiate their desire to bitch. They will bitch to enhance their self-importance, to remind the server of his/her insignificance within the universe, or to get a discount off the bill while masquerading as being mortally offended by such a suggestion. This group will decide upon a certain percentage of gratuity, based on some arcane guidelines (though not usually sinking below fifteen percent) and pay the server to the exact penny on their Gold or Platinum credit cards.

These two genres of restaurant goers are at either end of the customer continuum (with many others in between), but do share one thing in common: they are both absolutely oblivious to all the intrigue, politics, debauchery, romance, manipulation, fraud, collusion, and outright warfare that transpire behind the scenes of their favorite restaurant. Chances are the family sitting at table forty-one has no idea that their waiter is shagging the eighteen-year-old hostess after every shift, is hung-over from consuming a dozen stolen Coronas the night before, relishes eating the leftover meat off of his customer's plates, didn't wash his hands after expelling some foul gut rot mid-shift, plans to commit fraud on various credit card slips, and will be driving his beat-up Volkswagen absolutely hammered before the night is over. Perhaps ignorance is bliss, but I feel it is my duty to educate the customer on such matters and make the universe appear a little less queer. So, grab your anti-malarial pills and jump into the Land Rover, because we have a vast jungle to explore.

Chapter 1

Primates and Symbionts

"The city is not a concrete jungle; it is a human zoo."

- Desmond Morris

Swinging Servers...

The "front-of-the-house" staff consists of all the people seen during the dining experience, minus the few "back-of-the-house" vagabonds accidentally spotted while looking for the shitter. The front house staff are the beautiful species of the restaurant jungle and are largely hired on this single attribute. That's not to say these comely creatures are lacking the genes that encode for hard work, organizational skills, or some sense of urgency, but there is rarely the motivation to prove otherwise. For example, the cute hostess, who may be a complete sack of hammers (albeit light hammers with wonderfully curved handles) and who insists on *slamming* all the servers with a multitude of tables all at once, will never be fired due to her lack of innate ability. Rather, she will be allowed (nay, encouraged) to preen around the hostess stand chirping on about the day's *features* due to three very good reasons: (1) middle to lower management are dying to get into her pants (although they will ultimately fall short of boning her because they are all dorks and will invariably blow the small window of opportunity that was created by the tiny bit of power they shamelessly wield) in an attempt to disprove the commonly held view that they are all cheese eating, brown nosing, white bread eunuchs incapable of *closing the deal*; (2) the alpha-male waiters competing for the title of *silverback* are dying to get into her pants (and one will, late one night after three hours of well-rehearsed assurances and without a condom, but not until he lets the naive management boys eagerly promo her a bunch of strawberry daiquiris, thus getting her totally looped and distorting her judgment) and would attempt a bloody coup if she were ever fired before complete carnal knowledge was obtained; and (3) the job of a hostess is essentially mindless anyway, so it would accomplish nothing to fire her, but it would risk the morale and the delicate sexual balance of the restaurant by not finding a replacement equally as alluring.

Another good example is the hot waitress (or the politically correct "winsome female server"). Said waitress most likely has some natural beauty and big boobs, or at least creatively maximized medium-sized boobs. She may actually be a technically sound and tenacious worker, but the motivation to display these attributes is almost zero. Let's look at the tipping hierarchy to better understand this point. The following is a list of all the possible types of servers from highest average tip earners to lowest:

(1) The hot waitress who is actually proficient as a server and not a burden on the entire staff at all times. She will prance around the restaurant literally leaving people winded with her irresistible joie de vivre and outstanding bone structure, but she will also pitch in with some manual labor. These babes have unlimited potential within the industry.

(2) The hot waitress who causes absolute havoc behind the scenes due to her total ineptitude in all areas related to food preparation and delivery. She will end up being public nemesis number one, but damn it, she's so outrageously hot that the Greek tragedy is lost on all.

(3) The average looking waitress who is having a nightmarish shift and has the audacity to share this with all her unsuspecting tables, or worse, will actually cry in front of them. She will kick ass on sympathy tips and be let off early by the manager who fears the consequences of "that time of month." In the restaurant industry, menstruating can be as powerful as having Jimmy Hoffa and the Teamsters Union on one's side demanding shorter shifts, lighter duties, and plenty of understanding.

(4) All mid-range waitresses in terms of looks, abilities, and emotional stability. Nothing special here, keep reading.

(5) Any warm-blooded primate masquerading as a waitress with anything resembling mounds of flesh somewhere on the anterior aspect of their torso.

This would include transsexuals and the Malaysian she-he.

(6) Lastly, all male waiters, regardless of their charm, good looks, wine knowledge, food timing, or fire making ability. It just doesn't matter. This group has to scratch and claw (or steal) for everything they get.

Well, maybe the exaggerating is getting a bit profound, but the point is that female servers almost always attain greater tips than their male counterparts, regardless of their sweat equity. Why is this? Consider who pay the checks at most of the tables, most of the time: men. Now before Gloria Steinem (who was a waitress at the original Playboy Club, incidentally) flies into a rage and spontaneously combusts, let us play the role of armchair sociologist and put forth a fascinating theory. Here goes. As eating out at restaurants became much more common during the post World War Two boom, men almost always paid the check because not only were they the sole bread winners within their families, but they also made much more money than their female business associates. In addition, it was considered polite and chivalrous to pay for the lady at the table. Therefore, men of that era simply had more practice and understanding in the art of tipping, which became an acronym derived from: **T**o **I**nsure **P**rompt **S**ervice.

Many men of today still make marginally more money than their female counterparts, but obviously many more women hold down jobs that pay handsomely and many have grown up paying their own way, restaurant tabs included. Then why is it that twelve years of experience forces the conclusion that men are generally better tippers than women? Could it be that the women of the '50s passed on their lack of sophistication in the tipping department to their daughters, either genetically or socially? Did the "Generation Xers" watch too many episodes of *Happy Days*, *Gilligan's Island*, or *The Flintstones* as youngsters, thus internalizing aberrant sexual stereotypes? Both Charles Darwin and Sigmund Freud are surely laughing from the grave at such drivel. I think the answer lies in the fundamentally different strategies men and women employ to attract mates and deal with competition. Let's look at the four possible tipping combinations to illustrate this point: a male customer tipping a waitress, a male customer tipping a waiter, a female customer tipping a waiter, and a female customer tipping a waitress (note: this would be the heterosexual version).

A guy sitting at a table will survey his waitress regardless of who he is with. He may be sitting at the table with his beautiful family, having just made love to his vivacious wife that afternoon, and he will still steal glances at the waitress's jiggly ass, simultaneously trying to see evidence of thong panties and pondering his chances of taking her from behind in a toilet stall, at least on some subconscious level. Guys multi-task well in this way. Their neural pathways are well entrenched for such thought patterns. A possible explanation is that the vast majority of guys just cannot commit one hundred percent to one woman. Perhaps ninety-nine percent, but never entirely because the thought of being officially off the "playing field" and cut from "the team" is almost unbearable. This is akin to emasculation. And regardless of how miserable the guy was being single and playing the field before becoming attached, he will always have buddies in various stages of "single-hood" (i.e., divorced, just separated, casually dating, adulterous affair) continually reminding him of their utopian existence, consisting largely of grief-free, tantra-like sex. Rationally he knows this is bullshit, but the grass (or ass) always seems greener on the other side. Therefore, most men harbor an unrealistic perception of sexual dynamics, which causes them to continually search for something that doesn't actually exist within our space-time continuum. This doesn't mean that all men are dirty, dog licking, man-whores for having a wandering third eye. On the contrary, it may simply be a matter of ancient genetics, mixed with a fear of commitment, combined with peer pressure and bravado, interlaced with the excitement of the conquest, and complicated by low self-esteem. Consequently, that guy sitting at the table, especially if he is sans family, is gagging to impress the waitress. Does he do this by juggling his cutlery or listing his great qualities on a napkin? No, he does it with a very gratuitous tip. Gold bullion if he could. He wants to come across as important, as successful, as totally fucking loaded. After all these decades, most men still think money is their best lure and will shamelessly use it as bait to attract as many of the fish in the sea as possible. In the sea of restaurants, the hot waitress gladly accepts the bait. A twenty-five to thirty-five percent tip is not uncommon in this situation.

Scenario number two starts with the same guy at the table, but now he's contemplating the alpha-male waiter who swaggers up, squats down, and flashes at least one hundred and forty pearly whites. This would be an obvious case of competition. And much like the rules of engagement between two male chimpanzees, if the waiter averts his eyes, whimpers, and displays his wet anus, then the two will get along famously. If, however, the waiter appears at all cocky, threatening, condescending, better looking, more muscled, or quicker witted, then the guy at the table thinks, "Screw you, shit eater." This controlled hostility begets a psychological jousting contest and much posturing between the two, but doesn't necessarily end with the waiter getting stiffed. The guy at the table may decide to assert his dominance by pulling out his Corporate Gold Card and tipping large, which kind of rubs the waiter's nose in it, but most waiters would gladly take a clump of shit on the end of their nose for that kind of money. Conversely, the guy might leave a below average tip and some patronizing advice on how the service could have been better, which will burn itself into the waiter's brain and fully justify the chunky mass of spit that will appear in the guy's coffee the next time he shows his grotty face in the restaurant. And although a little poorer, the waiter will rejoice for days as nothing satisfies a vengeful mind more than watching some asshole unknowingly consume some of your body fluids. Not surprisingly, this situation is the most precarious and thus exhibits the biggest tipping range, from ten to twenty-five percent.

The third scenario is the most interesting because of the catch-22 that exists with waiters serving women. On the one hand, most waiters love interacting with their female customers (on all levels, or at least on all fours), but on the other hand, they are absolutely maddening to serve and comparatively cheap tippers. If there was any justice in the world, women would be forced to tip the most because they are much more demanding and require more attention, but obviously, in the restaurant jungle, justice is an extinct species.

Let's imagine a woman sitting at a table. Even if she were there with other single women, the mob mentality still would not convince her to want to mount and grind the waiter's midsection. The vast majority of women are not consumed with the thought of picking up and bedding their waiter while dining at a restaurant. Women appear to be more pragmatic (in that they primarily want to consume food and beverage while at a restaurant), more loyal (in that they are committed and reasonably satisfied with the slug they left at home), more sensible (in that they realize waiters are not *Fortune 500* members), and have a bit more decorum (in that they realize picking up a waiter at his place of work is a little tacky). Still, having said that, many female customers like to have fun and flirt with their waiters, but it is much more subtle and sophisticated compared to their male counterparts. For example, a woman might make an appreciative comment about her waiter's tie, or she might pretend that she recognizes him from some mythical place, which will lead to some innocent probing and name exchanging. It's all quite clever and rather pleasant banter, but the veteran waiter knows he is not getting laid or much loot so he presses for a drink order and tries to move on. Unfortunately, much indecision usually ensues, as some women apparently have no idea that beverages can be obtained in eating establishments. They appear totally dumfounded by such a proposition. Therefore, they must consult each individual taste bud, calculate the pH balance of their stomach, take inventory of their waistline, and then weigh this information against the overall mood of the group before they can narrow it down to a pot of herbal tea or a frothy cocktail. Meanwhile, the waiter can feel the droplets of perspiration form on his brow ridge as he stands at his tormentor's table. He can feel his shirt sticking to his hairy back and his pulse become erratic. He can see his other tables perishing from malnutrition and dehydration, his section starting to resemble the Ethiopia of the '70s. In the waiter's mind, though, the real tragedy is not the loss of life around him (as he would take a twenty percent tip from a week-old corpse), but rather the collective ebbing away of his tips due to the growing dissatisfaction from all his other tables. So not only will he make below average money from his table of indecisive women, but because they insist on monopolizing his time and forcing him to scurry about the restaurant like a rodent searching for low-fat alternatives, he will lose some of the guaranteed money from his tables headed by men. This absolute nightmare is commonly referred to as a kick in the camel toe.

On rare occasions, the woman does want to convey her sexual interest to the waiter. Unfortunately, it's not quite as simple as lifting up her dress, bending over, and showing him her bright red, gleaming estrus. This is done in chimpanzee society with stellar results, but humans, sadly, have evolved beyond such straightforwardness. Thus, the woman might hint at a club she'll be at later, or leave a note filled with oblique innuendo on the back of the bill, or actually leave her phone number. Pretty tame compared to the leering, drooling, and interrogation that the waitresses have to endure from their male customers, but it can still develop into an uncomfortable situation for the waiter. Incredibly, though, the woman at the table thinks she can substitute some of her expected gratuity with strategic displays of her cleavage and a litany of subtle flirtation, and still have a shot at bagging the waiter. This is akin to paying a divorce lawyer with chickens. Unfortunately, flattery or poultry just don't compare to cold, hard currency. Not surprisingly then, this tipping scenario is relatively predictable at ten to thirteen percent. Such a pity.

The final scenario, involving a waitress serving another woman, is not as volatile as one might expect. There seems to be a certain neutral position that is achieved when two descendants of Eve encounter one another in a restaurant's Garden of Eden. The woman will still assess the waitress's foot wear, her attempt at a manicure, her eyebrow-plucking ability, the firmness of her ass, and the potential for varicose veins, but won't usually cut her down too mercilessly without provocation. If, however, the waitress is superior in all categories and intentionally flirts with a man who may be with the woman, then the truce is revoked and full metal jackets may be required. Hell hath no fury like a bitchy female customer scorned. Regardless, the tipping scenario remains utterly predictable at ten to thirteen percent, because that's just how most women tip, regardless if they are horny or scorned.

While on the topic, let us briefly discuss what would be considered a reasonable gratuity within the confines of a mainstream restaurant. Well, since tipping is an unspoken art and often a continuously evolving one, it's difficult to approximate without incurring the wrath of North America's service industry who rely on the generosity (or naiveté) of the general public for a substantial portion of their livelihood. And keep in mind, a tip is essentially a gift, a reward for service above and beyond the call of minimum wage duty, an act of kindness that has the potential to reconnect human souls, or at least get a guy laid. Therefore, as a general guideline, a tip of fifteen percent of the total check before taxes is quite adequate, assuming that one's server is attentive and striving to accomplish their core purpose. The tip should not be negatively affected if the food is appalling because this variable is beyond the server's control. However, the way in which they deal with it is well within their control, so their tip can justifiably depend on the merits of how they manage the complaint. If a server goes well beyond the call of minimum wage duty and actually contributes in a positive fashion to the overall dining experience, then twenty percent should be considered along with some overt solicitation.

☺ ATTENTION: THE FOLLOWING USEFUL INFORMATION MAY MAKE SERVERS MUCH MORE MONEY

Interestingly, a recent survey conducted in a large U.S. city revealed that customers tip more when: the check comes on tray, the weather is warm and sunny, they are paying by credit card, or they have a discernible penis roaming within their boxer shorts... (just thought I'd add my two cents). Believe it or not, customers also tip more if a waitress adds a smiley face on their check. However, when a waiter adds a smiley face, it has the opposite effect. Hmm, are we all that damn transparent?

Flighty Hostesses and Nimble Bussers...

Even with the above tipping information in mind, there are still many hostesses who adhere to the practice of sitting men in waitress's sections and women in waiter's sections. Although this exercise is gleefully supported by the customers, the waitresses, and a few naive rookie waiters, the veteran waiter understands that he is being royally shafted by such an arrangement. After all, he values a table of middle-age businessmen or male professionals who have a penchant for wine above all others. A distant second would be an upper middle class family, with no dependents under ten years of age, headed by a guilty Dad who feels he is somehow inconveniencing the waiter. To secure such treasured patrons, the veteran waiter has to either develop a sexual liaison with the hostess (which is nearly impossible to successfully manage long term), or bribe her with exorbitant tip outs and the occasional strawberry daiquiri (which is a much wiser strategy according to Machiavellian manifesto). Waiters who subscribe to this latter method often find themselves vacationing in Cancun and driving older BMWs in fairly short order.

The world of the busser is not any less convoluted. In fact, the busser's job description can be the most nebulous of any position in the restaurant. Bussers can take on a plethora of roles, including: food runner, bar assistant, messenger, informant, puke cleaner, private investigator, roofer, landscaper, and monkey boy in addition to their more traditional role of cleaning and setting tables. A well-trained, experienced busser can be invaluable to a server as they can essentially mask the fact that a server is ridiculously inept or a lazy dog fucker. Brutal servers can monopolize bussers to the point that they might as well be their own personal valets. This is not entirely detrimental to the bussers as they do appear busy (which is crucial to impress management) and can gain valuable experience, which bolsters their position when they try to become servers. For example, a young busser who can open and pour a bottle of wine is worth his/her weight in pennies (usually no more than $1.30, thankfully).

When a busser is monopolized, the other servers tend to become somewhat bitter. After all, there is usually only one busser scheduled for every four or five servers, which means on a busy night in a medium sized restaurant there are only two, maybe three bussers working the floor. If one or more of the servers is a total fuck-stick and requires the full attention of a busser to survive, the night can go very wrong, very fast for most of the serving staff. The only people insulated from such a snafu are the most veteran servers because they are the most self-sufficient. This is due, in part, to the fact that veteran servers are generally excellent time managers, which enables them to take all their own food and beverage orders, run all their own food, and clear most of the plates and glasses from their tables. Consequently, the veterans only really need the bussers to wipe and set their tables, but when said bussers are scarce, they don't even get this basic service. Therein lies the cruel irony for veteran servers: they are the most efficient, and they tip-out the most (because they have a reputation to uphold and because political patronage doesn't come cheap), but they often receive the worst service from the support staff. Invariably this will annoy the veterans, but it really concerns the vigilant little bussers because they realize that the brutal servers will eventually be fired, which will create an opening that is difficult to secure without the support and lobbying of the remaining veterans. This is where the busser must walk a political tight rope, much like Senator Ted Kennedy has done since the Chappaquiddick debacle.

In short, once of age, a busser's primary goal is to become a server at any cost, but he must prove his desire to management (in terms of kilocalories burned per shift) and his willingness to do various favors for the veterans (work related or not) before he is promoted. This paves the way for beautiful, symbiotic relationships to develop between veteran servers and ambitious bussers, that is, until a busser is regarded as possible competition. When this occurs, the busser will receive the fate of the cheeky, adolescent chimp who tries to mount the alpha-male's consort: he gets cuffed in the gonads and shit is flung in his general direction.

Because bussers are often privileged with sensitive information and are enjoyed by the servers as one would enjoy a pet ferret, they do not occupy the lowest branch on the front-house forest despite the fact that they make the least amount of money, are usually the youngest (ranging from fifteen to nineteen years of age), and are often forced to do the most demeaning tasks. Instead, the bottom branch is usually reserved for hostesses because they are the most replaceable (unless they have absolutely "show-time" looks). Generally speaking, hostesses don't work as hard as they claim, have a distorted view on how vital they are to the success of the restaurant, and are constantly nagging management to become waitresses, despite their obvious lack of aptitude. Fittingly then, hostesses can best be thought of as the tropical birds of the restaurant jungle: soft, colorful, and cute, but annoying to listen to after a while and almost no caloric value if caught and eaten.

In contrast, hard-working bussers are absolutely essential to the success of a restaurant. They get dirty in the trenches, they fill in the gaps of labor, they are versatile and resilient, and they get paid minimum wage. Moreover, the ability and speed with which a busser can clean and set a table is directly related to the length of time a customer waits in line, the total number of customers that can file through the restaurant, and the customer's overall impression of the restaurant's cleanliness. Bussers are, therefore, most analogous to primitive tarsiers: small, wide-eyed, and usually solitary (i.e., not getting laid), but very nimble amongst the trees and willing to be nocturnal if need be.

There is also a catch-22 that exists in the busser's world, though. If a busser does his/her job better than any other busser who has ever walked the Earth, then that busser is regarded by management as much too valuable to ever promote to the serving ranks because the black hole that would form in the bussing universe would cause matter to become anti-matter, electrons to become protons, and the other bussers to move at less than the speed of light. This must never occur in the busser's universe. Accordingly, said "uberbusser" receives a lifetime membership (or sentence) to the "busboy's club," with no access to the squash courts or the executive server's lounge, if you get the metaphor. Of course, management will never see fit to pay uberbusser any more money for his/her outstanding efforts, but this is a fitting outcome for someone so stupid and shortsighted. There is simply no need to be the hero and sabotage one's future by showing up other co-workers. In distinct contrast, the truly clever busser will work hard (but not too hard) and cultivate alliances with key servers, but he/she will always keep focused on reaching the promised land of serving. The reasons for this goal are essentially threefold: (1) being a server is considered much cooler than being a busser and exponentially increases one's chances of getting laid, (2) servers make at least three times as much cake as bussers, and (3) servers are exempt from cleaning up vomitous or unclogging toilets. Without doubt, these are all fabulous perks.

Once within the serving ranks, however, the ex-busser has to sink or swim in crocodile infested rivers. And unfortunately, the water wings must be removed when one leaves the kiddies pool. If the ex-busser ends up as a deficient server then they are simply fired; flicked off like a week-old scab. Demotions back to the bussing ranks are exceptionally rare, as they tend to cause unbearable humiliation and unspeakable name-calling. The same holds true for hostesses who aspire to become waitresses. Although, if a hostess is fiendishly hot and tanks as a waitress, some manager will invent some ludicrous position in order to keep her. This is how the title of "Director of Fun" came to be. Sad, but so very true.

Slithering Bartenders...

"Bartenders are Gods," proclaims a t-shirt advertising cranberry vodka. This may be true for Tom Cruise in *Cocktail* and a few other booze slingers within the club scene, but the mainstream restaurant bartender is much more mortal. This difference between Heaven and Earth is based on volume. Bartenders at clubs pour infinitely more drinks, which results in blistering speed and over-inflated tips ($200 or more per night). Granted, they are rarely challenged by much more than an imported beer at the back of the cooler or an extra lime in a vodka and soda, but these bartenders are all about quantity, not about being certified mixologists. Frankly, they are most comfortable pouring shots of tequila. The restaurant bartender, on the other hand, is forced to be more knowledgeable about his/her craft because of the clientele that frequents the restaurant and/or corresponding lounge. Patrons from the restaurant side are more apt to order wine, blended drinks, and cappuccinos, which are much more time consuming and finicky to concoct. Lounge patrons prefer to saddle up to the wood and ponder which of the fifty beers on tap they should order, or debate which of the fifteen single-malt scotches is smoother. Either way, the restaurant bartender is destined to do twice the work for half the money. A closer look at the average time spent preparing a customer's drink compared to the amount of tip per drink is rather telltale:

(1) Club bartender: spends approximately five seconds needlessly flipping and spinning things, then five seconds pouring a highball or opening a beer (for a total of ten seconds) and receives a fifty cent tip.

(2) Restaurant bartender: spends approximately thirty seconds bitching to the bartending gods for his/her lot in life, then one hundred and twenty seconds blending a daiquiri, or making a cappuccino, or drawing a pint of Guinness (for a total of two minutes and thirty seconds) and receives the same fifty cent tip. Houston, we have a problem here.

It is because of this big discrepancy in money that restaurant bartenders tend to get a little antsy about moving on to the club scene. Not much empathy is doled out from the waiters, however, because any job that involves associating with hot lounge waitresses while having almost zero contact with the kitchen is regarded as idyllic. Besides, the modern bartender's icons are Tom Cruise and Ted Danson, whereas the waiters are stuck with the likes of John Cleese and Jerry Lewis, who are decidedly less sexy. Clearly then, the waiter's public image becomes tarnished when compared to the bartender's. Consequently, jealousy can sometimes rear its ugly head and cause animosity, which is best settled on the baseball diamond, basketball court, or ice hockey rink. This is because sports are the great equalizer for guys. Simply put, the best athlete will always garner the most respect regardless of his ability within the restaurant, and the lesser athlete consequently kowtows like a small Chinese Mama-san and yields the right of way. This time-honored tradition is clearly a remnant from when rudimentary male mammals bashed heads and ran around in a fury trying to impress possible mates with their dominance and flare for the dramatic. For these reasons, being regarded as a restaurant alpha-male (be he a waiter or a bartender) is not easily accomplished because one must be a talented overall athlete, quite proficient at his job, and a real mack with the ladies. This menagerie of traits is known as the "ultimate trinity."

It is interesting to note that the bartender is the only restaurant employee who makes money from both customers (via gratuities) and staff (via tip-outs), so he/she is in a position of great influence. Below is a quick summary of the money trail to better understand this point.

(1) Bussers: receive minimum wage from the restaurant, plus tip-outs from the servers (ranging from a half to one percent of their ring outs) which is divided by the number of bussers working each shift.

(2) Hostesses: get about $2 over minimum wage from the restaurant, plus tip-outs from the servers (about half a percent of their ring-outs) which is some-

times split between two hostesses. Although, the only reason why a restaurant should have two hostesses working the same shift is if they are Siamese twins attached at the skull and sharing the same brain, making it nearly impossible to separate them. But then again, most hostesses do offer living proof that they can survive with only half a cortex.

(3) Servers: receive minimum wage from the restaurant (with no chance of ever receiving a raise), plus gratuities from customers, minus tip-outs to bussers, hostesses, bartenders, and the kitchen. In this way, servers act like the neighborhood Godfather as they bankroll everyone else in the restaurant.

(4) Bartenders: receive at least $2 over minimum wage (can anyone provide rationale for this?) plus tip-outs from servers and lounge waitresses (at least one percent), plus gratuities from lounge customers.

From the above then, it's obvious that the money is squeezed from the hapless customers, funneled through the servers, and then distributed to the entire staff. So if a server averages fifteen percent in tips during a shift, he/she will pocket only eleven percent as at least four percent is relinquished for tip-outs. Unfortunately, servers do not have the good fortune of being tipped out by co-workers who can appreciate their efforts, so there is always a risk of tipping out a disproportionate sum. For example, it doesn't matter if a server's customers were all cheap bastards over the course of a shift, because the support staff would all expect to be tipped out as per usual. The bartender, on the other hand, is in the glorious position of being tipped out by the serving staff, which sets up an interesting situation. For example, if a lounge customer was to tip a bartender poorly, there might be some pouting and a small tantrum in the beer cooler, but there is really nothing that can be said or done to rectify the situation. But if a server tips out a bartender poorly, the reproaches are limitless. The bartender has the option of verbal or physical abuse, but often chooses the simple act of payback.

Payback can entail ignoring the server's special requests, intentionally losing some of his/her drink orders, delaying the making of all special coffees (although this tactic is used indiscriminately to deter all staff from ordering the bartender's most loathed beverage: the cappuccino), or revoking "free drinking status," which is often the most devastating. Losing this status can be a real social hindrance because one invariably falls below the level of drunkenness of one's comrades while drinking after a shift. This can be painful for three reasons: (1) without a constant flow of free alcohol into the bloodstream, everyone at the table suddenly seems quite hideous, showing far too much tooth and gum, and spewing forth pieces of wet nacho chips with each chortle; (2) without the cerebral dulling achieved by shot after shot of free Sambuca, everyone at the table ceases to be clever and, in fact, appear to be talking out of their assholes; and (3) attaining a higher state of drunkenness actually requires hard earned money out of pocket. Needless to say, the wayward server gets with the program in fairly short order and begins to tip-out large.

In essence, the bartender has the most power amongst the front house staff because he/she controls the distribution of the almighty firewater. He/she can barter the booze in exchange for higher tip-outs from the servers, to get free food from the kitchen, to get into clubs around town, and to grease the wheels of any prospective romance. This can reach shameless proportions, but bartenders are not known for their subtlety. Surprisingly, the servers will not always consume their entire nightly allotment of free booze in one sitting; rather, they will shuttle it to their friends who are expecting (nay, demanding) some preferential treatment. And without the bartender's generosity, all the servers can normally manage are free sodas and milkshakes. This is considered pretty weak, especially when a waiter is pretending to be the "Big Man on Campus" to all of his lecherous buddies. Overall though, the barter system benefits both bartenders and servers and is another fine example of symbiosis, but it's because of this leverage that bartenders are analogous to python snakes: sociable and passive enough from afar, but upon closer inspection, they are actually quite cunning and inclined to snatch and squeeze the life out of as much of the restaurant jungle as possible.

Some serpentine bartenders clearly get carried away with abusing the system, though. This is commonly referred to as barefaced **scamming**. It's not that bartenders are any less ethical than servers, it's just that there is much more opportunity to rip the restaurant off while working behind the bar. Keep in mind that the bartender is the person who orders the booze, stocks the booze, sells the booze, collects money for the booze, and accounts for the booze. If bartenders are sounding like the Wall Street traders of the early '80s, it's no coincidence because there are no watchdogs, no safe guards, and no supervision behind the bar (undoubtedly, Michael Milken was a bartender while in college). Consequently, there is almost nothing preventing a bartender from selling a customer a drink and pocketing the money without ringing it in. The only practical deterrent would be inflated liquor costs, which could alert the managers. But, the clever bartender combats rising liquor costs by: (1) running an otherwise efficient bar with minimal breakage and waste; (2) being selective as to who receives free drinking status; (3) substituting restaurant booze with bottles from the liquor store (remember, pocketing forty shots of vodka @ $3.50 a pop clearly offsets the cost of a $28 bottle from the liquor store); and (4) underpouring absolutely every drink that leaves the bar, as one eighth of an ounce skimmed off all drinks can really accumulate. If these measures fail to quell the inflated liquor costs, the bartender has one last option at his/her disposal, but it takes fortitude and a certain amount of thespian-like panache. He/she can take an empty liquor bottle (preferably one that contained vodka because of its clarity and relative lack of odor), fill it with water, set it on the bar as if it were a bottle of actual vodka, inconspicuously knock it off the bar sending it crashing to the floor, and then pour a few ounces of real vodka on the broken mess (for authenticity) before the startled managers arrive on the scene. This can work surprisingly well as long as the manager does not fancy him/herself a descendent of Sherlock Holmes. To increase the chances of successfully pulling off this caper, the bartender must appear angry for being so clumsy, appear concerned about the effect the breakage will have on the liquor costs, and he/she must dispose of the evidence post haste. If the manager is duped, then forty ounces of liquor are instantly written off, the liquor costs drop by a point or two, and the bartender's job is saved for another week. This cannot be relied upon very often because the bartender's reputation can eventually be called into question, but the most cunning of bartenders will find a way to blame the "accidents" on bussers or bar assistants and avoid suspicion altogether.

☺ ATTENTION: THE FOLLOWING INFORMATION MAY GET YOU A GENEROUS "BUY-BACK"

For a bartender to enjoy abnormally large fiscal returns during any given shift, customers need not always be outright scammed or looted. On the contrary, if liquor costs are under control, some humanitarian bartenders will occasionally single out a well-behaved, discerning, generous stranger who is sitting at the wood and decide to lavish him/her with a premium beverage at "no charge" (which is referred to as a buy-back) in hopes of acquiring an even larger gratuity from the flattered customer. Thus, buy-backs are an implicit agreement between the bartender and the customer to put something of value in each other's jeans at the direct expense of the restaurant. This is another classic "win-win" scenario. To better your odds of scoring buy-backs, be relaxed, show some respect, tip well on your first couple of drinks, and never thank the bartender so effusively that other lounge customers take note and demand the same treatment, or worse, the bar manager takes note and lavishes the poor martyred bartender with a premium shit canning at no charge. On second thought, be as effusive as you possibly can...

There are two stages to an interaction between a server and a bartender every time a drink is ordered. The first stage is totally impersonal as it involves a server standing at a distant computer terminal and browsing and extensive list of alcohols before selecting a drink and sending his/her order electronically to the bar. And I must say, it's simply amazing how often this electronic message is mysteriously altered while traveling within the fiber optics. Regardless, the bartender then retrieves the chit from his endlessly chattering printer and either makes the drink without a fuss, or sets the chit aside and prepares for battle. Grounds for battle include: ordering any drink that involves a blender or the espresso machine, forgetting to modify a drink that needs a modifier for its completion (salt or no salt on the rim of a Caesar, for example), tagging a drink with too many modifiers (lime margarita, tall, no blend, on the rocks, extra ice, side of lime, for example), or just plain not being liked by the bartender.

The second stage of the interaction is much more personal because it involves being face to face with the bartender while picking up the drink. This can be tricky and, as such, requires good timing and a neutral disposition because a bartender can blow a fuse at this stage even if he/she had no issues with the original drink order. For example, there is no point in a server running directly to the bar once an order is placed because the bartender is always a few drinks behind and does not appreciate the added pressure of a server staring him/her down like a puppy anticipating its Puppy Chow. Reactions to this can range from the restrained, "It's gonna be a few minutes" to the profane, "You just ordered that fucking drink, so piss off." Conversely, if a server is in the weeds, he/she may be grossly delayed in picking up drinks from the bar. This is not a major issue with drinks that have a lengthy "bar top life" such as wine and highballs, but it can be disastrous with blended drinks and beer. Nothing looks worse than a margarita that's ninety percent liquid with a one-inch skiff of ice floating on top, or a pint of draught with a stringy, evaporated head on it. As a result, these drinks will need some refurbishing from the none-too-happy bartender before they can be delivered to the impatient customer. Practical servers can restore the heads on pints by sticking a straw in the beer and swirling, but even they are helpless with expired blended drinks. The bartender's reaction to this can range from the mildly chastising, "I'll reblend it this time, but not next time" to the flippant, "Too fucking bad, just get this shit off my bar, pronto!"

Even if one's drink order and timing are impeccable, the bartender is very sensitive to even the slightest criticism or suggestion. For some reason, the bartender never appreciates the fact that virtually every member of the serving staff has consumed such a cornucopia of alcoholic beverages in their short careers that they are often leading authorities on a variety of alcohol based products, surpassing even the bartender's vast knowledge. But be that as it may, when face to face with the bartender, a server should never question the ingredients of a cocktail, request a different type of glass, comment on the quantity of ice in a drink, ask for a frostier beer glass, inform the bartender that he/she is out of garnishes, or offer to help in any way (unless it's to unload the ubiquitous glass wear from the dishwasher). These areas are considered taboo, on par with incest, cannibalism, and bestiality.

If a bartender does have an issue with the original beverage order, then no amount of good timing or etiquette can dissipate the rage that often erupts. Sometimes it's even beyond the server's control, as customers don't know which drinks are on the bartender's blacklist and can inadvertently put their server in jeopardy by ordering them. For example, some jackass at a table of six might decide upon a cappuccino. Hence, "Oh, that sounds yummy!" is usually the chorus that echoes from the table. The server is then faced with coming to terms with six cappuccinos. At this point, veteran servers have two options: (1) they can apologize to the table for the espresso machine being "on the fritz," but offer to bring six complimentary regular coffees, thus trying to capitalize on people's tendency to be cheap and placated by anything complimentary; or (2) take the six cappuccinos in the ass as a scolding enema, but try to make the most of it by up selling six shots of Baileys to go with them. If the latter, the veteran server will receive a stern look from the bartender, but there will be some understanding of the circumstance and some appreciation for turning a $4 coffee into a $7 "special coffee." Inexperienced servers, however, will gladly order the six cappuccinos because they think that increasing the table's check will automatically increase their gratuity. This type of thinking is naive and shortsighted, because said servers will arrive at the wood to the sounds of, "Hey rookie, this isn't a fucking Starbucks, so get with the program." Next, the cappuccinos will then be mysteriously delayed for about twenty minutes, which will irritate the six customers who are invariably late for the premier of a foreign film festival, which will ultimately compromise the server's tip. Nice going, Cherry.

From a bartender's standpoint then, the best servers are the ones who: tip-out the most (this is first and foremost), don't abuse their free drinking status, order the easiest drinks to make, modify the least number of drinks, pick up their drinks in a timely manner, remain absolutely quiet while at the wood (unless it's to comment on some glorious gibbon that's swinging from the forest undergrowth, or to reveal detailed carnal knowledge of a cute hostess), and are able to appropriately garnish their drinks. Bartenders loathe servers who can't garnish a drink. It may be the least significant in terms of what makes a server valuable to a bartender, but it can be a major pet peeve of most bartenders. In short: Caesars, margaritas, Cuba Libres, Tom Collins, Mexican beers, vodka and sodas, and gin and tonics require a wedge of lime; Bloody Marys, Long Island ice teas, and some draught beers require a lemon; creamy tropical drinks, daiquiris, and sangria require either a pineapple or an orange slice. It's as simple as that. Don't ever say I didn't warn you.

Finally, lest you think that bartenders and servers are constantly antagonistic to one another and clash like steroid raging titans, they are often of the same mind when it comes to categorizing customer's personalities according to the drinks they habitually order. If pressed, the two sides will invariably concur with the following observations:

(1) Women (including all varieties of cougar):

Ordered Drink	Personality Traits
Beer	Low maintenance (i.e., no big hair or flesh colored nylons) and down to earth; she likes pool and actually knows the rules to American football.
Blended Drinks	Annoying, flaky, and demanding; she knows the difference

	between shiatsu and acupressure, but not between football and lawn bowling.
Wine	Conservative and sophisticated; a real social climber who might allow you to climb aboard after a few carafes of house merlot.
Wine Coolers	Thinks she is trendy and sophisticated, but actually is a trollop with no clue; has inferiority complex about entry-level intelligence.
Highballs	Fairly mature and discerning, especially if ordering a premium vodka on ice; usually an abrasive lawyer if in a business suit.
Rye Whiskey	Beyond mature, bordering on hardened; almost always from a small town and with a history of dating absolute losers.
Baileys	A bit of a tart who is battling a weight problem, therefore, emotionally unstable and dangerously unpredictable.
Shots	Either trying too hard to fit in with male pals, or looking to get totally hammered then naked; might consider consummating a budding relationship in an alley behind the restaurant.

(2) Men:

Ordered Drink	Personality Traits
Cider	Probably under-aged and hoping desperately to get laid before graduating from high school (without matriculation, of course).
Domestic Beer	Starving students or chronic underachievers who spend their Saturday nights trying to flip bottle caps into stained coffee mugs, which effectively eliminates any possibility of getting laid.

Premium Beer	Considers himself a beer connoisseur and is pretending to be particular about getting laid.
Imported Beer	A pretentious yuppie wannabe who will assume the lotus position and roll on a flavored condom if he ever has the slightest chance of getting laid.
Bitter	A relatively old fart who genuinely likes good quality beer and is hoping to get laid before the effects of his Viagra wear off.
Guinness	A try-hard hooligan who has probably never been to the U.K., but will eventually get laid one way or another.
Wine	Somewhat cultured, but hoping the wine thing will boost his tarnished image and help him get laid.
Port	Thinks he is quite sophisticated, fantasizes about young boys, and always chooses masturbation over the enormous effort it would take to get laid.
Vodka	A sardonic and extremely horny bastard who would unhesitatingly shag a warm scarf.
Rye Whiskey	Becomes strangely altered upon intoxication and doesn't give a shit about anything and will throw a punch at any one who gets in his way of getting laid (see rye guy).
Cheap Tequila	Spends too much time in the gym or on the oil rigs up north and likes fighting almost as much as getting laid.
Crantini	Generally well dressed and flamboyant with a trendy hair cut, these pansies will get laid alright, but by what gender?

Chapter 2

Beasts of Burden

"Heaven sends us good meat, but the Devil sends cooks."

- David Garrick

Dish Pigs and Grease Weasels...

The back-of-the-house staff is an interesting collection of characters. It's difficult to define them as they represent one of the most diverse groups of people on a demographic pie chart. Most seem to be anti-establishmentarianists. That is to say, they are suspicious of big business, they embrace anarchy, they monitor quietly from afar, they are pessimistic and brood about the future, they have a tendency to be nomadic, they are much more open-minded to tattoos and dope, they favor longer hair and shorter skirts, and they drive shitty cars with awesome sound systems. These are fun people generally. And if not fun, at least genuine. In short, they are the antithesis of the front house yuppies and proudly revel in their role as underdogs. And aside from harmless dope and mainstream tattoos, they obviously don't have much in common with the front house staff, although a dozen pitchers of stolen beer after a shift can go a long way in promoting understanding and goodwill.

One gets the impression that the recipe for the back house staff is one part '70s headbanger partially frozen in time, one part computer nerd lightly salted with the idea of becoming the next Unabomber, and one part first generation immigrant fully strained because they were previously mechanical engineers who garnered some measure of respect in their native lands. This motley crew is then mixed thoroughly and put into a sweltering, greasy environment for eight hours at a time while being roasted by management and carved by the servers. If the back house staff were a menu item they would be Triple X Chile on a crusty roll.

The back of the house (or kitchen area) is roughly divided into three main areas: the dish pit, the prep area, and the line. The poor bastards who choose the kitchen as their vocation invariably start in the dish pit. If the term "dish pit" evokes visions of medieval torture, it is by no accident, as it has claimed its share of victims and maimed many more. No one knows who named it so aptly, perhaps some prophetic Frenchman circa 1770 when the first public restaurant opened in Paris. Regardless, a couple centuries later, the conditions are essentially unchanged. Imagine an 8x8 foot area inundated with a ton of plates, pots, pans, kitchen gadgetry, coffee mugs, and cutlery all caked with some sort of food byproduct in various stages of decomposition. Of course, the servers and kitchen workers are supposed to scrape off the food from the various items, but they are often distracted from this task by the omnipotent fear of falling in the dish pit area. Falls are not that common, but represent a constant threat as the tiled surface of the dish pit is always covered with an industrial slime that could fell the most sure-footed mountain goat. One wrong move in the dish pit could put a server's shift (or life) in peril. Imagine wearing a crisp white shirt one instant, then being covered in the most ungodly, primordial sludge the next. One could not appear anywhere in public, let alone serve tables with such a befouled garment. Therefore, servers have three options if they are felled in the dish pit. (1) To feign an injury that would prevent them from continuing on with serving tables. A sprained wrist or a strained lower back are solid and defensible choices. This is not a bad way of getting out of a shift if a server is having a shitty go of it and is not otherwise hurting for cash. But, the server would be wise not to be spotted "busting a move" until three in the morning at some local club. (2) To beg, borrow, or steal an unblemished shirt from someone of similar stature. This task is easier for females to accomplish because waitresses often arrive at work in fashionable street clothes before changing into their working garb. Consequently, there is usually a Coco Chanel quality of wardrobe to choose from. Waiters have far fewer options, unfortunately, because they often walk in to work looking disheveled and schleppy in their ill-fitting uniforms. Ultimately, they may be forced by management to wear some dorky patio shirt in a size far too small, which was last considered cool when *Mork and Mindy* was a hit on television (in other words, the Paleozoic). Make no mistake, this does affect one's tips adversely. Or (3) to spend twenty minutes feverishly scrubbing the shirt in a sink. This is an exercise in futility because the dish pit sludge quickly fuses with the cotton fibers, and twenty minutes spent away from one's section is disastrous. The best bet is to burn the offensive shirt (during a small ceremony in the alley, behind the dumpsters, under a full moon) as a sacrifice to the dish pit gods, and then simply move on.

Without question, watching servers slip and fall is a highlight for the people who work in the dish pit. These people are commonly referred to as dishwashers, but are sometimes labeled **dish pigs**. Admittedly, this is a derogatory term and is not appreciated by the "flatware sanitation engineers." This is unfortunate, because any job that forces one to run around in slop like a pig, sweat profusely like a pig, eat dinner hurriedly like a pig, and squeal in protest like a pig, begs to be termed dish pig. This should, in no way, be taken personally as it is not a reflection of the dishwasher's disposition or physical attributes - just commentary on how brutal the job position is. It embodies high school frosh, boot camp, and minimum security prison all at the same time. However, if the dish pig can survive a couple months of heat exhaustion, stabbing back pain, and grotesquely pruned hands, he/she will most likely be promoted to the "prep area." Tragically, though, the long, slithery tentacles of the dish pit demon occasionally grabs hold of some dish pigs' heads and constricts mightily. The enormous pain will often make the poor dish pigs delusional. In their altered state, some believe there might be some future in selling their soul to, and dancing with, the dish pit demon on a full-time basis. There just isn't though. These poor beasts of burden can misplace years of their life in the dish pit if they do not attempt to move up the kitchen ladder. Overall, fatality rates in the pit can climb as high as eighty percent.

Once out of the dish pit, one need not wear Ralph Lauren and Sperry Top-siders to work in the prep area. Prep area is short for **prep**aration of food **area**, not preppies lounge, although some do take on a superior attitude and keep their collars turned up once liberated from the dish pit. The prep area is much more hospitable and the job of prep cook can be fairly bearable if chopping crudités is your calling. New prep cooks are notorious for being overly proud of their kitchen whites (complete with a paper chef's hat), which they receive with their promotion. But much like the busser's primary strategy, though, the prep cook should always have his/her eye on the front line, where actual cooking procedures are practiced. Unfortunately, working on the front line increases the hazard level ten-fold. The following is a list of the top hazards in the kitchen per position, with medical complications in parentheses:

(1) Dishwasher: inhaling particles of industrial pink detergent (mild brain infarct and seizures), or being passed over for promotion to prep cook (shock, temporary paralysis, and suicidal tendencies).

(2) Day prep cook: covertly licking the dessert spatulas (fissured tongue, hyperactivity, and mild bloating).

(3) Night prep cook: removing the highly caustic guts from baby squid in preparation for calamari (partial loss of fingers and a leper-like appearance).

(4) Line cook - deep fryer: deep-frying chicken wings and dry ribs (face blisters looking remarkably like acne vulgaris and permanent retinal damage from splattering grease).

(5) Line cook - grill: relighting the grill after a power failure (spontaneous external combustion) or overcooking the manager's dinner (psychological abuse and facial contusions).

(6) Kitchen manager: getting a stain on his/her custom embroidered chef's coat (massive coronary).

Once on the line, the newly promoted line cook is faced with the daunting task of penetrating a very rigid hierarchy. One does not walk onto the line, head directly for the grill, and start cooking $18 sirloins; let's not be foolish. There are a multitude of "stations" to learn and master first, ranging from "fryer" to "pastas," before one can grab the tongs and grill meat with the confidence of a fat Texan. Initially, the new line cook is given cheap stuff to fuck-up and overcook such as potato skins, garlic toast, and salads as this is all part of the learning curve. Unfortunately, much of the sub par product ends up on the customers' plates and not in the garbage bin where it belongs. It may be disguised under extra cheese or sauce, but the telltale signs are always there: edges that are burnt, insides that are raw, portions that are scanty, and far too much seasoning. In other words, welcome to the world of the eighteen-year-old line cook: heavy on the hormones, light on the culinary skills.

The caveats of stocking a kitchen full of adolescents are fairly evident, mainly: they can't cook, they can't possibly appreciate fine food, and they don't take pride in their work. In clear contrast is the typical restaurant patron, who is middle class, in their thirties, and has experience in consuming and preparing a wide variety of dishes. These people have spent quality time with their BBQs, woks, food processors, and convection ovens. They know what macaroni and cheese to Mandarin duck should look and taste like. Yet strangely, they pay good money for "Y Generation" slackers to butcher their food (no pun intended). Obviously, the general public pays a premium for the convenience of dining at a restaurant, but should one not expect his/her food prepared at least as well as the average North American backyard barbequer could have done it? And by world standards, that's not asking very much. Again, this is not malicious commentary on the integrity and moral fiber of the young people who work in the kitchens across North America, but rather a simple observation of the typical teenager. It is the rare teenager who has gotten his/her act together enough to develop confidence, maturity, and pride in what they do. It is rarer still to find these individuals in the underbelly of a restaurant's kitchen. But yes, an ancient coelacanth was found off the coast of South Africa, so maybe there's hope.

The advantages of hiring such pubescent individuals should be obvious too: they are cheap like borscht and they won't sue for wrongful dismissal. Restaurants thrive off slave labor as the servers and bussers often do no better than minimum wage, and the kitchen staff only does marginally better at around $2-3 above minimum wage (plus a free meal every shift at most restaurants). This meager sum is often enough to attract keen, young workers who prefer to avoid the fast food scene, but usually isn't enough to keep them for more than a year or so. This is bad because continually training new staff is time consuming and expensive. To combat this dilemma, all restaurant management gurus eventually figure out a way to increase the kitchen staff's salary without paying them any more per hour. Seemingly a paradox, yes? Well not really, because those crafty corporate bastards invariably decide to restructure the percentages of the tip-out pool. Thinking they are descendants of Robin Hood, they will steal from the "rich" (the servers, hostesses, and bussers who are all chauffeured around in vintage Bentleys) and give to the "poor" (the kitchen staff, who do actually live below the poverty line). For example, if a server was accustomed to tipping out one percent to the hostess, one percent to the busser, and one and a half percent to the bartender (for a total of three and a half percent), the new scheme might have him/her tipping out a half percent to the hostess, three quarters of a percent to the busser, one and a half percent to the bartender, and one and a quarter percent to the kitchen (for a total of four percent). Therefore, from the server's point of view, they are tipping out a half percent more per shift, which equates to between $3-6 out of their pocket. Not a life threatening reversal of fortune, but irritating nonetheless. From the hostess's point of view, their tip-out pool is reduced by half, which could equate to $20 less for each hostess per shift. This is tragic and can throw the lipstick budget for a loop, but the management team realizes how replaceable they are so they push the envelope. From the busser's standpoint, their tip-out pool will decrease by a quarter, which means about $7 less per shift per busser. This is cruel, because $7 can buy a lot of bubble gum and anti-bacterial face soap. Naturally, the bartenders remain unscathed by the changes, which just adds to their reputation for being lucky sons of bitches. This leaves the kitchen staff, who appear to be the big winners. Or are they? Let's take a closer look.

The kitchen people had originally made between $2-3 above minimum wage (depending on where they were in the hierarchy), with a remote chance of getting raises totaling another $2 spread out over a couple of years. They were also entitled to a free meal every shift, although this usually only amounted to a plain burger and cold fries. Under most revamped systems, the kitchen worker's salary is often frozen at about $3 above minimum wage and they lose their precious free meals, but they benefit from the raping and pillaging of the front house to the tune of about $8-9 each per shift. However, all mammals must consume a certain ratio of protein/carbohydrate/fat in order to survive, so the kitchen staff must buy their dinners at a cost of about $5 after the standard restaurant discount is applied. So in the end, the average kitchen guy is maybe $3 further ahead after each shift, but with no possibility of a future raise. This is a tough trade off, no matter how it's calculated.

The restaurants, on the other hand, manage to save money by: (1) freezing the kitchen wages and not granting raises beyond the first year; (2) not giving free meals each shift to every kitchen worker; and (3) retaining staff longer under the guise of a higher salary and a more egalitarian system. In addition, as a final kick to the camel toe, the restaurants actually make a small profit from the meals the kitchen staff must purchase out of pocket to avoid keeling over mid-shift and lapsing into a hypoglycemic coma (which is to be distinguished from the comas induced by tainted heroin). So who's the real winner? The restaurants of course, because the restaurants always win at the expense of their docile employees. One need not be Mike Wallace with the crew of *60 Minutes* in tow to expose this situation for what it is: good old-fashioned sodomy.

It doesn't seem to matter if the restaurant management gurus are to blame for the increased tip-outs, because servers invariably blame the kitchen staff, which amounts to a classic case of "blaming the victim." Most servers reason that since the kitchen staff receives more money, they must have whined and bitched to management about not being paid enough. It's assumed that the kitchen staff had been successful in mounting a pay-hike campaign, while the servers had perennially failed at any attempts to change their minimum wage status. This type of reasoning is partially lucid, but it's the restaurants that are ultimately behind the changes due to the cost savings to them, not because they caved in to the lobbying of some merry band of kitchen characters. Besides, the servers conveniently forget to calculate their gratuities when comparing hourly wages with the kitchens. When gratuities are accounted for, the average server makes nearly twice as much per hour as the average kitchen worker. So in reality, kitchen staffers often do not rapidly close the economic gap when tipping pools are reconfigured, and the server's jealousies and hostilities are usually grossly misplaced. Regardless, it's these hard feelings layered on to the pre-existing incompatibility that initially created the term **grease weasel** in reference to the kitchen staff, deserved or not.

I doubt if such a sub-species exists in the wild, but it is such a sublime term to reflect a server's sentiments when some kitchen guy loses a table's order and then refuses to start making it until he sees it rung in again. Thus, "Look you fucking grease weasel, that order was rung in twenty-five minutes ago, but you stupid fuck-sticks lost it! Now toss that shit on the grill this fucking second before I toss you on. Jeeesusss H I'm fucked now, and I'm actually tipping you out for this?! Mother fucking soft heads," erupts from the depths of the server's soul and becomes totally cathartic. It just feels so much better saying it aloud. This situation is analogous to a heated discussion between husband and wife: the husband is pissed off and just has to get something off his chest, so he snaps and yells, nothing personal mind you, then he feels great and wants to move on, or have sex; but the wife takes it very personally, becomes overwrought, and wants to discuss it in great detail, over and over, and won't have sex until the problem is fully resolved. Of course, no self respecting server would ever have sex with a grease weasel, which is good because there are strict laws against bestiality (even when consensual), but the point is that the kitchen guy naturally becomes offended by such derogatory name calling and profanity and refuses to let it slide or to see it from the server's perspective. And the only rational discussion that ensues is the kitchen guy whining to management, instead of finding a quick resolution with the server. In the end, the customer suffers because their dinner has been grossly delayed, and the server's job is in jeopardy for verbal assault, but the kitchen guy smiles to himself because he just loves anarchy and fucking with the self-righteous, uppity servers.

Direct interaction between server and grease weasel is intentionally restricted by management in efforts to minimize the number of confrontations and death threats. Management accomplishes this by installing an **expediter** in the pass-thru, which is the area on the other side of the line from the cooks. The expediter's main functions are to act as a liaison between the servers and the line cooks, and to make sure that the food is presentable and reaches the appropriate destination in a timely fashion. It might sound like the weight of the world is on the expediter's shoulders, and it sometimes is, but he/she is dependent on **food runners** to be truly effective. In short, food runners deliver food for the expediter on behalf of servers who are unable or uninterested in running their table's food. Some restaurants do not employ food runners because they expect their servers to be responsible for running all their table's food (imagine that?). Other restaurants specifically schedule food runners for the purpose of running all the food. And still others rely on the altruism of their serving staff to pitch in with the collective food running when they aren't too busy. This latter scenario would be viable if human beings were all loving, selfless, and living in a '50s sitcom like *Leave it to Beaver* (as in, "Oh that Beaver, he's busy talking again to a young lady with a tight, angora sweater. Gee whiz, don't bother that little rascal, for I'll gladly run his chicken wings!"). Well, human beings aren't so benevolent by nature and most servers would let the Beaver's chicken wings go nuclear under the heat lamps before they would touch them. This is because every server has a different work ethic, philosophy, conscience, agenda, and level of commitment to "the team." In reality, most servers wouldn't give a shit if the entire restaurant staff was decimated by the Ebola virus (save one grease weasel to cook and one dish pig to wash), as long as their section was unscathed and bustling with big tippers. Forcing these autonomous types to do work that doesn't immediately pay dividends is playing with dynamite. In essence, it's difficult to convince some servers to help their fellow workers for the collective good when that usually requires spending time away from their section, which usually causes second-rate service, which usually translates into a lesser gratuity. The logical question from a potential food runner then becomes, "Why should I work harder and make less cake?" which is a point very well taken. Therefore, expediters are viewed with great scorn by the serving staff and are generally ignored like red-headed stepchildren. Consequently, the futile question, "Can I pleeeease get a food runneerrrr?!" can be heard echoing in vain throughout the pass-thru hour after hour, shift after shift.

Much like clueless hostesses, the majority of grease weasels are easily substituted and replaced. They are as inconsequential as fruit flies in a zoology experiment. They are not valued for their unique cooking talents, but rather as mindless cogs within the vast kitchen infrastructure. These people are not part of the middle-class demographic who wake up early on a Sunday morning to watch Emeril kick it up a notch on a helpless Cornish game hen stuffed with goat cheese and drizzled with a pear coulis; lets not be ridiculous. Rather, they sleep in all day until wakened by their unemployed roomate playing *Mario Brothers* on the Nintendo, then drag their sorry asses to the corner store for a microwaved burrito and can of Mountain Dew. This is why when they get to work, they are confronted with "paint by numbers" type instructions on all the various food stations. It eliminates the need for any original thought, culinary inspiration, or uniquely human trait. In fact, if lesser apes were indigenous to North America they would probably be working on the kitchen lines, smacking their lips and mounting each other, while trying not to burn the potato skins. And knowing the restaurant industry like I do, some financial analyst somewhere has already priced their import and training costs just in case. Perhaps a *Planet of the Apes* Cafe is in our future.

All kidding aside, the kitchen staff, as a collective, are obviously vital to a restaurant's success, which is why they are most analogous to indigenous beasts of burden: flatulent, stubborn, and not particularly clever, but without their shit for fertilizer, the jungle couldn't flourish.

Chapter 3

Ruminants and Sloths

"Those that can do; those that can't become managers."

- J.C. Mitchell

Various Sniveling Managers…

Managers come in a variety of shapes, sizes, and smells. Some are angular, slight, and sour, while others are round, obese, and musty. None are sweet and fragrant. Some are stylish, most are not. Some have carefully mapped out their career path and would call Machiavelli their hero, but most just get sucked into management and follow along as if they were sheep. Far too many believe that they are bolstering their precious resumes with such a job, when in reality most restaurant management positions end so disgracefully that they are best erased from all memory and parchment. Precious few restaurant managers have any training on how to actually manage people, and contrary to popular belief, this is not easily learned or innately understood. Charisma, vision, empathy, and leadership qualities are rarely displayed in the management ranks, making it nearly impossible to produce effective managers. Just think of "Captain Bligh" pulling all those shenanigans on his ship, the *H.M.S. Bounty*. Undoubtedly he became a restaurant manager after the mutiny.

The vast majority of entry-level restaurant managers come from the serving ranks. Why is this? Do entry-level managers make more money, garner more respect, have greater job stability, or get laid more than the servers? God, no. Are they more gullible and apt to bite onto the carrot dangled in front of them by upper management? Partially, yes. The most complete answer, however, lies in the fact that they were shoddy servers who would have gotten fired by knowing management (pardon the oxymoron) or gotten their asses kicked (physically or verbally) by other staff who came to regard them as an enormous ball and chain. But instead of going gently into the night, the lamoid server "volunteers" him/herself into the management trainee program, thus ensuring that he/she is not banished from the animal kingdom that has provided many flagons of grog, much camaraderie, and a few sniffs of genitalia. Without these vices and opportunities, life would be unbearable for the underachieving server as the restaurant has come to represent the Fountain of Youth, a Roman orgy, and Mom's kitchen all fused into a very alluring hybrid. Consequently, a thick and sinewy umbilical cord forms between the restaurant and the employee that should not be underestimated. And much like its function between mother and fetus, this figurative umbilicus really can supply life to many wayward souls. The server's biggest fear then becomes being aborted by having the cord severed, or in other words, being fired. It is this fear that propels an individual into a management job that will compromise friendships, propagate disrespect, and pay absolute peanuts. Of course, the whispered hints of possibly becoming a slothful General Manager and making $100,000 per year helps to ease the pain.

Aside from coming in various shapes, colors, and smells, managers are also fairly plentiful (therefore redundant) within a restaurant setting. This allows them to fully pursue their favorite pastime: sitting for hours on end in an overstuffed booth sipping coffee. Unfortunately, this leads to difficulty in differentiating the hierarchy that exists within a herd of lesser managers as they congregate around booths (much like herds of Cape buffalo gather near watering holes), because all of them dress equally as shabby. Few ever seem to learn that combining herringbone pants with a plaid shirt and polka-dot tie is a risky undertaking. Thankfully, the management fraternity has developed nomenclature that serves to delineate their profession without having to rely on physical markings. The following is a list of all possible managerial subtypes (sometimes all represented within a single restaurant) from most authority and compensation to least, and with an idea of what they actually do:

(1) General Manager (G.M.). Main responsibilities include: not letting the restaurant burn down, stammering on about the merits of fine wine during the G.M.'s wine seminar, developing a disapproving facial expression that can be instantly displayed, eating as much free food in front of the staff as humanly possible, endlessly bitching about high labor costs, making everyone feel about

as replaceable as the "Slurpee" cups at 7-Eleven, and playing a couple rounds of shoddy golf each week.

(2) Kitchen Manager. Main responsibilities include: not letting underage line cooks perish from third degree grease burns, developing a sarcastic disposition, throwing out as much viable food in front of the staff as humanly possible, endlessly bitching about high food costs, denying the accountability for infecting the local community with *E. coli* bacteria, and growing a little paunch with matching love handles.

(3) Night Manager. Main responsibilities include: eating his/her dinner at the height of the dinner rush, contemplating who to backstab or sabotage to become a G.M., fudging labor costs to appear more efficient, grossing-out all the hot waitresses with drunken proclamations of lust, and playing hours worth of *Snood* on the office computer.

(4) Bar Manager. Main responsibilities include: staying coherent on Friday and Saturday nights, accepting a plethora of free stuff from the beer reps, not getting addicted to cocaine, endlessly bitching about high liquor costs, developing ways to systematically under-pour all customers, and attempting to minimize the bartender's shameless scamming.

(5) Day Manager. Main responsibilities include: stroking the ego and/or penis of the G.M. while lunching together, breathing impossibly putrid coffee breath on all those within a ten-foot radius, irritating the local business people who have only forty-five minutes for lunch with an ill conceived "networking approach," and spending hours pouring over the *Auto Trader* after the G.M. leaves to play golf.

(6) Assistant Night Manager. Main responsibilities include: alienating all the servers who were previously his/her friends, trying to catch all the servers using the scams that he/she was using just months prior, fucking up the night schedule for all those who book time off, pretending to know much more about wine than he/she actually does, and endlessly droning on about the economic value of hot cloths.

(7) Assistant Day Manager. Main responsibilities include: deflecting criticism that his/her day staff is inferior to the night staff, refusing to run any food during the lunch rush on principle, scheduling people who have already been

fired or quit, critiquing everyone's lack of shirt ironing skills, carrying around a very officious looking day-timer, and conducting numerous one on ones with the front house staff.

(8) Director of Fun (seasonal). Not actually a managerial position, but it demands explanation. Main responsibilities include: organizing events that hinge on consuming copious amounts of liquor so that the staff can become incestuous with one another, developing theme days that are largely ignored, kissing the manager's ass who saved her from being fired as a waitress or hostess, and trying to get laid by the local beer reps.

The Stages of Gestation...

As a general rule, managerial candidates start their gestation in the underbelly of the kitchen (in an attempt to learn the various food stations while looking totally ridiculous in ill-fitting whites), and then begin life as full-fledged snivelers under the title of "Assistant Day Manager." This is of no real importance, not even warranting personalized business cards, but it is a starting point and a crucial part of the development process. Let's review the entire thirteen-stage process to better understand.

Stage 1: a particular server is ostracized for being shitty and annoying.

Stage 2: said server avoids being fired or pummeled above the shoulders by volunteering for the managerial ranks via some over-hyped training program.

Stage 3: not coincidentally, middle management has already become disenchanted with the bogus promise of power and riches and thus desperately want to hire an assistant to slough their menial tasks onto.

Stage 4: at the same time, the G.M. senses middle management's restlessness, but doesn't give a shit as he/she knows that a continual source of raw meat is needed to stuff through the managerial meat grinder.

Stage 5: the above-mentioned ostracized server is then unanimously "promoted" after much smoke is blown up his/her bowels about his/her tremendous leadership qualities and potential within the company.

Stage 6: training then begins in the kitchen (including a few horrifying shifts as a dish pig) and consists of ridiculously early mornings and long, greasy hours.

Stage 7: gradually the newly promoted trainee realizes he/she has never started work at six-thirty in the morning before or ever made less money.

Stage 8: the newly promoted trainee either quits (which is fine because he/she was a pathetic bed shitter anyway and living on borrowed time) or trudges on to face a battery of training manuals filled with food costs and outdated pictures.

Stage 9: if the trainee withstands the rigors of the kitchen, then he/she is birthed as an assistant day manager, which temporarily restocks the management team and makes it viable again because he/she can usefully deflect or bear the brunt of the G.M.'s erratic bouts of rage and sexual aggression. Hooves and a multi-chambered stomach then soon begin to form.

Stage 10: in time, the newly appointed assistant day manager realizes that in order to have any chance of climbing the managerial ladder he/she must compromise all integrity and brown nose like never before. An unpleasant complication of this servility and whoring is mild hemorrhaging from the anus, but if said manager's self-esteem quickly rebounds, then the blood often coagulates and simply flakes off.

Stage 11: such brown nosing, servility, and whoring causes the entire staff to revile and plot retribution against the new assistant day manager, which forces him/her to seek refuge within the safety of an over-stuffed booth for many hours each shift.

Stage 12: said manager either realizes he/she has no right being a manager of any sort and mercifully quits, or trudges on because far too much time has been invested and the remote possibility of making $100,000 per year as a G.M. and evolving into a three-toed sloth is worth risking life and liberty for.

Stage 13: if the latter scenario unfolds, then the development process continues, but the resilient little manager has survived the initial brunt of it.

From the initial posting of assistant day manager, one progresses through the meat grinder and ends up as an assistant night manager. This change from a diurnal to a nocturnal existence often requires large doses of caffeine or "little blue pills" to stay awake until the wee hours of the morning. The position of day manager is next if one has morphed into a total ass kisser. This change back to diurnal hours usually necessitates melatonin or copious amounts of beer in order to fall asleep before midnight. The title of night manager follows once enough allies have been secured and enemies fired. By this time, the cud-chewing night manager can avoid sleeping the day away by simply scheduling his/her assistant manager for all the closing shifts. The sloth-like existence of a G.M. is the ultimate prize for those able to stab enough backs, slander enough reputations, cover up enough inadequacies, and sip enough coffee within the confines of some booth. Of course, much luck and timing are needed, but remarkably scant managing skills. Making the situation even more daunting is the total lack of job security. Any manager can be fired due to some performance shortcoming, some sexual indiscretion, or an excessive amount of debauchery (thus, there is never a shortage of reasons). Also, if the restaurant is a franchise of a large chain, then even the G.M. can fall victim to politics, economics, or whimsy. If it isn't, consider that the average life span of a non-franchised restaurant in North America is less than three years, which is not much time to make it through the managerial meat grinder and lay claim to the pot of gold. Consequently, the chances of ascending to the top of the heap are unlikely for most males, and merely theoretical for females. This is why Gloria Steinem ended up a feminist and not a G.M. of a restaurant.

Being a manager is not quite as cushy as the above may make it seem. On the contrary, there are some dangerous pitfalls and health concerns to be aware of. For example, G.M.s are most susceptible to inguinal hernias, gout, and Type II diabetes because of the obesity stemming from their growing affluence. Lower back strains from weekends of excessive golf are also problematic. Night managers must combat alcoholism, insomnia, and venereal diseases from cavorting with their staff into the early hours of the morning. Day managers have trouble with chronic halitosis and caffeine-induced headaches from enormous consumption of coffee, eyestrain from reading magazines and newspapers in the dimly lit office, and chaffed penises from excessive mammalian rear entry. Kitchen managers suffer from high cholesterol, heartburn due to grazing too quickly, and severe cramps due to the pressure their tight hound's-tooth pants put on their little paunches and matching love handles.

Finally, it should be noted that some wannabe managers take courses based on hotel and restaurant management. Hurrah for them. Whether or not these individuals develop the skills to become better managers is open to fierce debate, but it is clear that they are no more popular with their staff. In other words, same shit different tie. I suppose one could argue that ruminants and sloths make important contributions to the jungle, but I've yet to see any glorified in a Disney cartoon or grace the cover of *National Geographic*.

PART II

REARED IN THE JUNGLE

"An adventure is an inconvenience rightly considered.
An inconvenience is an adventure wrongly considered."

- G.K. Chesterton

From a fourteen-year-old's perspective, a restaurant can be an exciting, dynamic place and "Trader's Inn" was no exception. It had been refurbished in the early 1970s to resemble a Medieval Inn, not that anyone bothered to research what that might have been like mind you. Be that as it may, Trader's Inn eventually morphed into a large, dark, maze-like collection of three dining rooms, a lounge, and a nightclub by the late '70s. Two of the dining rooms shared the same ambiance and decor: high ceilings, exposed dark timbers, fireplaces, high back velvet armchairs, kerosene lanterns, lead goblets, copper water jugs, antique locks on the walls, and powder kegs on the floor. It possessed a King Henry VIII meets Captain Hook feel. The third dining room was more of an atrium in that it was much lighter and more open and, consequently, always seemed a little incongruent with the overall theme. Nevertheless, all three dining rooms were continually full as Trader's was one of the more popular restaurants in the city for the better part of two decades.

The owner of Trader's was an immigrant from Poland who started out as the restaurant's janitor sometime during the mid '60s. And being of eastern European ancestry and weaned on unfiltered cigarettes, he must have been compelled to buy a couple of cigarette dispensing machines and strategically place them around the restaurant so that he would never be too far away from his precious fags. Well, apparently many other people stumbled upon these machines and pumped gold florins into them in exchange for their death sticks, because in fairly short order he was in a position, along with a silent partner who was a line cook, to buy the entire restaurant. Or so the inspirational story goes. Regardless, I'm sure the good news spread all the way back to Krakow, where the headlines undoubtedly read, "Local Kid Shuns Communism to Become a Rich Bastard."

 We called him the "Vagrant," and were quite justified in doing so because: (1) he looked, dressed, and smelled like he lived at the Greyhound bus terminal and slept on a layer of newspapers that were previously used for wrapping battered fish and chips and then urinated on by a very territorial Blue Heeler; (2) he had this grunge rocker's ability to make his hair look perfectly matted and greasy regardless of the time of day; and (3) he would randomly appear and stand in the kitchen, talking with the Chinese cooks while simultaneously appalling all the new front house staff who assumed a street urchin had wondered in off the street and was demanding scraps of meat in exchange for not infecting everyone with hepatitis B, and then he would skulk away (with some actual scraps of meat) and not be seen or heard from for months. Only his pungent scent would linger and remind the veteran staff members that their fearless leader had appeared to survey the troops.

 The Vagrant had a very nice home in the city, one that resembled Trader's actually, but he preferred to stay at his cabin and occasionally commute back and forth within the confines of an old, rusty Jeep Wagoneer that burned oil and left the stench of gasoline on you if you ever had the misfortune of riding shotgun. He had three kids with his first wife, "Tina," who was a fixture at Trader's during the lunch shift. She worked the cash register, which was tucked away near the dish pit, and dabbled in some incidental accounting. Her real purpose, however, was to insinuate in her thick Polish accent that you were either (1) grossly negligent in accomplishing your tasks (whether it was offering the outrageous sum of two creamers with a pot of tea or having the audacity to replenish the Portuguese bean and sausage soup before the last drizzle was reduced to charcoal), which she thought was robbing her of some potential profit; or (2) mischievously designing diabolical ways to scam the restaurant, which was undoubtedly robbing her of profit. Most of us eventually became exhausted from trying to prove that such scrutiny and suspicion were unwarranted, so we decided to stop trying so hard and prove her right on both counts, as you will eventually read.

Trader's was known for its prime rib, salad bar, and steaks (in that order). It was also known, for a short period of time, as the "key swapping party headquarters," at least to the city's swinging couples during the experimental '70s. But providing people with beef, not discarded interchangeable spouses, was what Trader's did best and was the reason why most people showed up night after night. They came mostly for the prime rib, which was very good, but not quite the "best in the world" as Trader's claimed. Yes, there was a thriving cattle industry in the region. Yes, there were sharp knives to butcher the cattle with. And yes, some Chinese guys were taught how to load the pieces of dead cattle into a slow cooking oven. But so what? Was there a restaurant in any industrialized nation that couldn't have obtained the product and the technology to create prime rib that wasn't too disagreeable to the palate? We're not talking about food that must be scoured for during particular seasons in the Loire Valley, then carefully prepared, sautéed, and parched by an elite Parisian chef, then complemented perfectly with black truffles and baby organic carrots in a foie gras mousse, then finally presented on fine china with the balanced eye of an aesthetic genius. No, we're talking about opening a huge convection oven, slicing off a one-, two-, or three-inch cut of prime rib, throwing it onto a plain white plate, and dumping some watery, brown juicy on it, which would immediately drain off the meat, encircle it, and begin to evaporate under the blazing heat lamps, leaving rings of crusty juicy that could actually be used to organically date when the plate was put up. Of course, an inexhaustible source of juicy could be used to "freshen up" the beef if the waiter was enjoying a cigarette somewhere and simply didn't want to be bothered.

Sometimes the meat would be served with plain rice or a baked potato, but it was usually ordered a la carte because all meals included the mighty salad bar, which people would graze on with absolute disregard for the holding capacity of the human stomach. Then, once bloated from the early digestive stages of crudités, cheese, fruit, and beans and sausage from Portugal all combined into an incongruent bolus, a large chunk of brown protein would arrive at the table with a few rings of evaporated juicy around it, indicating that the waiter had either ordered the meals about ten minutes too early, or was puffing on a butt somewhere and lost track of time. This wouldn't faze anyone at the table, as they would resume their feeding frenzy on the beef with little regard for the girth of the impending morning's defecation that would invariably test the extendibility of their anal tissues. Then, while barely conscious, some coffee flavored ice cream pie would find its way to the table and somehow (perhaps by osmosis or phagocytosis) end up in the gullets of the nearly overdosed victims. Finally, an industrial sized winch would fall from the ceiling and be attached to the distended customers in order to haul them out to the parking lot where they would somehow navigate a course home. This was considered fine dining, *Michelin Guide* be damned.

As blasphemous as it may sound, I can attest to the fact that I've most definitely tasted better prime rib than that served at Trader's. It was marinated in some delicious garlicky concoction, then flamed on a Mesquite grill with rosemary and thyme, then served with wild mushrooms and little roasted potatoes. In short, it was wonderfully considered and prepared, which is in clear contrast to the assembly line attitude that existed at Trader's. But Trader's was not so automatic with the people because it served the best prime rib this side of Alpha Centauri (contrary to propagandist rantings), but rather because the place had immense character. In essence, Trader's combined a good, consistent product at a price that was somewhat affordable by most, in an atmosphere that encouraged total over-indulgence. I mean sitting in a chair that resembled a throne, and in a room that inspired images of medieval gluttony, would cause even the most restrained patron to beckon for more flagons of grog and another side of boar (or in this case, a twenty-four-ounce cut of prime rib which just added to the folklore of Trader's). "Off with her head!" or "Let them eat cake!" could be heard from those who took the medieval imagery a bit too far.

I had been introduced to Trader's at a very young age because the G.M. of the restaurant just happened to be a relative through marriage. I will refer to her as "Medusa," partially because she had long hair that she took such unwarranted pride in, but also because she was a seducer of men who would scheme, manipulate, and back stab like no other human being I have ever encountered. Consequently, while in her kingdom known as Trader's Inn, she inspired considerable fear and loathing, which she undoubtedly relished with much aplomb. And like the Vagrant, Medusa had also started at Trader's sometime in the late

'60s and had to scratch and claw her way up the ladder, often leaving scars on the backs and buttocks of her various suitors. To her credit, she was a strong willed woman with a keen intellect, but was about as unscrupulous as a Machiavellian whore. And believe me, this depiction is not influenced by any psychological in-law angst; rather she was simply a living, breathing dragon who caused much ruin, both physically and emotionally, to nearly everyone and everything that crossed her path. Thus, she makes a bloody good villain within the context of my adventures, especially when it came time to leave Trader's, as you will also eventually read.

By the time I was fourteen, Trader's had become quite familiar to me as Medusa would take us there for every birthday, holiday, and special occasion that would provide an excuse to retreat back into her domain where she could wield her power like Mary Queen of Scots. And by God, she would have more people flustered and kissing her ample hindquarters than old Mary ever did. I would order my usual (escargot, fillet Neptune, and mocha pie all washed down with a couple of "Shirley Temples") and just sit back and watch the procession of ass kissers and well-wishers fawn all over her. Our waiters on those fateful nights, who were usually chosen beforehand by Medusa, would have a perpetually frozen smile on their faces in order to mask their apprehension that something was about to go awry. Invariably something would be wrong with her dinner, despite the fact that the waiter was giving us his full attention and had informed the cooks that the incoming fillet mignon was Medusa's and had better be fucking magnificent. Everyone in her little kingdom was making her their top priority, yet there was always some culinary indiscretion that would put her off and be impossible to remedy. I eventually realized that her shtick was to be perpetually unsatisfied, plain and simple. This might have been amusing, watching Trader's become a Chinese circus every time we were there, but this was also her persona with my family outside of the restaurant, which became extremely tedious to say the least.

While back in the real world, collecting $10 a week in allowance was just not cutting it during the summer after I turned fourteen. I was on a waiting list to deliver the local newspaper, and had tried delivering flyers in the mean time, which was a pathetic evaluation of how much your time is worth at that age. If I really hauled ass, literally trotted, while pulling my red wagon laden with worthless flyers, I could flirt with the $1 an hour level for a grand total of $45 per month. Ditch diggers at the height of the Great Depression probably fared better. Needless to say, I retired without a pension from the junk mail industry with nary a hint of regret. But as grade nine approached and the pressure mounted to look like an Ivy League hopeful, I began a relentless assault on Medusa to hire me as a "salad boy" at Trader's. Surprisingly, she succumbed to my pleading and my adventures within the restaurant jungle were underway and rightly considered.

Chapter 4

The Vegetation

"Welcome to the jungle, we've got fun and games."

- Axl Rose (*Guns 'N Roses*)

The Salad Bars...

Although I had ruminated at the salad bars for years, I had no idea what was required to stock and maintain them. I guess I assumed they were just large, fast-growing gardens that were sustainable despite the constant grazing by people who were determined to get their monies' worth and justify the cost of their prime rib. I was clearly wrong. There were people needed to refill them and these people were labeled "salad boys," which was not a sexist term because during my three-year watch over the salad bars only one girl had worked with us (albeit briefly), and she was the Vagrant's daughter. Therefore, for all intents and purposes, the salad bars were the domain of boys, and any young girls who worked at Trader's did so as bussers, although they were called "desk helps." Rarely was there any cross over between the two positions, which was a shame because some of the desk helps were quite cute and occasionally made tips (which was never a privilege extended to the salad boys) if the domineering hostess believed it was warranted. So the little desk helps sat perched near the hostess stand folding red linen napkins, glancing around for tables to clean and set, and gossiping about the salad boys. The salad boys, on the other hand, had the times of their pubescent lives and created their own social order without the supervision of any adults, as if they were living on an island like in *Lord of the Flies*.

The salad boys' only real mandate was to stock the two salad bars, one of which was in the original, darker dining room (which we termed the "Death Star"), and the other one being adjacent to the newer, lighter dining room (which we called "Planet Hoth"). They were required to do nothing else. They didn't run errands for the hostess, or help the bartender stock the bar, or clean and any tables, or help the waiters run food, or have to kiss any ass whatsoever. It was as though they were members of a very powerful union that carefully outlined their job description and were told to never deviate from it. It seemed nice and simple. That's not to say, however, that stocking two World Class salad bars was a walk in the park. On the contrary, the customers expected a great deal from their salad bar experience and the boys had to deliver in the face of many obstacles, but the pressures of perfection always took a back seat to having a good laugh, often at the expense of certain deserving targets. This continual baboonery would occasionally merit some harsh chastising by the night manager, but salad boys were never fired for bad behavior or poor performance. It was as if, once on the schedule, the salad boy achieved tenure and were impossible to get rid of, which is analogous to those lazy curmudgeons in the university system who call themselves professors. This job security allowed the salad boys to be cheeky little shits and live to tell about it.

The Initiation Ritual...

I don't remember much about my first shift as a salad boy. I was suddenly cast into a world that I was familiar with only as an outsider looking in; like a kid running away to join the circus based solely on what he saw while in his seat, with his Mom, under the big tent. I found myself behind the scenes in a big way and no one was there to hold my hand, which was fine because I was fourteen and needed my right hand for other dubious deeds. Fortunately, that first shift was an orientation and I wasn't expected to do any salad bar related work, because my head was wildly spinning from all the introductions, the tour of the kitchen, the job description, the quick lessons on bread, cheese, and fruit cutting, the low-down on who were friends and foes, the gossip on who was shagging whom, the etiquette on how to obtain a Shirley Temple virgin cocktail, and the endless stories from the veteran salad boys meant to impress me. Wow. Clearly, I had much to learn aside from simply stuffing crudités into ceramic crocks before I was accepted into the salad boy fraternity. That much I knew. What I didn't know was that the "initiation" was being planned and fast approaching.

When I was officially added to the schedule after that first shift, I joined four other salad lads: "Marcel," who was a tall, *Dungeons and Dragons* playing type, and the Vagrant's eldest son; "Todd," who was an acne-riddled chronic masturbator and best friend of Marcel; "Keith," Medusa's eldest son, who was a perfect hybrid between Michael J. Fox and Christian Slater, but with a stutter and bigger ears; and "Len," who was the eldest of us all and apparently the most celebrated salad boy who ever lived according to *The Bible*, *The Torah*, and ancient Hindu scripture. Len was a legend in his own eyes and those of his loyal admirers. "Len this, Len that, blah, blah, blah" was all I ever heard. I can't remember who his connection was to initially become a salad boy, but looking back, he now reminds me of the title character in *King Rat*, which is a story about an undistinguished American soldier caught in an atrocious P.O.W. camp during World War II. The King, as he was nicknamed, was a nobody before he got captured, but became the most powerful man in the camp because of his ability to bullshit, network, and prosper from the black market. Basically, the crux of the story was that the King didn't want the Allies to liberate the camp from the Japanese because he had attained such status and couldn't bear the thought of becoming a nobody again. This was the case with Len (and Medusa too): Trader's Inn was their little P.O.W. camp where they ruled the roost and prospered at the expense of those around them.

It was a Friday night, and Len and Marcel tepidly welcomed me to my second shift. Normally, there were only two salad boys working the busy nights (Fridays and Saturdays) and only one working the other nights, but because I was the rookie, I was meant to shadow the veterans and learn the ropes. I had dressed in some smashing preppie attire: purple button-down oxford, khakis with a braided leather belt, and Top-siders with plaid socks. I didn't realize that clothes of this caliber were inappropriate for handling food in a fast-paced environment for six hours, as they became an instant magnet for all grease-based food products that fateful night. As such, it was the last time that I dressed to impress as a salad boy, which was fine because we didn't have an official dress code (ah, that wonderful union again). The only dress code stipulations, and these certainly weren't rigidly enforced, were no blatantly ripped jeans or open toed sandals. As a result, the salad boy had evolved into the most casually dressed employee in the restaurant, which contributed to management's reluctance to have us in the public eye. This was just fine with us, and our labor union, because less time spent in the public eye meant more time spent in the far reaches of the restaurant, exploring and pissing ourselves laughing.

All was going pretty well as my second shift progressed. I was learning where most things were and was being treated with due respect and consideration, because everyone knew my direct connection to Medusa. But this didn't afford me any special status within the fraternity, because the one thing that all salad boys had in common was that they were all related to someone powerful within Trader's, or were a buddy of someone who was. This was one of the main reasons why salad boys were never fired. It was a classic case of nepotism. Another reason was that although we were low "men" within the restaurant hierarchy (inexperienced pubescents making minimum wage), we were in charge of orchestrating the mighty salad bar sonata, which was an integral part of Trader's success. Therefore, management didn't want to mess with a good thing by rocking the boat. Consequently, we had more lives than a black cat on Halloween.

So as eleven o'clock approached, we started our closing duties, which involved dumping the garbage. The dumpster was behind the restaurant at the end of the loading dock, which was up against the rear kitchen door. In order to dump the garbage then, one had to walk out the rear door, down the loading dock (which was about seven feet above the asphalt and about ten feet in length) and heave the garbage bag into the dumpster, which was level with the end of the dock. Naturally, I was the one hauling the garbage while Len and Marcel were on the loading dock behind me making sure that I had the mental and physical abilities to launch forty pounds of garbage into the night. I remember thinking it strange that these two insisted on walking so close behind me, which caused an image of some wayfaring captive walking the length of a pirate's plank to his death to flitter across my cerebrum. Well, as Spiderman would say, my spider senses were tingling as I hurled the garbage bag and instantly felt two pairs of hands on my back trying to propel me into the dumpster. Apparently this was the time-honored salad boy initiation ritual: pushing a comrade into the abyss of stench. Well, luckily I had four advantages in my favor that prevented me from swimming in Trader's Inn detritus: (1) I had played sports my entire life and was not oblivious to the possibility of an initiation, especially when the team is lead by a punk like Len; (2) from playing sports, my reflexes and agility were certainly above average; (3) the dumpster was fairly full with refuse that night, which was largely contained in plastic garbage bags; and (4) I was wearing my finest preppie gear, and was absolutely determined not to ruin those glorious garments. Consequently, with my sympathetic nervous system in high gear, I managed to keep my feet under me as I hurtled through the air, and was able to land in the dumpster standing upright. After a moment's hesitation to find solid footing, I then sprang out of the dumpster, a la Jackie Chan, and landed on the asphalt about seven feet below. For an instant I felt like a lithe jungle cat and hissed for effect. Len and Marcel were astounded by my performance, as I was the first salad boy to emerge from his second shift unsoiled and smelling of Drakar Noir, as opposed to stinky rubbish. Unfortunately, it wasn't until I was safely on the train home that I discovered a small collection of slimy fish eyes within my jacket pocket (which must have been carved from the discarded heads of the nightly fish special and covertly placed in my jacket as a back-up initiation). Those sneaky, cagey bastards, I thought, as I admired their moxie. Regardless of the slimy orbs covered in pocket lint, though, that night was a small victory and it marked the last time that initiation ritual was ever attempted, because I was running the show the next time a salad boy was hired and I opted for less pedestrian tactics.

A Real Crock of Crudités...

Not too long after I began, Len turned eighteen and made his bid to become a waiter. In most other restaurants, an eighteen-year-old wanting to become a waiter would not be a major issue, but at Trader's it was almost unprecedented. For starters, Trader's was a very popular restaurant that could pick and choose the cream of the waitering crop because there was so much plunder to be had, at least in the early years. For example, in the late '70s, servers were consistently walking home with $200 or more per day in tips. That equates to over $50,000 per year virtually tax free because servers, then as now, claimed a very small percentage of their tips on their tax returns. So while in total defraud mode, a full time Trader's server in the '70s would have made about $5,000 a year in wage and claimed about ten percent of his/her wage in tips, which would have equaled $500. The tax return would have read $5,500 in income for that year. In reality though, that server would have made $5,000 in wage plus $45,000 in tips, or about $50,000 for the year. Not bad for the late '70s when you consider a deluxe Custom van with an eight-track player and shag carpet was a mere $6,000. Waiters of that era were living high in more ways than one and competition was fierce to get aboard the Trader's Inn gravy train.

As the '80s gained momentum, though, a recession gripped the region and dramatically reduced the gluttony that occurred at Trader's. People were not so willing to frequent a restaurant of Trader's caliber and reputation for excessiveness. Instead, frugality and moderation became the mantra of the day. Naturally, the servers at Trader's made less money, but stayed on for the most part probably hoping for a reversal in fortune. This never really occurred because as the economy picked up, the number and types of restaurants substantially increased. People in the city suddenly had many more dining options, which they exercised, much to Trader's detriment. Still, it remained a decent place for a server to make a living, but it held on to the rather undeserved reputation as one of the top gratuity-making restaurants in the city. Consequently, Trader's attracted servers who were generally more aged and experienced, with many ending up working there for ten or more years. The age of the servers ranged from about twenty-four to forty-two, although most were between their late twenties and mid-thirties. It was quite a grizzled jungle community.

As one can imagine then, the atmosphere was not conducive to allowing a young hot shot to flourish and, as a result, Len had a tougher time than he foresaw cracking the waitering squad. In essence, there wasn't much room on the schedule for him as none of the alpha-male waiters would relinquish any busy shifts, and he tried too hard to fit in, and the kitchen didn't like him, and he couldn't master the semi-formal waitering approach. He was simply doomed in his new environment, much like his literary counterpart, "King Rat", was. This was all very tragic, but what can you expect when an adolescent gazelle wants to play with the lions? A bloody, mid-day carnage, that's what.

I didn't take too much pleasure in Len's deconstruction because he had grown on me over the previous months. He was basically a good guy at heart, but acted and looked like a "Rico Suave." He had poker straight, dirty blonde hair that he bisected with a center part and tried to feather back with very little success, much like his idol, Tom Petty. He wore metal framed, oversized aviator eye glasses with a bit of a tint to the lenses. He loved to wear light colored dress shirts with ridiculously low thread counts, unbuttoned far too low in order to display a flimsy ten karat gold chain that lay against his hairless chest, speckled with pimples. He drove an older Monte Carlo that was amateurishly detailed. He dealt low-end drugs like pot and hash, and sold car audio equipment that was obviously stolen. He would illegally record music onto blank cassettes for $5, which I indulged in and thoroughly enjoyed on my Sony Walkman; he had a way of mixing *Martha and the Muffins* with *The Police* that sounded just right. In fact, he was usually the D.J. at his high school parties, which I wasn't invited to because I was in grade nine and far too preppie for his crowd. But, Len was OK and, in the final analysis, probably deserved a better fate. He struggled as a waiter for a little while, then got a job selling home electronics, if memory serves, and fled the restaurant jungle altogether. In short, King Len was liberated from the Trader's Inn camp, and found that he was no longer everyone's hero.

Shortly after Len left the salad boy fraternity, Marcel followed suit. I can't remember the reason, but no one was especially sad to see him go. He wasn't a whole lot of fun and you never knew if he was writing secret reports to the Vagrant, such as, "Salad boy Number Two stuffed fourteen grapes into his mouth while in the cooler, then sucked back a Shirley Temple while loitering in the basement. This kid is a damned, dog fucking preppie! Suffering Jesus, Dad, do something! Over and out." Well, we didn't need our activities or sexual preferences reported back to the higher powers, so we said, "Be well" to Marcel and bid him a tearless goodbye. That left Keith, Todd and myself to keep watch over the salad bars, which we did with uncommon flair.

Before I arrived on the scene, the salad bars were adequately stocked by the likes of Len et al, but no one seemed to take much pride in their work. They made sure nothing became too depleted and that things looked reasonably fresh, but that was about it. When I first had time to ponder the situation, my initial instinct was to stock the hell out of the salad bars for two simple reasons. First, having all the colorful veggies piled inches above the rims of all the crocks, and the creamy salads mounded and sculpted, and the fresh fruit trays creatively designed and heaping, looked absolutely amazing. It was a true symphony of colors and textures that could captivate the most obtuse of people. Servers and hostesses who worked at Trader's for ages and had walked by the salad bars thousands of times before would suddenly stop after we were finished stocking them and say, "Wow!" That's why I can understand the attraction to cooking. There is a deep pleasure derived from working with food and creating something that is able to dazzle all the senses, not just the taste buds. But the more important reason was that cramming all the resources we had at our disposal into the salad bars meant that they could withstand the hordes of locusts that continually assaulted them for longer periods of time. This meant that we could engage in baboonery and slothfulness until we were weak in the knees and giddy from it. Thus begot the era of the super stocked salad bars.

That first summer at Trader's, before grade ten, was glorious. I was working three or four times a week and looked forward to the Friday and Saturday shifts because there would be two of us scheduled. One guy would work from five to ten at night, the other from six to eleven; so there would be at least four hours of riotous overlap. Once the second guy got there at six, we would flip a coin to decide who would work the Death Star's salad bar and who would work Planet Hoth's. The dark side was preferred because it serviced only the one dining room, and you could access it from all four sides. It was simply less work. In fact, you could tell who had which salad bar at the end of the night merely by the number of empty Shirley Temple glasses above the prep area: the dark sided salad boy's consumption rate would be at least twice that of the other salad boy. On the other side of the restaurant complex, the better illuminated salad bar fed two dining rooms: Planet Hoth and the other dark dining room above the nightclub. In addition, the salad bar was a little smaller and accessible only from one side. As such, it was much more work and hassle. Upon winning the coin toss then, the victorious salad boy could never quite contain his elation and would often imitate the chimpanzee's routine of unbridled pant hoots with prodigious chest puffing and lip smacking. He would then amble off towards the dark side and prepare himself for a night of leisurely work and mass consumption of virgin cocktails.

Our prep area was in the kitchen, but our domain was either around the salad bars or in the basement fooling around. Therefore, we were a mongrel breed, an abomination: half front-house staff and half back-house staff. It was as if a horse had inseminated a donkey and out we came; we were like the mules of the animal kingdom, produced from an unnatural coupling, incapable of sustaining our subspecies due to infertility. We had no right to exist according to Darwinian Laws of Natural Selection. Yet we not only existed, we absolutely flourished. We would lurch around the restaurant, having to defend our unsightly appearance by quoting *Elephant Man's* John Merrick: "I am not an animal, I am a ... salad boy." It was a cruel existence, but it was our fate and calling. I just hope that freaky "King of Pop" isn't interested in our skeletal remains.

Our prep area was crammed in between massive fume hoods and a tiled wall that housed a multitude of kitchen gadgetry on metal scaffolding. Two human bodies could not pass one another in our work area without turning their shoulders. We had a 2x6 foot rectangular wood cutting counter in there and had access to two knives that were sometimes the sharpness of fifteenth century samurai swords, and other times about as sharp as garden hoses. To test their sharpness we would tap the blade on the edge of the wood counter; if it sank a couple of inches into the hard wood then we were screwed because bloodshed could be expected at some stage of the night, but if the knife literally bounced off the wood we were still screwed because we would be futilely hacking at everything like Paul Bunyan and be paralyzed with hand cramps by the end of the night.

We spent about half our time in the prep area, cutting things, eating things, drinking things, and trying to look busy. It was the safest place to be if the salad bars didn't need any attention. Of course, "needing attention" was a subjective assessment. It didn't matter if the entire restaurant was astounded by the quality, quantity, and cleanliness of the salad bars, our night manager would notice something and whip himself into a frenzy over it. We called him "Mussolini" as he was a full-blooded Italian and second in command, under Medusa. He was on the shorter side, balding at the crown of his head, perpetually tanned, quite hairy (especially on his upper back), and fairly svelte. He always wore a dark suit, a ring on his left pinky, and a meticulously maintained moustache. He so rarely uttered words of encouragement to us that when we heard something that could have been interpreted as positive, we naturally assumed it to be sarcastic. In all honesty, he was the biggest, most relentless fucking ball breaker that I had ever come across. He would get in your face, curse you, then stare you down, or he would yell and threaten your job in front of other staff, or he would just stand there in total disbelief that such a dog fucker was ever hired and slowly shake his head in amazement while the veins in his temples pulsated. We all despised him for the tyrant that he was and for hampering our good time. He scared us too, because he would often complain to Medusa and bring her up from the basement offices to lecture us about something petty. We knew it was irrational, but we sometimes feared for our jobs, and these were jobs we didn't want to lose.

Mussolini would ride other people's asses occasionally too, but we were his favorite whipping boys because we could be found quickly if he felt a tirade coming on, and we were too young to protest his inhumane tactics. But being the age that we were, we would still get the giggles if two of us were stuck in the prep area getting shit on. Often he would be standing at one end of the prep area yelling at us or pleading, "Come on guys for Christ sake, this isn't a fucking Club Med. If you two can't get your asses in high gear I'll have to find others that can.

That salad bar is a disaster, guys! I mean we're nearly out of potato salad for God's sake!" while the two of us would be standing absolutely still, looking down at the counter trying to drown out his frenzy. All it would take was Keith to slowly take his hand off his bread knife and almost imperceptibly start to raise his middle finger in quiet protest to start us quivering with concealed laughter. We would be squinting our eyes, flaring our nostrils, blowing air out of our noses, clenching our abdominals, biting our lips, anything to keep from exploding with gales of laughter. It was all we could do to find something to slice in order to get our mind off the hilarity of the situation. We sometimes had to resort to pneumonia-like fits of coughing to disguise the chortles and giggles that were rising up and out of us. Mussolini would then mercifully storm off, leaving us to collapse onto the floor, dry heaving and gasping for air. This brings us to our first managerial tip:

****

MANAGERIAL TIP #1: Do not take on the role of the ranting asshole as your managerial style. A manager's position in a restaurant is just not that important in the grand scheme of things and will most likely end in disgrace or disaster any way. Therefore, treat your staff with respect, even the young ones, because some of them will become important people in society and otherwise think of you as that ranting, no-good asshole. Consequently, these important people will not hire you or befriend you in the future, and in fact may actually seek revenge against you for all the times you shit on them, which I would strongly encourage them to do if any are reading this.

****

Keith and I could find something humorous at the Pope's funeral, that's just the effect we had on each other. We did have a history outside of Trader's, though, because Keith was Medusa's eldest son. As such, we played together as infants, but he later went to live with his Dad and we lost touch. The Trader's Inn salad bar essentially reunited us, but proved to be our only connection as we lived in different neighborhoods and attended different schools. But every Friday and Saturday we would pick up like we hadn't missed a beat and proceed to have a blast. He was senior to me at Trader's by a handful of months, and thus was in a position to show me the ropes when I first arrived. When I think back on Keith, I always envision him chewing on some lettuce, a stalk of celery, or cube of cheese, which I think helped him conceal his stutter. Not being able to get the words out could always be blamed on a mouth full of food, which was a convenient excuse and one that helped him save face. That was fine, and we let him get away with it because he was a decent kid. He didn't really have a nickname back then, though, which strikes me as strange now, because anyone who had ears like Keith's and nibbled on as much shit as he did should have been called "the Rabbit." I'm amazed we missed such an obvious moniker, so for the sake of this chapter he will henceforth be referred to as said creature.

One of the first orders of business that the Rabbit imparted to me was how to obtain a Shirley Temple from the bartenders. We all loved this sweet nectar of the gods and needed a couple per night just to function. The sacred ingredients were 7-Up, a juice mixture (containing at least some orange juice and bar lime), a splash of grenadine, then topped with a carcinogenic maraschino cherry. What a gorgeous drink, especially to a fourteen-year-old's sugar craving palate. I was introduced to this liquid ambrosia when I first visited Disneyland as a five year old, and I was immediately hooked. California always seemed to have weird and wonderful things to offer when I was young (like Mint Juleps and "silver dollar" pancakes), but the Shirley Temple was perhaps its greatest export. The problem at Trader's, though, was that a "Shirley" took a little longer to make and cost the bar more in terms of product. Consequently, the bartenders could be a little uncooperative when asked to make one. The Rabbit explained that before one could boldly ask for a Shirley, one had to perform a physical task for the bartender that, thankfully, was of a nonsexual nature (although I would have accepted the role of "devoted catamite" to get a Shirley some nights). The most common task was to haul cases of beer up from the basement and load them into the small coolers behind the bar. This afforded us the privilege to request the Shirleys. The best way to approach the bartender was during a slower period obviously, but common sense was not always so common. Then once at the wood, the most agreeable, least offensive query seemed to be, "Er, sorry to bother you there, big guy, but could I trouble you for a shout of Shirleys?" A simple enough question, but it was successful for three reasons: (1) it was submissive without being sniveling; (2) the term "big guy" suggested that he was our hero and was a formidable foe if messed with; and (3) the term "shout" is Australian slang for a round of drinks, which we used to conjure up the glorious memories of their travels in "Oz," as nearly all the bartenders had been there or were planning to go. It worked as smooth as silk. Hey, we salad boys could be deceptively clever and calculating when we had to be.

I was a tad nervous the first time I embarked on a "Shirley Run." My mission was to bring back two tall Shirleys without being spotted by Mussolini, and then hide them above the prep area behind boxes of crackers. If Mussolini found the Shirleys he would invariably pour them out (oh, the horror of witnessing that), then lecture us on inflated bar costs as his superficial temporal veins threatened to burst from his skull. But we just didn't care, it was worth the risk. So I set out for the bar as stealthful as I could be, armed with the "query" and some light small talk. The Rabbit had suggested that I approach "Spam" the bartender and enquire about his brother's weight lifting ability, which was meant as a light barb because Spam was pudgy and weak. So I arrived at the wood, effectively stated the query, and as he was pouring the Shirleys, I said, "Hey man, so I hear your brother can bench 285." Spam slowly looked up from the fresh Shirleys, leveled his eyes on me, and replied, "My bro is paralyzed from the neck down, you fucking little prick."

"Oh," I croaked through a suddenly dry larynx, needing that damn Shirley more than ever.

"It was a motorcycle accident, two years ago. Now get the fuck away from my bar, dick wad," he barked, showing some froth at the corners of his mouth.

I turned away from this scene of humiliation, completely mute, and skulked back to the prep area empty handed, feeling like a large, musty sack of shite. As I approached, the Rabbit could see my ashen face and was instantly doubled over with a spasm of laughter, literally banging his palm on the counter trying to intake air. No guffaws bubbled out of me this time as I thought of ways to inflict searing pain on the bastard: a karate chop to the clavicle? a sidekick to the throat? an eye gouge? rat poison? Revenge would be mine either way. Then I noticed someone peering around the fume hood with a mischievous little smirk on his fat, Spam-colored, sweaty face. Ah yes, the sting had been on. The joke was on me and I hated being the butt of jokes. I realized that the chances of Spam having a crippled brother were about as likely as me having a vagina and moonlighting in a traveling freak show as a hermaphrodite. Which is to say, not very likely. As a consolation for being psychologically traumatized, I received two Shirleys with extra toxic cherries, but they tasted pretty bitter going down due to the bile that was lingering in my throat.

When revenge had to be sought, it usually centered on sabotaging the offender's beverage. My favorite retaliation was switching someone's regular Coke with one saturated with black pepper (which had to be added first, then the ice, then the Coke or else too many of the pepper flakes would float to the top and alert the victim) and sticking in a straw filled with Tabasco sauce. That first big slurp, normally meant to quench the thirst and recharge the sugar rush, would pack enough of a kick to bulge eyeballs and trigger the gag reflex. In fact, the retribution got so out of hand at times that we all ended up abandoning the use of straws as a safety precaution, and began marking our beverages so we would know if they were tampered with. The Rabbit, for example, liked to align his drink directly in front of a certain line of grouting between the tiles in the wall. But I knew this and often used it to my advantage when he thought he could mess with me. We didn't usually contaminate any Shirleys with these poisons, though, partially out of divine reverence for them, and partially because they were so difficult to replenish once fouled. However, the Rabbit experimented for a short time by substituting onion juice for 7-Up, thus creating mock Shirleys, but most of us could detect the pungent onion before we indulged in a sip, except for the perpetually congested and ridiculously named "Jonathan McAllister-Haycock."

Jonathan was one of a handful of ephemeral salad boys who came and went without much acclaim under my tutelage as salad bar custodian. He was raised as the only son of a divorced female lawyer, who obviously refused to relinquish her proud Scottish heritage on her doomed wedding day, and in so doing condemned her children to a life of hyphenation and mispronunciation. He really was a well-mannered, articulate little toad, but hopelessly anal retentive, naive, and continually battling impaired sinuses. As a result, he would unfailingly take us at our word, be unable to detect our overt sarcasm (e.g., "Here you are Jonathan, my good man, I thought you might enjoy a lovely Shirley. Hope it's not too tart there, old boy, better take a big swig just to be sure"), and be too stuffed up to detect any foul play. The Rabbit was the first villain to offer Jonathan a tainted Shirley, and to our surprise, he gratefully accepted it. He must have drunk half of it over the course of five minutes before he started to appear a little green around the gills. Keep in mind; he was drinking onion juice (which was liberated from the sliced onions and oranges at the salad bar) with bar lime, some orange juice, and a squirt of grenadine. Not a pleasant cocktail to be sure, but Jonathan's congestion must have sabotaged the workings of his taste buds and sense of smell. Well, to make a long story short, he disappeared for a while without a trace, then turned up looking haggard and belching up fumes that smelled more like stomach bile than Spanish onion. Needless to say, he did not accept another gratuitous Shirley from the Rabbit, which was fine with us as we were certainly willing to consume his share.

Shirley Temples were not the only beverage that we consumed while at work. We also had a penchant for virgin Pina Coladas, cherry Cokes (cola with grenadine generously added), and the occasional beer. All were considered contraband by Mussolini, naturally, but we pushed the envelope and refused to settle for regular soda pop. Unlimited soda pop would have certainly satisfied most kids, but we were very discerning when it came to our fluid intake. Of course, the consumption of beer was the most precarious thing we could do as salad boys. We were clearly underage and it was clearly theft, two excellent reasons to fire us if caught, but we never were. We had coded terminology to veil all our dangerous missions, which we thought helped our cause. For example, if one of us thought it was time for a shout of Shirleys, we would say, "Surely, you must be rather parched." Or if we fancied a virgin Pina Colada, we would ask, "By the way, how's your penis doing?" But, if we were feeling especially daring, or we were going out after work and needed a little liquid courage (which was more common when we were seventeen), we would ask, "Did Harmon Killebrew go yard last night?" Harmon Killebrew was a ball player who was known for his home run hitting ability, and his name phonetically was "kill a brew," which is slang for, "to drink a beer." Needless to say, we thought we were quite clever with all the double talk and cloak and dagger stuff.

Harmon Killebrew only entered the conversation once the salad bars were well stocked, which afforded us the fifteen minutes or so we needed to escape to the basement and pound back a warm beer. Trader's basement was huge and contained the washrooms, the Vagrant's office, Medusa's office, a cash-out area, the prime rib coolers, a bakery, dry storage, and beer storage. One of us would head down there under the pretence of getting some chick peas or something from dry storage, while the other would go down a different set of stairs, concerned with some other vital aspect of salad boy business, and we would congregate in the middle, amongst the verboten long necks, stubbies, and silver bullets. I didn't even like beer, especially the tepid variety, but that was far from the point. We would each select a can of beer that was as close to five percent alcohol as possible, raise our mini flagons in a toast to getting laid before high school graduation, then gulp as hard as we could while testing our throat's capacity to sustain carbonation burns. I often couldn't tolerate the pain, either in my throat, or my stomach from the assault of the expanding suds. In fact, I don't believe I ever successfully pounded an entire beer using that method, although we learned another method that reduced the amount of time one had to suffer. It involved poking a hole near the bottom of the can (with a pen, usually), putting our lips over the opening, and then quickly pulling the tab while holding on for dear life. Apparently this latter method was based on some pressure gradient/gravity principle, because the beer would absolutely explode out of the can and straight down one's esophagus. It was like trying to drink from a fire hose. To survive the ordeal, you had to abandon any attempt at swallowing and just open your throat and let the warm beer scream down it. The first time I accomplished this feat my stomach felt like it was in labor, and in a way it was, because I gave birth to a burp so big I saw the Rabbit's hair flutter from the turbulence. Then came the afterbirth, in the form of some regurgitated beer that I expelled onto some boxes with a retching cough. It was a sweet victory at last. And while we were never actually severely drunkened by this diversion, it always seemed to make the shift pass just a little quicker. After we finished the beer birthing, we carefully disposed of the empty cans and scurried back upstairs, continuing the charade as salad boys, but feeling much more like men.

Aside from the prep area, we spent the next largest chunk of our time either at the salad bars restocking, or in the cooler refilling the buckets since much of our work was essentially transferring the pre-cut crudités and pre-made salads from the walk-in cooler to the salad bars. We did this by scooping said items out of their bins and into old plastic buckets, which we stacked onto metal carts and wheeled out to the salad bars as the crocks became depleted. The cooler was a fun place to hang out and served as our private consultation room. Once that heavy metal door closed we were free to discuss a variety of sensitive topics, vent our rage by screaming foul obscenities, conduct grape eating contests, and deal drugs to the waiters (as was Len's business). But it was also the first place Mussolini looked for us if he had to purge a tirade, so we had to always pretend to be doing something legitimate because we had no warning if he was about to enter the cooler. On more than one occasion I had to suddenly swallow a mouthful of grapes as Mussolini rattled the cooler's door, which felt like swallowing a Mike Tyson fist (albeit without the ear nibbling) every single time.

Our only direct dealings with the public was when we had to wheel the metal carts, laden with teetering columns of plastic buckets, out to the salad bars to restock them. We would emerge from the kitchen looking much like homeless people, I suspect, by pushing our carts and dressing the way we did. My favorite top was a bright yellow T-shirt from a bar in Whitefish, Montana. On the back, in lettering that would have been visible from a great many feet, it proclaimed, "Boogie till ya puke." No one seemed too offended by this, management or otherwise, but it seems rather inappropriate now, because not only was I advertising the merits of another eating establishment, but I was summoning visions of regurgitation, which can't be very savory while trying to digest your dinner. Oh well, salad boys weren't responsible for cleaning up body fluids anyway, so I would have been oblivious to any of the shirt's ill effects.

Once at the salad bar, it was a struggle to fill the crocks because the customers always seemed to be in some catatonic state induced by the task of having to mound as much cellulose on their plates as gravity would allow. Building an Eiffel Tower out of croutons and celery would have required less consideration. As such, the customers would invariably start with a small edifice of lettuce on their plates, which was a mistake because it was the least valuable item, but occupied the most space. As they progressed down the trough and encountered hardier, more valuable foodstuffs, their faux pas would usually become evident. The dilemma going through their flustered minds must have been along the lines of, "Hmm, I'm paying $21 for my meal, but I've wasted half the space on this damn salad plate with worthless lettuce that I can't put back. Jesus, Mary and Joseph, I must find some room for the cheese and fruit in order to bloody well justify my expenditure." Of course the simple solutions would have been to grab two plates worth of food, or make a second trip back to the salad bar. But no, social pressure often won out over practicality. It seemed that the stigma attached to making a second trip back to the salad bar would have been far too much to bear, and the coordination of filling two plates simultaneously would have obviously required unearthly dexterity. Consequently, neither strategy was hardly ever employed. Instead, people shuffled along the length of the salad bar clutching on to their plates, which supported a collection of crudités that resembled the leaning Tower of Pisa, nearly spellbound in concentration. Needless to say, communicating our intentions to these zombies was challenging. After all, we were there to fill their precious salad bar with fresh stock, which should have garnered looks of appreciation and words of praise, but instead we got looks that queried, "Who are you, feral boy, and why are you wearing that wretched yellow T-shirt while trying to butt in front of me?" We felt like responding, "Madam, we are cherubs who have descended from the heavens in eager support of your rampant gluttony, hoping to expedite your passing from this Earth. Please indulge in our gifts copiously so we can soon claim your bloated carcass." Instead, we tried to squeeze in between them and replenish what we could without being cheeky or caustic, but some nights we couldn't keep pace with the unbridled feasting or handle the outright stupidity. The salad bars were just too big to be tamed at times.

At the height of their grandeur, the salad bars contained as much biodiversity as some small rain forests. These included: carrots, cauliflower, sliced tomatoes, celery, radishes, broccoli, beets, chick peas, baby corn, alfalfa sprouts, grated carrot slaw with raisins (!?), bean salad, potato salad, ambrosia salad, rotini salad, macaroni salad, onion slices with oranges (!!?), coleslaw, cottage cheese, spiced crab apples, pieces of cactus (!!!?), sliced ham, processed cheese, croutons, bacon bits, various buns, slices of French, Rye, whole wheat, raisin, and Pumpernickel bread, cubes of Gouda, Swiss, and Cheddar cheese, grated Parmesan cheese, steak soup, French onion soup, Portuguese bean and sausage soup, cantaloupe, honeydew melon, watermelon, green and red grapes, strawberries, pineapple, and tossed lettuce with your choice of French, Italian, Roquefort, or Ranch dressing. It was a beast to be sure, but it certainly didn't rob us of all our energy or time. Our mottos while at work were, "Clean minds or clean bodies, take your pick" and "All work and no play makes for dull salad boys," consequently, "job stress" was a totally foreign concept to us.

Once the salad bars were stocked and Mussolini was considered safely preoccupied, we set out to accomplish buffoonery in some distant biome of the jungle. The basement was a common destination because of its lack of habitation and vastness, which were probably the same qualities that enticed the French to send their convicts to the jungles of South America originally, and this simile was not lost on us as we disappeared below ground each night. Of course we were hooligans more so than convicts, and we chose to explore the basement as opposed to being condemned to die there, but I like the imagery of two salad boys wondering the jungle in search of adventure, so the simile shall remain. Regardless, the basement housed the sacred offices, which were vacant for long stretches of time. Luckily, the Rabbit managed to find out the door code to the manager's offices, so we often just walked in and made ourselves at home. Once inside the cramped entrance, Medusa's desk was immediately in front of us, which wasn't a familiar sight to most employees because one was only summoned there to be fired or shit on, and if it was the latter then you vowed never to return. Overall, it was a nondescript little space and not much fun (although we enjoyed assaulting her chair with absolutely noxious farts), so we would turn to the left and enter the Vagrant's office. His domain was the size of a small apartment and contained many of the same amenities. There was a well stocked bar that housed a fridge and sink, a chesterfield or two, some eclectic art work, a private washroom, and an awesome saltwater fish tank that was built into the wall. The Rabbit and I would lounge on a plush chesterfield, stare at the impossibly thin tropical fish drifting in the tank, and dream of someday becoming rich bastards like the Vagrant. What type of cars would we drive? Porsches naturally, after being told there was "no substitute" by Tom Cruise in *Risky Business*. How big would our houses be? Big enough to contain indoor tennis courts so we could play tennis or ball hockey year round. How attractive would our wives be? On par with Farah Fawcett because she was the hottest of the group on *Charlie's Angels*. Would they have sex with us? Not if we didn't get some experience soon, we lamented. These were the profound thoughts that were dancing within the minds of us all, and we certainly believed we could eventually top the Vagrant in all areas (at least his retched wife and that Wagoneer were easily improved upon), although none of us have yet managed to obtain anything nearly as sublime as that saltwater tank.

  Another pastime that was performed in the basement was hauling up boxes of prime rib from the meat coolers each week. Again, this was not mandatory, but we did it for a handsome payoff. The reward in this case was a prime rib dinner that could be eaten and savored after our shifts ended. We would get a one-inch cut of prime rib, a baked potato, and some garlic toast in exchange for about ten minutes of backbreaking work. Very fair remuneration in my opinion at the time, as the fear of chronic low back pain was still a few decades away. The only catch was that it was a one-man job, which commanded only a single prime rib dinner. Consequently, the coin toss for this hearty treasure became very serious, as you can imagine. So serious, in fact, it caused treachery to flourish within the salad boy ranks. Originally, the prime rib was carried up on either a Friday or Saturday night, meaning that the two scheduled salad boys would be vying for the job. The Rabbit, however, began convincing the kitchen that it would not be too deleterious to bring the prime rib up on a Thursday night, which he (not coincidentally) worked all by himself. I could picture the Rabbit finally nibbling on something with caloric value, looking like he was a rather large eared hyena scavenging the remains of another creature's kill. It took the rest of the fraternity a couple of months to catch on to his little scheme, but I had to applaud his resourcefulness and desire to be carnivorous. In the end, our little feud was settled amicably by the cooler heads of the kitchen staff, who were all Chinese and much wiser than us.

The People's Republic of Trader's Kitchen...

When I first set foot in Trader's kitchen (sometime before I actually became a salad boy), I was surprised to find that the entire staff was of Chinese ancestry. This seemed incongruous because Trader's was the prototypical "meat and potatoes" restaurant and, at that time, had nothing on the menu that even faintly resembled Asian cuisine. I am not claiming that Asians are incapable of cooking North American fare (far from it), but it's intriguing how they came to reside at Trader's in such force. I suppose I'll never know their migration and settlement patterns, but I do know that having them in the kitchen made for a much richer salad boy experience. Their patriarch was the kitchen manager, "Barry," who was a gentle, patient, exacting man somewhere between forty and one hundred years of age. He considered himself a direct disciple of Confucius, I assume, because he was always offering us his philosophies, codes of conduct, and suggestions on how to be less wasteful in the kitchen. This is a man who would roll up his kitchen whites and stick his entire arm into a steaming heap of kitchen garbage to pull out a piece of cantaloupe rind that had a skiff of edible fruit on it, then slowly shake his head while walking over to our prep area to say something like, "Boy, boy, this no good heh. See, too much here, too much. You cut better with sharp knife, this way now heh," and then proceed to show us some intricate method of cutting a melon (no doubt learned in the hills of Guilin during the Japanese occupation when one melon had to be shared between three villages, a pack of wild dogs, and a small herd of Mongolian horses) that left behind rinds that wouldn't have interested a sewer full of starving rats. Needless to say, Barry was frightfully efficient and an absolute stickler for waste, which I believe are qualities present in all Chinese people who were actually born and raised in China. I say this because I've traveled to China since my days at Trader's and witnessed how they live and subsist. These are people who probably originated the entire concept of recycling and display an immense talent for capturing every possible calorie from the Earth's bounty. They will pull things out of the ground to eat that are best classified in the West as either roots, weeds, firewood, or rocks. We don't allow these items to reside in our flowerbeds let alone stomachs.

As an illustration, years later while traveling in China, I fled the safe confines of our hotel in Beijing and insisted on an "authentic" Chinese dinner in some family run restaurant. I ended up receiving pieces of pure pork fat in some sticky brown glaze (embedded with perhaps a few striated fibers of pig muscle), long greens that looked like the tops of green onions but tasted more like corn husks, lightly fried lotus root that was gracious enough not to produce a taste, plain brown rice that was thankfully identified as such, and local beer preserved with trace amounts of formaldehyde that my taste buds had no difficulty affirming. Simply said, it was the worst dining experience of my life as my occipital lobe refused to recognize most of it as being from this planet. In fact, it was even less recognizable to my stomach and bowels, which expedited its evacuation from both ends simultaneously about an hour later. And I have no doubt that we inadvertently fed the owner's family for a week thereafter because we left more than half of our dinner behind. Unfortunately, the Chinese buffets that I was accustomed to in the West were but a distant, cherished memory at that point and were not encountered anywhere in the China that I bore witness to. Oh chicken balls in red sauce, how I missed thee! But more to the point, China was not a place of abundance or extravagance during much (any?) of the twentieth century, and produced people who exhibited certain traits out of absolute necessity, such as frugality, determination, efficiency, and a sense of being part of something more important than oneself. Of course Communism was the driving force behind the shaping of such characteristics, and say what you will about Marxist ideology, but it did create a certain resiliency within its comrades. What other group of people would have marched forty-eight-hundred miles in support of a dumpy little guy named Mao?

Not surprisingly then, aside from Barry, everyone else was considered an equal within Trader's kitchen. There was "Flippy" the grill man, whose job it was to grill filet mignons, top sirloins, and New York steaks. He literally flipped meat with metal tongs for the better part of a decade; they trusted him with nothing else. I heard that after I left he won a partial share in a lottery, then moved to Hong Kong to gamble it all away. There was also "Lou," who cut the slabs of prime rib, plated them, and coordinated them with other food items. In modern terminology, he was the "finish man" and "call man" combined. He was a squat little guy with shaggy black hair and snaggled teeth who would talk trash to you in Cantonese if even slightly provoked. He looked and acted like a grumpy Wildebeest, and remains at Trader's to this day, twenty-six years after he began. There was also little "Rosie," who prepared most of the appetizers, such as escargot and braised shrimp. She would make us the best garlic toast any of us salad boys had ever or will ever consume, but would also spit in your eye if she felt disrespected. And there were about a half dozen other Asian characters who I can't recall the names of, but no one could forget the "Mamas," who were a crew of three women somewhere between sixty and one hundred and forty years of age, who ruled the dish pit with iron fists and wandering hands.

The Mamas were dishwashers who inhabited an 8x10 foot tiled dish pit as if it were their cage. They only ventured out for the collective meal at the very end of the night. Two of them would work in there at a time, moving in a way that zoo animals sometimes do: rhythmic and repetitive, but in a slightly psychotic, cheerless way. And true to my above-mentioned stereotyping, they were efficient, waste conscious, and seemingly tireless. As salad boys, we only had to enter the dish pit and interact with the Mamas about ten times per night, which was a good thing, because they gave us the creeps. It seemed that every time one of us was in the dish pit to collect the clean salad plates and bowls, the Mamas would converge on us like used car salesmen. Now do understand, they were well meaning ladies, but not many teenagers enjoy being stroked by their mothers, let alone old Chinese dishwashers. They would stroke our forearms and our necks with their aged, pruned, clammy dishwasher hands. Our necks for God's sake! Is there no sanctity for a salad boy's body!? And while they were grooming us like horny old primates, they would coo broken English at us. Of course, the Mamas only knew about six English words between them, which meant we would hear the entire gamut of their vocabulary when they issued phrases like, "Ah good boy. Big boy heh, pretty boy son-son," or "Ahh, pretty boy heh. Mama-san best big son." I didn't like it one bit, the stroking or the cooing, but nothing could be done to stop it. We tried to placate them with colas (much like Coca-Cola has done to the entire Third World), which they quickly became over-reliant on, but this just seemed to increase their appreciation and fondness for us. In fact, nothing was more amusing or heartwarming than when we would give them their colas, because they would react like they were being handed a bag of heroin in the middle of the Bangkok International Airport. Their eyes would grow large and they would nervously glance around to see who was monitoring their good fortune, then they would quickly grab the colas and hide them behind some buckets and shoo us out of the dish pit while whispering, "Good son, yes-yes." We didn't mind doing them favors, it was their way of showing thanks that we took issue with.

It wasn't just the Mamas who had a thing for touching us. The entire Chinese kitchen staff thoroughly enjoyed being tactile at our expense. I guess it was just their friendly nature, but next to having my pimples commented on at that age, I liked being touched by the greasy fingers of a stranger least of all. Well, that's not totally accurate because they weren't exactly strangers. In fact, we knew them extremely well in some ways; we knew their favorite sayings, their mannerisms, their temperaments, and their talents and deficiencies within the kitchen. On the other hand, we had no idea what their real names were, or how old they were, or who was married, or who had kids, or where they lived, or what cars they drove, or what their ambitions were, or anything personal whatsoever. It was a strange social dichotomy. And adding to this sense of mystery was the fact that none of us ever saw any of them anywhere in the city other than the kitchen at Trader's Inn. For all we knew, they could have slept in a little room in the basement that had wall-to-wall bunk beds. Maybe they were all Kung Fu celebrities from Hong Kong, or the sole surviving relatives of China's Last Emperor. We really had no clue, which I suppose was partially due to them being private people, and partially due to us not taking more of an interest as kids of that age tend to be fairly self-centered. Once at work, though, we knew as much as we had to know about one another to get by, and this included knowing who was most awe struck by our ability to haul prime rib up from the basement.

Barry and Flippy seemed most impressed by our Caucasian boy-strength. So much so, in fact, that they felt compelled to fondle our biceps and shoulders to make sure they were authentic while we were carrying the boxes of beef. Again, none of us enjoyed these physical transgressions, but these were the people providing us with the coveted prime rib dinner, so we weren't too vocal with our objections. We tried to carry up the beef when Barry and Flippy seemed preoccupied, but I swear they could sense our over-exertions and materialized out of nowhere to witness the spectacle. However, it wasn't as if we were dead-lifting thousands of pounds of meat; on the contrary, the heaviest boxes weighed maybe one hundred pounds, of which we would carry one at a time up the fifteen or so stairs. It just wasn't an Olympic caliber performance. Invariably, though, once at the top of the stairs, Barry would be there to greet us with an approving smile and then proceed to survey the tension within the striated muscles of our upper limbs. He would then offer, "You strong boy heh? You Arnold Schwarzenegger!" which sounded more like "Yoo Ahnod Swasanagah!" then he would laugh and chatter in animated Cantonese (is there any other form?) to everyone in the kitchen, probably saying, "We could have used these precocious, turd-eating grasshoppers back when we had to carry the Emperor on his throne from the Forbidden City to the Southern Provinces. Imagine having such green eyed devils as sons!" Everyone would then look at us in wonder, with little Rosie probably thanking Buddha that she had not birthed such Goliaths, and nod in agreement with Barry's musings.

Well, Goliaths we were not. At that time, I stood five feet, eight inches tall and weighed one hundred and sixty pounds, the Rabbit was five feet seven and weighed one hundred and forty pounds, Todd was even more of a girlie-man than us, and Jonathan never even had the privilege of carrying up the prime rib so his insignificant physical dimensions don't warrant mention (except the disturbing fact that he was hung like the runt of a gerbil's litter). We were clearly not giants by any standards other than theirs, which sometimes proved nourishing for our fragile adolescent egos if you could get beyond the sensation of having greasy fingers clasped tightly to your upper arms for a few minutes each week. I could, and ate a considerable amount of prime rib as a result.

Aside from their stroking, poking, and clasping us at every opportunity, the other habit that stood out as excessive was their gambling. I've never encountered a people more anxious to tempt fate and play the odds. Lou was the bookie for the entire restaurant, and for a guy who looked about as athletic as a Jim Henson Muppet, he could give you odds on the most obscure sporting event. If there were a cricket match between two small villages in northern India, he would know about it and give you the odds and point spread. Incongruently, the N.F.L. seemed to be his specialty, which always attracted wagers from the cocky waiters who considered themselves "weekend warriors" (although "burned-out, hung-over, promiscuous, weekend couch slugs" would have been more accurate). At that time, I couldn't have joined in the gambling fervor even if I had wanted to because I had no idea how to decipher their incomprehensible vernacular. To my rather unsophisticated perspective on wagering, one would choose a favorite team to win, then find someone who unconditionally favored the opposing team and might actually part with the princely sum of $5 in the unlikely event that your team won. But to Lou, gambling translated itself into words like, "I take Raiders by six points, heh? You like? What you say? Ok, Ok, seven points and give two to one odds, heh? Ah good man, you too smart for me son bitch! Same like last time, $200 heh?" Which meant if the Raiders outright lost or only won by six points or less, Lou would lose $400, and this was just one of a dozen bets he would make over the course of a Friday night. Much legal tender would hang in the balance at any given moment, which was remarkable considering Lou's modest salary. Nevertheless, he was convinced that he had to carry a billfold containing well over a $1000 at all times. On more than one occasion we dreamed of him accidentally dropping that billfold near our prep area, which would have allowed one of us lucky bastards to give Mussolini an "atomic wedgy" up the ass, then promptly retire from the crock filling business. Yes, we literally dreamed of this.

Enter Buddy and Renny...

By the time I was in grade eleven, life was pretty grand. I had outgrown one of the worst haircuts to ever besiege the head of an adolescent, my acne epidemic had been officially downgraded to a minor outbreak, I was dating a tall, blonde Slavic knockout, my tennis game was coming along nicely, and I was making enough money from salad boying to keep me in the fashion circle. To be specific, I was making about $180 per month in exchange for working every Friday and Saturday night. That was good money in those days when you consider that most of my friends were receiving a $10 honorarium every week as an allowance. Of course most of my friend's parents were wealthy beyond belief, so $40 a month can go a long way when cars, bikes, insurance, sports equipment, and clothing are all purchased for you carte blanche. My Mom and I, on the other hand, were not members of the aristocracy so we had to be more frugal and that $180 each month allowed me to buy the clothes that I wanted without having to cajole or justify to any great extent. Looking back, the salad bar provided me with quite a bit of financial freedom and most likely eliminated some of the strain that parents are forced to endure in order to keep their kids looking like Beau Brummell wannabes.

Grade eleven was also the year that I solidified some great friendships, and in addition to Matt, I fell in with some mates by the names of "Buddy" and "Renny." Buddy, socioeconomically, was much like myself. He was raised by a single mom on the periphery of a very posh neighborhood. He was a funny, gregarious character, who was a little chunkier than the rest of us and loved to relate grandiose stories and exert his physical dominance whenever possible. I initially became acquainted with Buddy because his girlfriend, "Buffy," was best friends with my girlfriend, the Yugoslavian supermodel. The four of us played tennis a number of times that year and two important events came from it: (1) Buffy and I started dating and became a fairly hot item over the next two and a half years, and (2) despite the brutal cuckolding, Buddy and I became top notch mates which eventually earned him an invite to be the new Trader's Inn salad boy. This was a touchy issue because Matt was next in line to join the salad boy fraternity, but the timing was off and Matt had a job as a busser at another restaurant when the opening at Trader's came about. Needless to say, Buddy was appropriately excited by the offer and left his position as an assistant pizza cook post haste in order to join us.

When Buddy joined us at Trader's it was a fairly momentous event because, next to myself, he was the most competitive bastard I had ever come across. This is a kid who literally wrapped his brand new Prince "Woody" tennis racket around a pole when I beat him in straight sets one afternoon (which wasn't that often) and screamed, "You didn't win, I lost! So fuck it and shut up French fry!" Well, most might not understand the distinction there, but I knew what he meant. He was the sorest of all losers, sometimes making John McEnroe look like John-Boy Walton by comparison. Fortunately for him, he didn't lose that often at anything, mainly because he was so competitive and such a remarkably good natural athlete (especially considering that he had precious little coaching in any sport). But it was this competitive nature of his that blessed us at Trader's because it seemed to push us salad boys to the next level. Thus begot the era of the hyper-stocked, creatively maximized salad bars.

Working with Buddy was, at times, a total panic. He would always try to upstage the salad bar you were restocking, which was often to the direct detriment of your salad bar because there was a limited stock of certain foodstuffs in the restaurant. For example, we were limited to one crate of strawberries per week, which often meant that we would run out by Saturday night under normal circumstances. Well, when Buddy started as a salad boy, one of the salad bars would be barren of all strawberries by Thursday night because he would horde all of them and create a massive fruit tray that wouldn't have looked out of place on Carmen Miranda's head. He had no interest in allowing the other salad boy a chance to offer his customers the entire spectrum of Trader's food stock. If the other salad bar was reduced to stale breadcrumbs and soggy lettuce, while his offered delicacies from around the globe, he wouldn't have thought it at all inequitable. In fact, some nights we had to hide things in the cooler so we could ensure their availability later in the night, or actually steal things from his salad bar so ours didn't look second rate by comparison. Pathetic perhaps, but true. Buddy definitely threw down the gauntlet, which forced us to raise our level of performance, but having to battle Mussolini, the customers, and then ourselves proved to be very fatiguing at times.

  What Buddy lacked in equitable resource distribution, he compensated for by sharing his ample supply of shenanigans, which proved to be pure comedy at times. So in addition to coaxing various virgin cocktails from the bartenders, pounding back warm beer in the basement's storage area, gorging ourselves in the prep area, conducting various experiments in the food cooler, lounging in the Vagrant's office, saturating Medusa's office chair with sulfuric fumes, and exploring the outer limits of the restaurant, we took to tormenting a select group of people whom, we unanimously decided, sincerely deserved it. One such target was "Crash."

  Crash was a waiter who was in his early to mid-twenties at that time. He was slight of build and of average height, with short brown hair that was starting to thin out on the top and recede at the temples. He always wore a black vest over a white shirt and plain black tie, but sabotaged his own attempt at elegance by donning tight black polyester pants that had become blindingly shiny due to an inordinate number of dry cleanings and by lacing up cheap, black running shoes that were encrusted with dish pit sludge. Even more of an indiscretion was his decision to first grow his hair out in the back and fasten it into a tiny nib of a ponytail, but then to cut it short except for a long, wispy piece that became his "tail," which he occasionally braided. As well, his hairy, simian-like body must have been composed entirely of fast twitch muscle fibers because I had never seen anyone who was so jerky in their movements or who had such a cache of nervous energy. So not only did he run around like a savanna baboon in mating season, but he was also a total stress case who was on the verge of an eruption, a melt down, or both at any given moment. It seemed that the basic act of waitering pushed him to his limits, perhaps beyond the point with which his biological or emotional coping mechanisms could tolerate. As evidence, he was always perspiring, his face was always flushed, his speech pattern was usually in warp drive and interlaced with little staccato bursts of laughter, he was prone to episodes of sudden frolic (like whipping our asses with a hot cloth), and then he would slip into states of irrational panic and senselessly argue with the line cooks over the whereabouts of some forgotten order. Looking back, he was clearly manic and quite possibly insane.

Even as salad boys we knew it wasn't just the basic act of waitering that drove Crash to such idiosyncratic behavior, because there were many other waiters who appeared relaxed while on shift as they puffed on their fags and drank coffee laced with Kahlua and/or Sambuca. In fact, our initial impression of waitering was that it was a pretty tolerable way of making decent money and probably less work than stocking the salad bars (we would later refine our notions considerably). But be that as it may, our issue was with Crash's core personality (and that ridiculous braided tail that hung from the nape of his neck as if he were Rapunzel waiting for one of us to ascend it and choke the shit out of him), as he was simply impossible to co-exist with.

For reasons that were unclear at the time, Crash usually worked the dark dining room that was above the nightclub. Consequently, I remember him constantly running up and down those stairs with reckless abandon. He would pile plates of prime rib on his left arm, grab a couple of skillets containing sautéed asparagus or mushrooms with his right hand, and race out of the pass-thru, past our prep area, and disappear up the stairs like a man possessed. Or we would see him skidding down the stairs struggling with a bus pan full of dirty plates careening around other servers toward the dish pit, where he would dump the bus pan and dash off somewhere else. In hindsight, I suppose there would have been less hostility towards Crash if he had been a totally self-contained madman, but he wasn't. He always managed to create hassle and havoc for those around him. For Lou and the kitchen guys it was Crash's poor food timing and abundant forgetfulness; for the Mamas it was the plethora of unloaded bus pans from the upstairs dining room that arrived courtesy of him; for the other servers it was Crash's virtually nonexistent body awareness as he constantly crashed into the front house staff at every intersection (thus, his nickname); and for us salad boys it was a long list of indiscretions that eventually forced us into a retaliatory mind set.

Crash's primary mistake was being condescending to us. Although we were only in our mid-teens, we didn't enjoy being thought of as little worker bees just waiting to complete the latest menial task for the larva spewing Queen (after all, we had our Moms who did a great job of reminding us of our servile roles within the colony). Crash, obviously, was naive to our powerful union that demanded nothing more from us other than baboonery, slothfulness, and generalized canine humping. He didn't quite seem to realize that he had no real leverage on us, other than what he assumed to be superior man-strength and adult intellect. So when he would say things like, "Hey little buddy, come give me a hand running this order, pronto," we were perfectly within our human rights and those outlined by the Geneva Convention to reply, "Hey, my name isn't Gilligan you tail braiding spazz. I can't even see you because I'm blinded by the shine from your pants. And I bet underneath those things you're wearing a pair of pink panties riding so far up your ass that it's created a camel toe. Besides, I'm busy sucking back a Shirley." Now, there aren't many places on this Earth where a sixteen-year-old could get away with such outrageous verbal abuse of a twenty-three-year-old, but Trader's was our bastion of safety. When you consider it, what options did Crash have for retaliation? He couldn't have beaten us up because (1) we were considered helpless adolescents by the rest of the staff, (2) we were related to the higher powers within Trader's, and (3) our collective boy-strengths could have easily neutralized his overrated man-strength. Nor could he have used his superior adult intellect because (1) his frontal lobes were far from superior, and (2) even the most clever of adults cannot compete with adolescents in the fields of name calling and putdowns, because junior & senior high schools are unrelenting training grounds for such skills. So Crash was basically in a no-win situation, but it took a surprisingly long time for him to clue in as he continued to tempt his fate with us. Our collective position was that we preferred to be left alone, but approached with respect and consideration if someone needed our assistance. Crash refused to accommodate even our most basic wishes.

Aside from the verbal abuse, we also ventured into the physical realm with Crash. We all had our favorite gags. For example, I loved to use the old "sign on the back" routine, of which Crash would be oblivious to for hours at a time. Typically, I would walk up to him and say with a lisp, "That's a lovely tail you have, Boy George," then pat him on the back in order to plant some smart-ass sign on him. My favorite sign read, "Pull My Tail and Hear Me Fart." I cannot describe the entertainment value that we received from observing Crash run around the restaurant with such proclamations taped to his back. It was comical beyond belief to our immature minds. Of course, we needed the help of the entire staff to pull the sign caper off, and because Crash irked everyone to such an extent, rarely would anyone let him in on the joke. It was usually a snickering table of his that informed him, and for all I knew he might have made some decent sympathy tips because of it.

Buddy, on the other hand, preferred the old "wet hot cloth on the ass" routine, which was a true classic. He would soak a hot cloth in water, then bunch it up in his hand and seek out Crash. The perfect opportunity was when Crash was occupied at a table or in the pass-thru carrying food, at which time Buddy would walk up behind him and push the drenched hot cloth firmly against his clenched buttocks. And although Crash's polyester pants (that were partially melted from the dry cleaning assaults) were not the most absorbent or porous fabric in the world, enough water would reach his gonch to ensure the formation of a rash by the end of the night. But believe me, a waiter does not need any help expediting the formation of a rash anywhere near his hindquarters as he already must contend with the omnipotent and infamous waiter's ass on a nightly basis.

And finally, the Rabbit preferred planting items in Crash's back pocket, for some bizarre reason. His object of choice was any spoon that had dried up Portuguese bean and sausage soup on it. Yes, strange, but true. The Rabbit would wait until Crash was carrying some plates through the restaurant, then he would slip the spoon into Crash's back pocket, which was a challenge unto itself because Crash wore his pants so tight. Sometimes Crash wouldn't feel the intrusion of the spoon, but most times he would and would have to wait until he dropped off his order before he could remove it. One of the stranger sights at Trader's, at least from the customer's point of view, must have been the night when Crash absolutely snapped and chased the Rabbit through the restaurant while holding the offensive spoon in his hand. Imagine the commotion caused by a waiter furiously running after someone, nearly at top speed, within full view of the customers. Without the knowledge that the Rabbit was a salad boy, the customers must have assumed that Crash was chasing some thief, or rapist, or some other undesirable. Needless to say, there were more than a few startled looks as the chase disappeared into the kitchen and down into the basement. Thankfully, not one of the patrons witnessed Crash catching the Rabbit and giving him a monstrous "purple nurple," which would have involved grabbing his pubescently engorged nipple and twisting mightily. All I managed to hear was a combination of high pitched squeals and shrieks, but I could clearly imagine Crash trying to savagely draw milk from the Rabbit's little conical breasts.

Ironically, it was the Rabbit who eventually bridged the gap between Crash and us salad boys. He did this by agreeing to haul the bus pans full of dirty plates from the upstairs dining room (which accumulated because there was only one dish pit in the entire restaurant complex and it was located on the main floor within the kitchen) to the dish pit in exchange for $5 at the end of the night from Crash. It was a win-win situation as Crash and the other waiters loathed carrying those greasy, filthy bus pans down the stairs, and the Rabbit needed the cash to make a small dent in the gambling debt he perpetually owed to Lou. In hindsight, it was this arrangement struck by the Rabbit that allowed us to be more assimilated with the waiters, which was important because all of us were within a year of making the risky transition from salad boys to either waiters or bartenders.

By the time our friend Renny entered the fray, all of us had become veteran salad boys, Buddy included. Renny was a tall, gangly kid, who had lots of freckles and the eyes of a giraffe, which is to say large, moist, and brown with impossibly long eyelashes. He grew up within a large Mormon family that was quite affluent because his Dad was a doctor. But "Dr. Don" was the only supposed "man of science" that I knew who would say things like, "The odds of us having evolved from a bacteria is the same as a tornado ripping through a junk yard and randomly assembling a fully functional 747 airplane," or even better, "Nobody has ever really proven that the earth is older than five thousand years old." How do you argue with a loon like that? As a high school kid I would try by countering that we didn't evolve from bacteria per se, but rather from primitive, single-celled organisms that contained a collection of mutating nucleic acids, and that I was fairly certain that scientists had carbon dated various fossils that were quite old, and … but he would be too busy trying to align my chakras or some such thing and disregard my rhetoric. Renny, thankfully, was not as wacky as his Dad, although he had his fair share of moral dilemmas to wrestle with as Buddy and I were considered "bad influences" because we paid absolutely no heed to the *Book of Mormon*. As far as we were concerned, any religion that caused your Dad to rant like a depraved heroin addict and forbid you to consume caffeine or have premarital sex was about as paramount to our lives as the Mickey Mouse Fan Club.

Renny was pretty much a spineless, push-over of an ungulate. He wasn't aggressive, demanding, decisive, or in any way dominant. He was simply too sensitive towards the feelings of others, which was noble, but it was also the bane of his existence. For example, during the four years that Renny and I were especially tight, I never knew of a girl who thought of him as anything other than just a "sweet friend." He was tall, dark haired, and boyishly handsome, yet he just couldn't get any action to save his life. Consequently, for a while we referred to him as "Eunuch" because we seriously doubted the presence of any sexual hormones coursing through his body, or any tangible gonads hanging between his legs. Now, he may have been a masturbating demon in the privacy of his own room, but you would have never sensed any ejaculatory urgency while in his presence. In fact, the situation digressed to an all time low one night as a group of us went for a late night swim in a local river after having consumed a few cases of fruity wine coolers. There were about eight of us, and my new Slavic girlfriend was too shy to disrobe in front of us all (I had barely seen her in anything less revealing than Gloria Vanderbilt jeans and a pink button-down at that stage), so she demanded that Renny hold up a towel while she stripped down to her panties, thus allowing him a private showing of her perky breasts. Now this may have initially seemed quite delightful from Renny's vantage point, but she was treating him as if he were one of her girlfriends which just seemed to underline how every female regarded Renny: as absolutely safe, reliably decent, and totally non-threatening. As such, the Spanish Inquisition's condemnation of "heretic" could not have caused him more anguish during those formative years. In fact, I think most adolescent males would rather have had the reputation of being impotent and uncircumcised, to be quite honest. And as far as I know, Renny remained without action until he married a fellow Mormon from Dallas at the age of twenty-four. Sad, really.

Buddy and Renny were such opposites in so many ways, and none was more obvious than their different demeanors while trying to restock the salad bars. Naturally, Buddy was more aggressive and charismatic, and usually had no trouble keeping his salad bar stocked even at the height of the dinner rush. The few people (usually obese women who were trying to quit smoking) who had the audacity to show him attitude while at his salad bar would get the business end of an expression that clearly imparted, "If you do not remove that pugnacious look from your face, I shall be forced to use these salad tongs to individually pluck those hairs from your upper lip that you have failed so miserably to hide with that preposterous choice of foundation. Now good day to you madam!" Buddy would make us proud and validate our position as salad boys whenever he unleashed such acerbic looks. Renny, on the other hand, couldn't quite gather the fortitude to drop the hammer when he had to. To Renny, facing the dinner rush crowd at the salad bar was like experiencing the running of the bulls in Pamplona: it was either run and live another day, or stand his ground and get bludgeoned. Renny often chose the former and applied that principle to most things in his life, with the salad bar being no exception. Sometimes the customers would actually be forced to grab items out of the plastic buckets on his metal cart, as if it was a new extension of the salad bar, because his crocks and bowls would be so depleted. This was the ultimate insult to a salad boy, but Renny was too oblivious to feel any shame.

As time progressed, the salad boy fraternity stabilized at four members: the Rabbit, Buddy, Renny, and myself. It was a truly glorious time and perhaps the most fun I have ever had while at a place of work. Consequently, our "happy-go-lucky" attitude seemed fairly infectious as most of the Trader's staff grew to enjoy us and looked forward to the numerous recounts of our varied adolescent adventures, which included everything from egging rickshaw drivers in the head, to sugaring the gas tanks of our sworn enemies. This forum turned out to be a valuable training ground for Buddy because he obsessed about telling stories as a Hollywood director, and somewhat for Renny as well, who dreamed of being a famous actor or model. In communicating our stories, though, we were cognizant of having to interject bizarre verbiage in order to be fully appreciated and accepted by the inner circles at Trader's. This verbiage was the Trader's English.

The Trader's English...

I didn't have the perspective at the time, but I have come to realize that most industries have a sort of verbal "short-hand" that is developed over time either out of pure necessity or absolute cacophony. An example of necessity would be the medical community's use of abbreviations or acronyms for various procedures and diseases to theoretically save time and reduce confusion, which is crucial if a patient is in a life or death situation. Case in point: "Nurse, we've got an MVA in the ER that's getting tachy. We need to check his BP before we stick him with an IV of ABC. Also prepare for a P to A chest film to rule out a

Fx and a CT to rule out a cranial bleed." An example of cacophony would be the stuffed suits within the banking/financial world who intentionally create abbreviated lingo so cryptic that we must use their services and pay their outrageous transaction fees to decode the most basic of concepts and procedures. Case in point: "Hello, I'm the VP of the VC division of ABC Bank, and we're rather bullish on the IPO of your dot.com start-up. In fact, if your P/E-to-growth ratio continues to linger below two, we'd love to include it in our hedge fund and offer our clients access to it through their R.R.S.P. portfolio." That's great, my little banking friend, but can you explain to me why I am charged a fee to deposit money into your bank and why none of the "personal banking representatives" even know my name after fifteen years of standing in line behind the elderly who cannot master the use of the little calculator, let alone the numerous banking options on your ATMs? Yeah, you get back to me on that.

The restaurant industry's quirky vernacular is a combination of the above-mentioned types because (1) employees are often in a hurry and must convey information quickly and concisely, but more importantly (2) it's vital for veteran employees to appear cool to all incoming staff, which serves to alienate all the new people from the mainstream modes of communication. Thus, new staff members must rely heavily on veterans just to be able to function, which seems to propagate a great deal of dependency and subservience. The unscrupulous veteran waiter will then have ample opportunity to capitalize on this power inequity by coercing the novice waiter to perform all of his back-breaking closing duties, or by maneuvering the novice waitress into the sack for a little late night bing-bang-boom. This latter scenario should seem very familiar to men of French, Greek, or Italian ancestry, as they have been capitalizing on the language barrier to lure exchange students and tourists into the sack for eons.

While almost all restaurants make use of standard terms like "slammed," "in the weeds," or "dish pit," each also has its own distinct dialect that is dependent on the creativity of its personnel, and on the most current cultural phenomena (i.e., movie, television show, commercial, or hit song). Generally speaking, the younger and more diverse the staff, the more colorful and humorous the lingo. Conversely, the older and more eccentric the staff, the more obscure and baffling the lingo. Looking back, Trader's was the source of some pretty absurd dialogue which most of us had to subscribe to if we wanted to be considered part of the "in-crowd." The salad boy fraternity did originate some of this, especially that surrounding the attainment and consumption of virgin cocktails, but the majority of the syntax was coined by "Big M," the most senior of the Trader's hostesses.

Big M was more of a caricature than anyone else at Trader's. She was a big, tall bird of British ancestry who would scale her accent depending on the situation. She sometimes sounded as if she was a blue-blooded pommey, and other times like she was trailer trash from Timbuktu. She had an attractive face that was framed by crazy blonde hair reminiscent of Loni Anderson's, but with an extreme case of "bed head." Trader's had held her hostage for about thirteen years at that point, which wasn't unusual by Trader's standards, but spending that amount of time in that kind of atmosphere could suck the aspirations out of Anthony Robbins. She was intelligent, funny, and charming, but she just didn't seem to notice that there was life with ample opportunities outside of Trader's. She rented a very modest dwelling, didn't drive a vehicle, and didn't have a lasting boyfriend. She seemed reluctant to be tied down or to grow roots despite the fact that she was the most popular and well-respected inmate in the Trader's prison. In truth, we really enjoyed her, especially Buddy, who developed a special friendship with her over the three years that he was there.

Big M was a hostess primarily, but also dabbled as a waitress and a sniveling manager depending on how much money she needed at the time. She wasn't especially ambitious, but she liked to travel to tropical destinations and work on her skin cancer, so a couple of times a year she would be in a panic for money and pick up as many shifts as she possibly could. This made her quite a valuable commodity within the jungle because she was versatile and had a desire to actually work. Consequently, she had many friends within the various social circles and grew to be fairly influential. In fact, I'm sure that Medusa used Big M on more than one occasion to keep informed of the latest gossip and to get dirt on the people who fell out of favor with her Highness, so that there were at least some flimsy grounds for dismissal. In this regard, Big M may have been somewhat of a Mata Hari, but we never knew for sure.

Buddy and I also weren't sure how old Big M was, but we assumed that she was well into her thirties because she began to talk more and more about her "biological clock" ticking away and her desire to rear at least one offspring. Most of the staff got a good laugh from that because they thought that Big M was incapable of looking after herself, let alone another member of our genus. Be that as it may, she kept on lamenting about her lack of fertility, but seemed to make more of an effort at being financially responsible. So when her "secret mission" eventually came to light it shouldn't have shocked everyone to the extent that it did. Apparently, Big M's annual trip to the Bahamas was really a mission to get pregnant by some random biped who would never be the wiser. So she went there and submissively mated with as many two legged beasts as she could under the guise that she was using birth control and would tolerate all mating rituals. In fact, when it became known that she was pregnant, she honestly didn't know what markings the newborn would have. But say what you will about the morality of Big M's decision, she was a true individual who saw her world (albeit small) through rose-colored glasses. Incidentally, when the rug rat was birthed she named him after Buddy.

Due to Big M's general popularity, unique sense of humor, and knack for impressions, she was a natural choice to be the ringleader of the Trader's Inn Circus. For the nearly four years that I was there, she was responsible for establishing what was cool and what was passé. For example, *Scarface* (a movie starring Al Pacino as a cocaine dealer) was quite popular at that time, so naturally all of Big M's cronies insisted on talking like Cuban gangsters. Consequently, the phrases, "Chew gottit meng" and "Foch yu meng," which were supposed to mean "You got it, man" and "Fuck you, man" respectively, became all the rage. At the very least, everyone referred to everyone else as "Meng," at all times. In fact, for a period of about six months, it was as if we had all become nameless, trash talking, thugs under the reign of Fidel Castro. Similarly, Eddie Murphy's parody of *The Honeymooners* was popular at that time too. As a result, it was considered cutting edge humor to turn to someone and say, "Norman, I want you, to come over here, and fuck me up the ass. Come on Norman, just slide it in me, give it to me real good. Do it now Norman, or straight to the moon, I swear to God!" regardless of who you were talking to. In essence, they were white, middle class servers imitating Eddie Murphy, who was imitating Jackie Gleason, who was pretending to be a 1950's bus driving New Yorker. It was humorous because it was utterly ridiculous the lengths to which they went to become accepted by their cohorts at Trader's, not because they were so uncanny with their impersonations and comedic timing. But most didn't make this distinction once they heard and became addicted to the soothing laughter that represented acceptance.

Big M got some tremendous mileage out of just a handful of words and expressions. One such word was "unigama," which was of Chinese origins and meant something so crude that little Rosie refused to give us an English translation. Nevertheless, that didn't stop almost the entire Caucasian staff from exclaiming it at every opportunity. If a food order was late, or a plate was too hot, or a waitress was showing some especially stellar cleavage, it didn't matter because one would exclaim "Unigama!" as if he were Bruce Lee in, *Enter the Dragon*. After a while, Big M then used the base of that expression to form other words. For example, if the waiters wanted some juicy to be poured on the prime rib, they would say, "Juicigama." If someone was pissed off at Lou the Wildebeest, they could hiss, "Louigama," at him. The derivatives were endless actually.

Another of Big M's favorites was "really." It could be simply stated, exclaimed indignantly, asked mischievously, casually queried, yelled elatedly, and used interchangeably as an adjective, noun, or verb. It was nearly as versatile as the word "fuck." In fact, I would argue that if combined, the words "really" and "fuck" accounted for about twenty percent of all verbal communication at Trader's during those years. Clearly we were not descendants of Shakespeare, despite the tales of tragedy with incestuous overtones.

Finally, Big M had her own hostessing vocabulary, which was hugely influenced by her British origins, and introduced us to terms like, "deuce" (a table of two), "four-top" (table of four), "cut" (a closed section), "chock-a-block" (a full section), "peckish" (a little hungry), "kit" (a waiter's apron), "a bloody good rogering" (a satisfying shag), and "fat bastard" (a defiant asshole). I'm not sure if she ever managed to get a dictionary named after her (a la *Funk and Wagnall's*), but she always kept us guessing.

New Year's Eve Cheer...

I had never ushered in a new year while under the influence of copious amounts of alcohol prior to turning seventeen years old. Before that, most of my New Year's Eve celebrations were spent at home within the company of my Mom's rather banal banking friends. I would relentlessly beat them at "Pong" (the original home video game) throughout the night, and then be glad to escape to my bedroom before the last chorus of *Auld Lang Syne* was bellowed out. New Year's Eve was not an occasion to be celebrated while younger; rather it was to be endured along side people fixated on *Meat Loaf's* debut album or the "wicked" styling of the new Ford Pinto. That all changed the year that Buddy and I turned seventeen and awaited the Trader's Inn celebration with baited breath.

Most of us salad boys had heard at least some of the stories from the previous year's celebration, and it sounded like pure, adulterous mayhem. According to the hyperbole-laced tales, it would have been nearly impossible to throw a more raucous affair without the help of the Marquis de Sade. So naturally our interests were peaked because our party going experience was limited to the occasional high school shag and various "wrap-up" parties for our sports teams. In fact, we were inexperienced enough to actually be nervous about showcasing our dancing abilities (or lack thereof) and had cursed ourselves for not practicing more in front of a mirror. Was it best to show some funky soul by break dancing, or stick with the white man's shuffle and be indifferently cool? Either way, the upcoming bash at Trader's was promising to be something well out of the ordinary.

The New Year's Eve bash was a tradition that went back many years at Trader's. Each year it was held within the Trader's Inn Nightclub, which was convenient for those pathetic few who seemed to spend all their waking hours within the confines of the restaurant searching for their lost youth. Adding to the excitement of anticipating vast consumption of alcohol and experiencing varying degrees of sexual promiscuity was the dispersing of the year-end bonuses. Only management and senior level employees received such bonuses (ranging from a few hundred dollars to a few thousand), but the rest of us peons were still excited by the possibility that the Trader's elite might buy a few rounds of drinks with their newfound wealth. This never really transpired because the elite either had gambling debts or owed money to their drug dealers, so the holiday spirit never quite touched all of us.

Buddy and I ended up going to the party without Renny for some reason (against the moral teachings of Joseph Smith and Brigham Young, perhaps?), so the two of us primped and preened at my house for the better part of two hours in preparation. We emerged with ridiculously feathered hair reminiscent of the band *A Flock of Seagulls*, and wearing some quintessential Ivy League attire that could have easily made the cover of *The Official Preppies Handbook*. If I recall, Buddy wore a pair of blue plaid slacks with a white button down and matching bow tie, all under a short, white cotton, tab collared jacket. It was a brilliant ensemble. I opted for a thick blue cardigan sweater over gray khakis, with a yellow button down and a baby blue plaid necktie. My penny loafers were glistening with ox blood shoe polish and intentionally contained pennies minted in 1968, the year of my birth. Clearly we wanted to set the fashion world on its ear that infamous night. Little did I know that my outfit would be reduced to a vomitous sponge by the end of the evening.

The party started out quite well. The music was loud and current, some comical styles of dance were showcased, and some intermingling of the various social hierarchies occurred. In fact, the New Year's Eve party was the only occasion during the course of the year that all of the employees mixed together socially, which was often good for some high quality P.F.O.s like, "That's just super. Good to hear. Well, I'll be sure to send you over some New Year's cheer. Right, sure, let's do some shots later. OK then, I'll save you a dance. I'll be looking for you too. Yes, I hear ya. OK now, fucking beat it." Each year the desperate were forced to consider chewing off a limb to escape some conversations, but it was all in the name of promoting socioeconomic understanding and goodwill after all. Buddy and I preferred to hang out with the younger, hipper servers, of which there were precious few. One such rarity was "Dude," who was a twenty-five-year-old skateboarder well past his prime, but trying to remain within that counterculture for as long as he possibly could. Dude was a shortish, mesomorphic burnout who loved his dope and his checkerboard patterned "Vans" (a type of slip-on canvas shoe popular with surfers and skateboarders). His hero was "Jeff Spicoli" from the cult classic *Fast Times at Ridgemont High*, for obvious reasons. Dude was a funny enough guy though, and he treated us as equals, so we generally enjoyed his company. He was a favorite customer of Len's when Len dealt drugs, so that's how we initially came to know him. As it turned out, Dude just happened to be a hit at that year's party because he brought a long, glass, drinking funnel that he referred to as the "Boot." The purpose of the Boot was to smoothly deliver a vast quantity of beer into your gullet in much less time than you would otherwise prefer. This was familiar territory for us beer pounding salad boys (unbeknownst to everyone else), so we looked forward to displaying our refined beer guzzling abilities.

Before we were officially introduced to the Boot, Buddy and I saddled up to the wood and asked Academy Award Winner, Spam the bartender, for a couple of double vodka paralyzers. This rich, creamy cocktail with vodka, Kahlua, milk, and Coke was Buddy's favorite, much more so than mine. They tasted a little like Coke floats, but with a bite, and we naively indulged copiously. I remember initially questioning our choice of beverage, as the cream had already appeared curdled within the glasses we were sipping from. Buddy wasn't too fazed by this observation, but I privately doubted if curdled milk would mix well with vodka, beer, tequila, Champagne, and Chinese food all within the acidic confines of our stomachs that night. Of course this type of sober reasoning was quickly replaced with a combination of inebriated misjudgment, reduced inhibition, and a dangerously amplified need for adventure. So we drank on and sized up our opportunities around the room, which seemed to be knocking louder and louder.

Joining us as the only "under-agers" at the party were a skittish gaggle of desk helps who were following Big M around as if they were her ladies in waiting. They ranged in age from fifteen to seventeen and were making a concerted effort not to consume any alcohol, which still didn't make the situation legal because they were in the confines of a nightclub surrounded by one of the largest selections of fermented liquid in the city. Admittedly, some of the girls were reasonably cute and proved to be a mild distraction, but Buddy and I thought we could do better if we could maintain our faculties and charm. Unfortunately, legality, morality, or plain good judgment didn't stop us from continuing to poison our bloodstreams and taxing our livers with an assortment of toxins. This seemed perfectly acceptable to all of the adult partygoers, including Medusa, who sat on her throne and appeared entertained by us as if we were her court jesters. So on a roll and eager to impress our benefactors, we were drawn to Dude's Boot.

The Boot looked like a giant test tube, except that it had a bulbous bottom. The premise was to pour beer into the Boot (it could have easily held a half gallon), then to put the Boot to your lips, tip it back and avoid drowning. The design of the Boot was such that it did not allow a bottleneck of liquid to form, unlike conventional bottles or cans, so that the golden fluid flowed the length of the glass funnel as if it were a raging tributary of the Amazon River. And because of its length, you could actually see the beer gathering momentum as it hurtled towards your pursed lips. So after observing the failed techniques of various impostors, Buddy and I wanted to display our Harmon Killebrew-esk talents that we had honed during the many hours spent in the basement. As such, we stepped into the spotlight and tangoed with the Boot, but much to our surprise, Buddy and I failed miserably at our first couple of attempts (primarily because the beer was cold and we hadn't anticipated this luxury) and we were forced to retreat back to our barstools with our tails between our legs. And there we sat until midnight, at which time we yelled "Happy New Year!" then kissed various waitresses (which planted a little seed and later set the stage for an anonymous salad boy to actually make-out with a twenty-four-year-old waitress with teased bangs, who chewed gum, and talked like she was a New Jersey bar slut), then tooted on some party favors, drained some flutes of champagne, and indulged at the Chinese buffet. The Boot had won the first couple of rounds, but not the prizefight.

Not too far along into the New Year, I found myself on the dance floor struggling to focus on the colorful scenery as the merry-go-round spun under me. I had faced this abyss before and successfully pulled myself back from it, so I wasn't especially worried. The trepidation began, however, when I was pulled off the dance floor and landed in front of Dude, and stood looking into his bloodshot eyes that were partially masked by enormously heavy lids. I noticed his mouth moving so I assumed he was trying to say something through his chapped lips and slightly yellowed teeth. Then more movement and sounds like, "Yeah, right-on bud. I said that you're the last one to conquer the Boot, man. Come on, give it another go Frenchy." Oh damn that little radical try-hard. He was essentially asking me if I was a man (i.e., waiter material) or a mouse (i.e., a turd eating salad boy). My answer would surprise him.

Unable to avoid the overt challenge, my only request was to have the Boot filled with tepid beer, which Dude eagerly complied with. So exactly twelve ounces of beer from a can were then emptied into the Boot, which inadvertently mixed with an ounce of the previous contestant's effort, which was more backwash than actual lager. This was the moment of reckoning and it caused me to reflect a little: I wasn't thirsty, I didn't need any more alcohol, and I didn't even enjoy beer, but yet here I was risking a meeting with my maker merely to ensure that my reputation as a salad boy did not include that of turd eating so that I could some day proudly call myself a waiter. Honestly, who fucking cared what Dude and the worthless collection of invalids around him thought of my potential during this lifetime? Well, I did apparently, so I grabbed that Boot and tipped it skyward. Consequently, the dike opened and the raging, golden water obeyed gravity and raced towards my parted lips. At the moment of impact, I forced my throat open and prayed that my gag reflex had been paralyzed by the near fatal levels of ethanol in my blood stream; it had, and I was thankful. Surprisingly, the beer didn't totally ravage my esophagus, although I had been too aggressive with tipping the Boot back, which caused the beer level to rise well above my lip and over my nostrils. In my stupor I actually sucked in some beer through my nose and avoided choking, which would be quite a party trick if someone could master it. Before I realized it, though, the challenge was over and I had joined the Parthenon of Beer Pounding Gods. I had successfully drained the Boot and stood victorious in near disbelief, with tears of joy (or from carbonation burns) running down my cheeks. I quickly let out a wail that would have made a banshee proud, then uncorked a belch that would have made Homer Simpson proud, then was gripped by a small spasm of sneezes that might have made one of Snow White's dwarfs proud. In short, all was good and I remember being deified. But then, an evil notion took hold in my brain so quickly that I was physically enacting it before my rationality filters could catch it. From all accounts, I apparently cocked the Boot in my right hand and launched a perfect strike into the brick fireplace that stood about fifteen feet away, as if I were a Sicilian Mafioso who had just finished toasting the Godfather. Needless to say, the Boot did not survive the launching. In fact, you could argue, at least metaphorically, that I used the Boot to christen the launching of a great new vessel from the "salad boy harbor;" a vessel that was to eventually set sail for the mystical "sea of servers;" a vessel that would come to be known as **H.M.S. WAITERMAN**. Looking back, perhaps it was that act of insolence, more so than any other, that propelled me into the Bermuda Triangle of the restaurant world, but I would hate to think that some burnout with checkered, canvas shoes had any sort of influence on my destiny. Oh well, just speculation.

Meanwhile, Dude definitely received my reply loud and clear, but took it on the chin like a man. And after the initial shock of seeing the Boot disintegrate into glass chards, we all laughed like lunatics. Dude did mention something about his prized Boot costing $60, but we laughed even harder. He also mentioned something about a celebratory round of tequilas, but I stumbled off to the washroom to avoid the toasting while saving face. It was while in the washroom that my saliva glands became hyperactive and it wasn't until years later that I learned the significance of this physiologic process: the human body increases its production of saliva to lubricate and protect the esophagus from the impending regurgitation of the stomach's contents, which contains a fair amount of hydrochloric acid and trace amounts of bile that can be quite corrosive to any mucosal lining. I didn't know this then, so I was still in denial even as I fell to my knees within a toilet stall. Amidst constant swallowing, I reasoned, "You can still pull yourself back from this, yes you can. Mind over matter. Yes, the mind is powerful. This can be done. You will not fucking puke, damn you! Please, don't let it be so! Shake it off, think positive. I can do this. Deep breaths. Maybe if I puke I'll feel better, though. A quick little yack then I'm back in the game. But puking really hurts, so maybe I'll just... ," then simply, "Aaaaaccchhh!" as I fell into the dark abyss of alcohol poisoning.

After five stomach emptying retches, the abyss felt pretty welcoming (or maybe that was just the cool porcelain of the toilet). I was still on my knees, having succumbed to exhaustion, with my right cheek pressed onto the rim of the toilet bowl as if it were my pillow. Yes, my facial epidermis was actually in contact with various droplets of urine that had either splashed up from the toilet water, or had been misdirected upon initial discharge. My face! God knows what else was lingering on that surface, but it was frighteningly close to my mouth. As I drifted in and out of consciousness, I remember repetitively focusing on a squashed cigarette butt that was lying near the base of the toilet and marinating in a similarly polluted puddle. It was at that moment that I fully comprehended the total lack of glamour that drunkenness bestows on its captives, for I had never felt so utterly pathetic. I was clinging to the rim of a fouled toilet bowl and spitting out small pieces of half digested Chinese food that still lingered in my mouth, while being unable to remove my eyes from a soggy, disintegrating fag. I clearly needed help, so I started calling out, "Buddaaay!" in hopes that Buddy would come to my rescue.

Someone eventually heard me and summoned Buddy, who then recruited a couple of other guys to carry me out of the toilet stall, but not until they had all finished partying. So I spent perhaps an hour in that fucking stall, cursing everyone from the first Homo sapien to experiment with fermenting fruits and grains, to Spam the bartender, who smirked knowingly every time he poured us a vodka paralyzer. Eventually I was seen to, and as I was hauled out of the nightclub and into the kitchen, I realized it was Crash and Mussolini who were dragging me along while my penny loafers acted as retardant brakes. What an ironic surprise that was. But instead of being thankful, sheepish, and/or humble, I thought it appropriate to be a straight talking little shit. So with all my inhibitions totally decimated, I slurred to Crash, "I hate to think what you did to me in that stall when my ass was exposed, you gerbil felching cheese ball," and then to the grinning Mussolini, "How'd you get so tanned through all that hair, you little monkey?" As rude as it was, they managed to refrain from tossing me into the walk-in cooler headfirst.

As we all stumbled out the back door, I noticed that Buddy was in front of me talking to some short creature with long hair. Well, it turned out to be Medusa, which was risky from a military point of view because the three least popular people at Trader's (take a guess who) were all within a grenade's radius. Thankfully no assassinations were attempted that night, because Medusa had graciously agreed to drive Buddy and I back to his Mom's house. This was good news because the last of my energy had been spent being a sarcastic dink to the fellas and all I craved was a mattress at that point. So we hopped into Medusa's Volvo and prayed for God's speed. Unfortunately, there remained a small clump of curdled milk in some distal fold of mucosa that wanted to be set free, so I looked for the appropriate depository. To my immediate right, there looked to be an open window, even though we were still well within the grips of a frigid winter. "How timely," I thought, as I purged my stomach one last time of its contents. But defying the laws of projectile physics, the stream of vomitous splashed against some invisible barrier and began to run down the doorsill and onto my absorbent knit sweater. I recognized this as not a good thing, but there was nothing to be done except wallow in my self-pity and murmur apologies towards the front seat as the sour odor of my mess filled the car. Then strangely, as we arrived in Buddy's neighborhood, he couldn't remember the location of his childhood home, so we inadvertently banged on his elderly neighbor's door (at three in the morning) and asked for directions, much to our chagrin. But we eventually stumbled home, like most resilient teens manage to do, and lived to experience a rare type of encephalitis commonly referred to as a "hang-over" the next day. Conveniently, Buddy's "forty-pound" alcoholic uncle was in town for a visit (named so because he was up to forty ounces of Canadian Club whiskey per day just to function) and provided us with some excellent home remedies, some of which I use to this day. Unfortunately, I was never willing to consider the possibility that the Volvo's window was rolled up that night, which was perhaps the first nail in my coffin at Trader's, because not only did Medusa have to clean up the congealed remains of my puke the following afternoon, but she realized that she was dealing with someone as stubborn as her and not as easily controlled by her treacherous manipulations.

In the final analysis, we made quite an impression at our first New Year's Eve party and the salad boy fraternity seemed to be better appreciated and respected as a result. And aside from initiating the early stages of liver cirrhosis, none of us suffered any ill effects from our actions, which surprised me because

I thought I could count on some retribution from the hot-blooded Mussolini. Instead, he ended up accepting a job at another restaurant a few months later, which made us deliriously happy and fuelled rumors that there was a power struggle between him and Medusa. Regardless, life at Trader's became more relaxed and we cruised on automatic pilot until the following summer at which time we graduated from high school and came to believe that we had an excellent shot at eventually becoming waiters. So we packed our bags and prepared to move up the jungle's hierarchy into the "canopy."

Before we leave the realm of the salad bars, though, there are some interesting points that are worth mentioning. (1) I'm not sure of the biochemistry behind it, but pineapple that sits on a fruit tray too long will eventually smell exactly like fresh vomitous. It won't taste like puke if you quickly put it in your mouth and immediately start chewing, but the odor is offensive enough to cause people to look to the ground searching for the offending puddle of spew as they walk by the salad bar. (2) The half-life of alfalfa sprouts is generally unknown as they can be left on the salad bar for weeks on end, undoubtedly providing a cozy home for billions of ambitious bacteria. (3) The pieces of steak in the steak soup were from the ends of the slabs of prime rib that were overcooked. The ends were eventually cut off and put in a bucket that the waiters continuously foraged through, either for their own consumption or for that of their canine pets. Consequently, on some evenings, the two gallon container of steak soup had less than two ounces of real steak in it. (4) I don't remember the crocks that contained the veggies ever being washed out. Therefore, there is a very real possibility that some of the items at the bottom of the crocks were there for years because we never let the crocks get less than three quarters empty. And (5) when fully stretched, the human mouth can hold about fourteen uncrushed green grapes, which is equivalent to a Mike Tyson fist without the handcuffs.

Chapter 5

Reaching the Canopy

"The higher a monkey climbs, the more you see of his ass."

- General J. Stilwell

The Transition...

As stated, the four of us salad boys proceeded to graduate from high school (not all as virgins, incidentally) and looked forward to the lazy days of summer. Buddy, Renny, and I had aspirations of going to university and becoming "professionals" of some sort, though, so we were anxious to make some money and embark on a tropical odyssey before we committed to at least another four years of school. I had approached Medusa about moving up from the salad bar ranks, and to my amazement, she mentioned that perhaps we could try our hand at waitering, even though we were not of legal age to do so. But legality never seemed to be a priority at Trader's, which consequently permeated most of the policies and attitudes there.

Simply said, ignoring the law became commonplace at Trader's because adhering to it was at times unprofitable, and at other times inconvenient. Here are some examples. (1) The minimum wage at that time was $3.65 per hour, but all of us received only $3.60. Why? Perhaps it was an insidious way of saving about $2,000 a year, or perhaps it was an innocent mistake by the accountant that got carried forth week after week (and year after year), but that single oversight was an insult to all of us and would play a significant role when I was later bid adieu. (2) Most of the servers worked split shifts during the course of the day that often exceeded eight hours, which should have qualified as overtime, but Trader's counted the split shifts as two separate shifts and avoided paying overtime wages. (3) Employees who were fired (justifiably so or not) never received their mandatory two-week severance pay, which effectively saved the restaurant thousands every year. (4) We never got the compulsory breaks that were stipulated by the local Worker's Board. Granted, this was also the policy of most other restaurants in the city because of the inconvenience of it, but it still pissed us off. (5) All of the servers had to pay a one percent stipend to the Vagrant based on their ringouts each shift. This amount was capped at $10 per shift (but it always totaled $10) and went directly into the Vagrant's pocket, which was a pretty shrewd way of making approximately $60,000 tax free dollars every year. This continual "thank you for allowing us to work at your restaurant" stipend caused much bitterness and actually provoked the staff to rip the restaurant off at every opportunity. And (6) although we obviously thought we were lucky bastards at the time, we should not have been allowed to get drop dead drunk at various Trader's sponsored events or even work as waiters before we turned eighteen, which was the legal age to partake in such activities. But at the time, we drooled at the prospect of increasing our income ten-fold and would have been the last punks on Earth to complain about abuses of the child labor laws. After all, it wasn't as if we were seven-year-olds and working in a coal mine at the height of the Industrial Revolution for the occasional moldy potato.

    After hashing it out with Medusa, it was decided that Buddy, Renny, and I would progress through the role of "lounge runner" before it was determined whether or not we were waitering material, and the Rabbit would work behind the bar as a "bar assistant" and train to work as the service bartender, which was fitting because his stutter kept him from being particularly smooth with the customers. We all thought this arrangement was exceptionally fair and actually believed that Medusa had our best interests at heart. I would later fervently recant this belief.

    The job of lounge runner was pretty basic. We essentially escorted people from the main lounge (which acted as a holding tank for people who were waiting for their table) to the hostess stand in one of the three dining rooms within Trader's. Sometimes we had to carry their drinks on a tray, which was supposed to improve our balancing and serving skills, but mostly we just carried their coats and made small talk. We were like adolescent butlers, really. As such, we had to dress better, which we didn't mind at that stage because we were tired of looking like salad bar tramps. Not surprisingly then, Buddy was soon dressing in his finest attire and forced Renny and I to follow suit. So within the course of a couple of weeks, I had gone from wearing soiled jeans and a cheeky T-shirt to button downs with bow ties, suspenders, and saddle oxfords. In fact, with my hair slicked back, I could have passed for the ninth Earl of Greystoke. And with our makeovers completed, some of the waitresses almost didn't recognize us and commented that we "Cleaned up real good," except for the spurned New Jersey bar slut, who just snapped her gum and lasciviously checked out our asses.

After a month or so of walking up and down the "cat walk" (due to it essentially having become a fashion show between us), Buddy and I were given instructions to memorize the ingredients, portions, and prices of everything on the menu and actually had a date scheduled to serve the management team so they could decide if we were ready to take the plunge. Renny, on the other hand, failed to impress anyone with his indecisiveness, unassertiveness, and general apathy, so he was left behind as a lounge runner and occasional desk help, making him the first of his gender to hold those positions simultaneously. Again, he probably didn't feel the shame he should have, but he sure did look like a pussy while folding napkins and gossiping amongst the flock of flighty desk helps.

Learning to Climb the Trees…

Our "dry run" as waiters in front of the management team transpired without incident, especially for me, because I had spent years watching the servers at Trader's as a kid, so all I had to do was be a good mimic. So after we made our favorable impressions, Buddy was sent to work on Planet Hoth, and I was scheduled for the Death Star. The Death Star operated much differently than Hoth, or most other restaurants for that matter. The most profound difference was that waitresses and waiters had to work together in pairs, forming serving teams. Consequently, the waiter's duties consisted of informing the tables of the evening's specials, taking the food orders, running the food, clearing most of the plates, and generally coordinating the entire dining process. The waitress, on the other hand, was primarily responsible for keeping the customers hydrated with potable spirits and liquids of a non-alcoholic nature. As such, she was referred to as the "barmaid" or "wine stewardess." Ironically, this approach was more intuitive to me because I had observed it in action for years, whereas the solo server strategy practiced within Hoth (and the restaurant industry at large) seemed much more cumbersome, and quite frankly it intimidated me.

Before I could officially take tables, I had to "shadow" a couple of the veteran alpha-male waiters for a week or so. I was assigned to shadow "Trojan" and "Ramses," who were both pushing forty years of age, had worked at Trader's for many moons, and were strangely particular about their lubricated prophylactics. While on the job, they both dressed like "Hans Solo" from *Star Wars*, but were about as communicative and cheery as his hirsute sidekick, "Chewbaca." However, they managed to show me the ropes without conveying too much cynicism about the job, the restaurant, or the industry, which was quite considerate of them (although I became quickly tainted soon thereafter). They made it seem so easy with their well-rehearsed greetings, droll replies, and cliché riddled farewells. Everything flowed well, the timing of things was nearly perfect, and as a result, the customers were able to relax and fully enjoy their dining experience. They also educated me on which barmaids were decent workers, and who were lazy parasites. They went on to recount the days when the tips were split 60/40 in favor of the waiters because their job was more demanding, but how cries of sexual discrimination caused the tips to be divided equally despite the fact there remained an inequity in work demands. In short, Trojan and Ramses did a decent job of training me, but there were some questions that they couldn't answer because I didn't dare ask them, and they were: "Why the hell are you guys still working here? Are you total losers who can't find anything else? Are you avoiding the responsibilities and commitment of a real job? Is the money simply that good here? Is the Vagrant blackmailing you with compromising pictures of the two of you fornicating?" But over time, I came to realize that some people enjoy the variety, hours, pace, sociality, and/or money of being a server and make a pro-active choice of being one without any feelings of regret, insecurity, or anxiety. They proudly become professional servers and probably laugh at the rest of us for paying exorbitant taxes, having to wake up early, being bored stiff, and not getting laid regularly. But having said that, I viewed waitering as a means to an end and just wanted to make some decent jack for a specific period of time and then get the hell out. Little did I know how easy the well becomes to return to.

Once the elders within the Trader's troop thought I was ready, my inauguration was soon upon me. But as much as I would like to relate a comical story of chaos, destruction, and general misfortune, I must admit that I can't recall a single thing from that first shift. Absolutely nothing comes to mind, presumably because of the powerful hand of terror that was gripping me. I guess I had to bury the emotional trauma that I suffered just to remain sane and reasonably functional. And while I don't recall any specific events of that harrowing night, I clearly remember why I was so scared. The reasons were threefold. (1) We were the first seventeen-year-olds in Trader's history to hold positions as waiters. Consequently, we had much to prove to management in terms of our maturity, commitment, and dependability. In essence, it felt like we were representing all teenagers, and failing as waiters might have compromised teenagers' job prospects everywhere. Well, not quite, but we did feel some pressure. (2) I didn't want to come across to the customers as a fraud and compromise their dining experience. For example, everyone has had the misfortune of being served by someone who was so overwhelmed, outclassed, and/or offensive that feelings of discomfort, pity, and/or malice dominate the evening to such an extent that the entire dining experience is ruined. I simply didn't want to be that server. And (3) because waiters worked with the barmaids, I didn't want to be a total buffoon and compromise their tips and, therefore, their modest livelihoods.

The barmaid sorority, as I later found out, had a distinct hierarchy of waiters whom they preferred to work with, which they based on certain qualities. According to them, the most desirable qualities in a waiter were: work ethic, organizational skills, rapport with the customers, ability to up-sell, a somewhat happy disposition, and honesty while dividing the tips. These desirable qualities were then thought to translate into an easier and more profitable night for the barmaids, but none of us waiters managed to acquire and master all of these qualities simultaneously. For example, when I began I'm sure my organizational skills and professional rapport with the customers were lacking, and my ability to up-sell was essentially non-existent, but my work ethic and sense of honesty were virtually unprecedented. In contrast, the veteran waiters, as they ripened, exhibited a noticeable decline in work ethic and honesty, while their dispositions became absolutely grotty, but they could up-sell pork roast to an Orthodox Jew. Consequently, out of the dozen or so waiters who worked the Death Star, I probably ranked tenth in overall desirability when I first started and climbed to possibly third by the time I was fired. A lesser quality that I did possess in spades, however, was the inclination to scrutinize the tip sheet, which most definitely cost me a higher ranking in the eyes of a few unscrupulous barmaids.

The tip sheet was a sheet of paper kept by the cashier at the cashier's station, which was tucked away in the kitchen next to the dish pit. Typically, when a customer paid their check, the waiter or the barmaid would collect the money or the credit card slip and drop it off at the cashier's station with a hard copy of the check. The cashier (who was Tina during the day, or one of Tina's friends at night) would then put it all into the till, but not before marking down the serving team's gratuity on the tip sheet. Consequently, at the end of the night the waiter would collect all of his team's tips in cash from the cashier, then proceed to calculate how much money was owed to the Vagrant (almost always $10), the kitchen (based on the number of the meals), the hostess (usually a flat fee between $5-10), and the charge card companies because Trader's refused to pay it on our behalf. Then the waiter would theoretically divide the remaining money in half and deliver the appropriate amount of cash to the barmaid, who was usually sipping a glass of white wine or a Caesar in the lounge and trying to solicit a foot massage or something more sordid. But the problem with this system was two-fold. First, we relied on the arithmetic and organizational skills of the cashiers, which were sketchy at the best of times. I don't believe that the cashiers ever intentionally scammed us, but I know for a fact that some tips would be left off the tip sheet, and others would be "accidentally" marked under the wrong serving team's column. As a result, the wise server would only hand in the exact amount of the check to the cashier and keep the remaining gratuity in his/her pocket as a safety precaution. And second, over the course of a busy night, a serving team would have accrued a few hundred dollars in tips, which basically served as a checking account for certain barmaids. For example, there were a few girls who would constantly buy cigarettes from the restaurant on account, which would appear on the tip sheet ledger as a negative $5, and conveniently forget to mention this to their serving partner. Granted, this was only $2.50 out of the waiter's pocket, but throw in a shot of Baileys or a glass of white wine, and it starts to add up. Suffice it to say, there were a few barmaids who took exception to some of our vigilant accounting techniques, but this could usually be dissipated with a foot massage or something much more sordid.

Before long, I began to better appreciate what it took to be a decent server. I agreed with the barmaids that work ethic, organizational skills, and a pleasant disposition were important traits, but not necessarily essential in order to become a highly competent server. For instance, I realized that work ethic and organizational ability are often negatively correlated; meaning that the harder one works the less organized one has to be in order to accomplish their tasks. Conversely, if a server is ridiculously organized (bordering on obsessive / compulsive) then he/she is not forced to run wildly around the restaurant to get things done and ends up looking like he/she would have plenty of time to have intercourse with a large-breasted quadruped. And in terms of personality, what a server perceives as a pleasant disposition can sometimes be interpreted as lifeless by some customers, or impertinent by others. Consequently, over the course of many years, I managed to boil the job of server down to its absolute essentials and found three distilled qualities at the bottom of the flask, which brings us to our first, and foremost, serving tip:

****

SERVING TIP #1: Yes, it helps if you are a hard working, highly organized, quick witted master of stress management who has a photographic memory, supermodel looks, and big boobs or pectorals, but these are not essential to become an extraordinary server. In actuality, you should focus on three vital qualities. (1) A sense of urgency - which means that you realize when you must bust your ass to get something for a customer, then actually bust your ass to get it. In other words, you must be aware and task oriented. For example, when a customer says that he is missing a carving instrument to cut his steak with, you must immediately walk to a cutlery tray and fetch a serrated steak knife for him, or, better, steal one off an adjacent table, but not take the long route past the cute hostess to inquire about her plans after work, then pick up your forgotten drinks at the bar, then drop off a butter knife to your hungry customer. No, that won't do. Instead, keep your head in the moment, be able to prioritize, and be prepared to break a sweat. (2) A keen ability to anticipate - which means that you can foresee a customer needing something, then actually bring it to him before he has to beg you for it, or remind you a dozen times. For example, if a customer orders some screaming hot chicken wings then you should automatically bring him a finger bowl with lemon and some extra napkins because he will definitely need them. You might also ask him if he needs a glass of water to douse the flames on his tongue. In other words, develop the ability to see a situation from another person's perspective, then act on it. And (3) a capacity for adaptability - which means that you can appreciate the social dynamics of a situation and then act accordingly. For example, a table of two love birds who are displaying their mating rituals do not need you doing your stand-up comedy routine for them. Conversely, a table of high school kids wouldn't appreciate your dry wit or white glove service. Therefore, develop a waitering persona that has some range and leave your own lame identity at home. This is why actors and entertainers often have the potential to be great servers, but usually self-destruct due to their various manias and insecurities.

****

Developing a waitering persona can be a precarious task. On the one hand, it can provide you with the freedom to say and do things that you wouldn't otherwise have the fortitude for. So while under the guise of another character, one is free to flirt shamelessly, scold brazenly, and carry on uproariously without the fear of customers or staff passing judgment on the inner you. On the other hand, it has the potential to unlock some latent, deep-seated schizophrenia or trigger a multiple personality disorder. Mental health concerns aside, my waitering persona eventually morphed into **WAITERMAN** who, as I stated previously, could have been my Tarzan or my Earl of Greystoke depending on your perspective. In essence, I needed **WAITERMAN** to hide behind, to be my sacrificial lamb, to take the heat for my mistakes, to allow me to be savage and unleash brutal honesty, to deflect the frequent blows to my super-ego, and to slough my anxiety onto because the most deleterious thing a server can do is internalize stress. I'm no Freudian, but I believe it's this internalization of anxiety that manifests itself into a truly dreadful type of dream state. Of course, I'm referring to the infamous waitering nightmares.

There is no question that the role of serving is stressful. Everything from the customer's demands to the dealings with the staff is ripe with potential stressors. Add to this the various biochemical stimulants derived from the mandatory drinks after work (or while on shift) and a greasy late night meal, and you might begin to appreciate the internal milieu of the server who lays in bed and futilely awaits sleep. When slumber does arrive, it becomes restless and chaotic. The imagery is vivid and lifelike, but lacking the social constraints of the real world. There is often something urgent that must be accomplished, but unable to be completed for absurdly restrictive reasons. Within a month of becoming a waiter, my subconscious had written, produced, directed, and filmed a full feature waiter nightmare that would rear its ugly head about three times a week if I was working full-time. When I later switched restaurants, a sequel was added to its body of work. Below is a synopsis of each waiter nightmare with some psychoanalysis as an added bonus in parentheses.

(1) Waiter nightmare number one began with me in a classroom. I am sitting in a desk with no clothes on and notice that my penis seems much smaller than normal. I am panicked because I must somehow leave the classroom and get to work, but I have ridiculously under-sized genitalia. I light a small fire in the desk next to me, which serves as a distraction, and then slip out of the classroom with a chalkboard eraser covering my privates. On the way to the restaurant I come across a bed sheet, which I fashion into a toga. No one seems to take notice of the toga while at work, but I feel more than a little self-conscious. Because I am late for work, my section has ballooned and spilled into the parking lot, which forces me to run around like a madman wrapped in a bed sheet. I then realize that my left leg is about six inches shorter than my right, and all of

my teeth have become detached from my gums but still residing within my mouth. Consequently, I am forced to hobble from table to table while trying to speak with a mouth full of loose enamel. I then awake from the nightmare in a panic, having soaked my T-shirt with sweat, and immediately reach for my mouth and genitals for reassurance (translation: I am an exhibitionist with deep fears of emasculation and dentistry, who has hedonistic tendencies, but needs to see a chiropractor).

(2) Waiter nightmare number two began with me standing at the wood of the service bar. I've made the mistake of ordering blended drinks and cappuccinos, which has not endeared me to the bartender. The wait for the drinks becomes excruciating because I can see the vindictive hostess seating table after table in my section, which is spreading as quickly as the fallout from an atomic bomb. I finally load my tray with the drinks and try to move on, but I notice my ankle is chained to the bar. The chain is able to stretch somewhat, but always falls short of my tables by five or six feet. Consequently, I am forced to toss my customer's drinks at them, some of which are caught, but most of which fall short and smash on the tile floor. Naturally there is no busser in sight, so I resort to cleaning up the mess while stretched out on my stomach. When I stand up and run to the computer to order about a thousand items, some officious manager type notices the stains on the front of my shirt and refuses to let me back into my section until I change into a patio shirt that just happens to be a size too small with a big silk screened picture of Don Johnson on the back. I then wake up, soaked with sweat and heart pounding, and begin to pray that the restaurant is awash in flames and burning to the ground (translation: I am a sadomasochist who enjoys subservient role playing and cross dressing, but harbors ill feelings for young hostesses who thwart my advances and has general contempt for authority figures).

It didn't take long to understand why the majority of the staff spent so much of their time at Trader's. Between the restrictive scheduling and the beckoning atmosphere, many of the staff found themselves unable to escape, as if the restaurant was a minimum-security prison (or asylum) that only occasionally granted day passes. As an example, most of us were forced to work split shifts, which meant arriving at the restaurant between ten-thirty and eleven in the morning, working the lunch shift until two in the afternoon, buggering off until about five, then having to work the dinner shift until eleven or midnight. Then once off work, the decisions became limitless: What were we having to eat? Were we sipping some cocktails or were we going hard? Were we staying at Trader's or exploring another jungle? Who was driving? Would any gibbons be swinging from the vines there? Consequently, we usually started our shenanigans when most people were deep in slumber, which made us functionally nocturnal (much like our primitive prosimian ancestors were, I suspect). In fact, most people at Trader's were deathly pale all year round because of the absence of any ultraviolet radiation exposure, which surprisingly didn't seem to cause a Rickets epidemic. Or maybe it did, which would have explained the bowed legs and ape-like posture most of them displayed.

In my case, I worked three split shifts and two regular night shifts during the week. But regardless of the previous day's shift, I would still struggle to wake up before noon on any given day (on Sundays I refused to work the brunch shift and slept in well past noon). However, once dull-eyed and greasy-tailed, I would drive to the restaurant and work the lame lunch shift for a measly $20 in tips. I then would have less than three hours off to run errands if I had any to run. If not, I would stay at the restaurant and graze on the salad bar while watching soap operas on the big screen television because three hours wasn't enough time to head home and accomplish anything productive (I hated myself for being concerned if "Luke and Laura Spencer" would ever get back together). As the evening shift approached, I would drag my ass into the kitchen and learn the evening's specials, which were usually some type of white fish and a strange cut of beef in a peppercorn sauce. Eventually, I would survey the night schedule and pray that my assigned barmaid was someone different from the lunch shift who didn't have a penchant for embezzling contraband cigarettes or house wine from me. Then I would straighten my brown knit tie, chew an aspirin, and prepare for the customers to shuffle in and make my life hell. Six hours of torment later, but with another $70-100 in tips within my pocket, Buddy, Renny, and I would start to plan our evening. Sometimes we would try to shmooze our way into the Trader's Inn Nightclub (as we were only seventeen), or use our fake identifications at a bar downtown, but if it wasn't a weekend shift we would usually just head over to Renny's house to watch a movie and eat pizza (while Dr. Don likely dreamed of a polygamous existence in Salt Lake City). Finally, at about three in the morning, I would haul ass home and go to bed, but not before I took a shower, worried about the impending waiter nightmare, and then prayed that the restaurant was awash in flames and burning to the ground so I wouldn't have to report to work the next day and continue the vicious circle.

Waitering was a love-hate proposition for me from the start. I obviously loved making much more money, the cooler status, the more dynamic nature of the job, and the omnipresent social opportunities, but I hated the basic act of "serving," the enormous amount of stress, the late night hours, and the dominating effect that the restaurant had on my life. Buddy, Renny, and I had grand plans for our lives at that point and we were fearful of the Trader's jungle becoming a boggy, quicksand-filled pit that was going to suck us in and swallow us alive, then shit us out as mere husks of our former selves without any ambitions or motivations. Well, not exactly, but we were certainly leery of its possible ill effects. As it turned out, Buddy and I initially succumbed to the restaurant lifestyle and ended up withdrawing from the university (although we would return the following year once we were out of Trader's evil clutches), whereas Renny procrastinated and missed the withdrawal deadline and was beleaguered with a transcript full of "Fs" that crippled his post-secondary plans for years afterward. In the end, we were lucky to escape with our anal tissues relatively intact and pliable, but many others were not as fortunate. A perfect example is that of an alpha-male waiter whom we called "Yankee."

Yankee was similar to Crash in stature and temperament. He would also bounce off the walls (which I would later learn was due to his cocaine addiction), but in a more controlled, cognizant fashion. People at Trader's liked Yankee more than Crash, even though he regularly offended the staff with his quick-witted, caustic comments that were often derogatory and overly critical. He was also a very bright guy with lofty ambitions: he wanted to be a brain surgeon. Literally, he talked about becoming a neurosurgeon, or at least a neurologist. Fair enough, we thought, as we had no reason to doubt his resolve. We were aware that precious few people in the entire restaurant had managed to obtain undergraduate degrees (Ramses was one of them), but Yankee was enrolled in a science program at the university and seemed different from the other waiters. The Rabbit, Buddy, and I got to know him fairly well because he dated Medusa's younger sister, "Elvira," who worked at Trader's as a lounge/nightclub waitress. In fact, Buddy and I rendezvoused with Yankee and Elvira during a trip to Mexico in '87 and soaked up some sun and booze with the two of them while contemplating various Mayan ruins. Initially I liked Yankee, and essentially looked to him as a role model because I also had ideas of becoming a doctor, but once we joined him as fellow waiters and got a better feel for his persona, the cracks in his armor began to show.

Yankee had a fairly dominating personality, which gave him a false sense of perspective. More to the point, because Yankee was often right (or bullied people into thinking he was right) he could never admit to being wrong or to misjudging a social situation. A good example was the time that a table of farmers gave him a poor tip. Now of course no server ever enjoys getting tipped poorly, but it is still entirely up to the discretion of the often uneducated customer, so one must develop thicker skin as a server. Yes, it is frustrating making a living based on what stupid people think you are worth at any given moment, but that's just the way it is. There is no point in taking it personally because most people do not know the guidelines for tipping, which cause some to tip poorly, but others to sometimes over-tip. Therefore, during the course of a shift, it usually evens out. The problem with Yankee, though, was that he thought he was owed at least twenty percent on every table and took it very personally when he didn't receive it. So one fateful night when a family of farmers left a seven percent tip (largely in coins), Yankee's substance-abused mind snapped while he was trying to scoop up said coins and noticed that their table was without any of the ornate salt and pepper shakers that were usually there. This served as the final kick in the camel toe to Yankee, so he ran out the door and into the parking lot where he confronted the oblivious family of farmers and said something along the lines of, "Look here hillbillies, it's bad enough that you insult me with this shitty tip, but don't think for a fucking second that you can get away with stealing those salt and pepper shakers!" He then proceeded to actually throw the coins at them and demanded that they return the shakers. When they pleaded absolute ignorance and innocence, and then finally became offended, Yankee stomped back into the restaurant cursing everything in his path while being oblivious to the fact that the desk helps had removed all of the salt and pepper shakers from the tables about ten minutes earlier and were cleaning them in the back. Justifiably, someone from the family phoned Trader's the next day to lodge a complaint against Yankee and demand that he get fired on the grounds of his outrageously shabby conduct. However, it was Medusa who fielded the call and made up some bullshit excuse on his behalf (strung out on crack, perhaps?) because it would have started a huge battle with her sister, Elvira, if Yankee had been fired. In the end, Yankee was suspended for a shift or two, which he managed to parlay into a quick holiday to Las Vegas, and then all was abruptly forgotten. Meanwhile, other less fortunate servers were being preyed on by Medusa for being a few minutes late for their shift, for not wearing a clean tie, or for showing up for work with a hangover. Unfortunately, that's the partisan justice system that often exists in the restaurant industry.

  To sum up my point, then, Yankee was a guy who was ambitious and bright, who thought that his goals were best met by going to university and becoming a doctor, but try as he might have, the sub-culture of Trader's wore him out and beat him down. He was initially well regarded and respected, but he slowly turned into an erratic, bitter, paranoid asshole. The many nights of drinking, snorting, and carousing melted his dreams quicker than an ice cube in the hands of Lucifer. And although Yankee crashed and burned brighter than most, he was just one of many who were sabotaged, derailed, or snuffed out. This brings us to our next serving tip, which is applicable for any prospective restaurant worker:

****

SERVING TIP #2: If you are a person who has ambitions of becoming something that requires quite a bit of training, studying, and/or productive time spent away from your much needed part-time job, then either avoid the restaurant industry altogether, or make sure you work at a place that has a disproportionate number of people with goals and ambitions similar to yours. This doesn't mean you can't shag the hostess after every shift, eat leftover meat off of customer's plates, commit fraud on credit card slips, experiment with various hallucinogens, drink stolen Coronas until you puke, or drive your rusty Volkswagen into a ditch, but at least there will be an almost imperceptible voice of reason lingering in the air reminding everyone that there are some important things that must be done the next day, and it's OK to do them. Or, put another way, make sure your restaurant party train is ambitious and headed for Grand Central Station in New York, not Platform One in Vladivostok.

****

Aside from learning the basic skills of the trade, my early education as a waiter also included learning some tricks of the trade. By tricks I mean methods of maximizing my yield and lessons on being opportunistic, or more to the point, being a proficient thief. I will stand by my premise within the definition of "scamming" in the glossary that absolutely all restaurant employees scam the restaurants they are working in to some degree or another. Whether it's breaking into the restaurant after hours to steal $25,000 in undeposited revenues, or taking home a small package of Orange Pekoe tea, the ability to scam exists within us all and the rigors of the restaurant industry will eventually promote its manifestation. The reasons for this are probably eloquently laid out in someone's criminal psychology dissertation, which is beyond the scope of this hack's diatribe, but I can definitely attest to its widespread existence.

I prefer not to climb onto a soapbox and proclaim scamming as either unethical or honorable, but rather to categorize it as either necessary or pathological. Reasons that would qualify it as a necessity might include: poverty, retribution, or emotional well-being. Pathological scamming is a different beast in that there isn't a conscious choice made to steal something for a defined purpose. Pathological scammers are compelled to steal due to some sort of chemical imbalance, and as such scam indiscriminately at all times. These are people who steal something as insignificant as a bottle of ketchup from the restaurant, then something stupid like a flashing hazard from a construction site near their home. Why bloody bother? If you are going to scam, do so because you are short for tuition, trying to increase your chances of getting laid, or correcting for some injustice that was perpetrated against you by management, but at least have a defensible, somewhat noble reason. At Trader's, there were a few pathological scammers, but mostly they scammed out of necessity and because they enjoyed playing the game. There was the petty stuff such as selling the ornate salt and pepper shakers for $10 each and pocketing the money, and then there was a much riskier scheme that required some clever planning. It was known as the "dummy scam."

During the early to mid '80s, computer technology within the restaurant industry was almost non-existent. Food and drink orders were either manually written down or somehow processed through an archaic looking till. This was time consuming, inefficient, prone to errors, and easily manipulated, but that's the way it was. At Trader's, each waiter was assigned four or five booklets of checks (with about fifty checks per booklet) at a time. Each booklet fell somewhere within a series of serial numbers, which was carefully recorded by management. For example, at the beginning of the week, a waiter would put in a request for more booklets of checks. He would then be summoned to the basement where Medusa or Mussolini would hand him four or five booklets and asked to sign some sheet to prove that he was given those particular booklets. He was then reminded that he would be charged $50 if any booklet or individual check within that series went missing. The waiter would then put his booklets in his locker and pray that nobody knew the combination to his lock and wanted to fuck him over. After the prayer was finished and his chest was crossed, the waiter would then proceed to stuff one of the booklets into his waitering apron and be ready for action on the floor.

The individual checks consisted of two sheets: a thin, white top copy that had a carbon backing, and a thicker, yellow copy that was referred to as the "hard-on." While at the table, the waiter would write the order down on some scrap paper then run to the back area and carefully fill out a check from his booklet. The table number, number of customers, and food orders with their corresponding prices all had to be written directly onto the checks. The waiter would then give the white copy to the kitchen with relatively little verbalization (or Lou would silence you with a Cantonese expletive that would make George Carlin cringe and throw it back in your face with some tepid juicy on it) and keep the hard-ons within his apron (no pun intended), which would later be presented to the customer for payment. Finally, the hard-ons were handed in with the customer's payment to the cashier, who filed them and recorded the gratuity on the tip sheet. Meanwhile, the barmaid would take the customers' drink orders and run to the bar where she would ring them in on a till using an entirely different check, then verbally order them from the bartender. When a table requested the check, the waiter would ask the barmaid for the total of the bar tab, then write that amount down on his hard-on and add it to the food total before he presented the check to his customers. I know it sounds pretty archaic by today's standards, but it worked smoothly and provided the waiters with an opportunity for a great scam.

To pull off the scam, a waiter needed a check that wasn't his, which was referred to as the "dummy." Obviously then, a check would have to be stolen from some unsuspecting, black sheep waiter (costing him $50, or at least a great amount of suspicion), or an entire booklet would have to be stolen from the office, which was a good scam unto itself because the individual checks could then be sold to other unscrupulous waiters for $10 each. Once a waiter had the dummy in his possession, he had to be very perceptive in order to execute the scam, and very careful not to let his barmaid in on it because he was already peeved at having to split the tips 50/50, so he was damned if he was going to give her a cut of the scam. The prime table to use the scam on was one that didn't want anything to drink aside from water, or one that had already purchased their drinks from the lounge while they were waiting for a table to become available in the restaurant. With no drinks to order, a bar tab would not be needed, which would effectively eliminate the bartender and the barmaid from the equation. That element satisfied, the waiter would then have to find out if the table was going to pay by credit card or cash, which was crucial because a credit card would have to be rung in and matched with the hard-on at the end of the night by the cashier. So typically, the waiter would say something like, "I'm sorry to have to bother you about this now folks, but we're having difficulty getting authorization from the credit card companies tonight, so it would be more convenient to pay by cash if that would be at all possible." If the table acknowledged that they would be paying with cash then the scam was a go and the waiter would begin to salivate at the idea of being $100 or so richer once the customers departed and their check was carefully discarded, which effectively eliminated any proof that they were there. From this point, there were only two hurdles that could trip the waiter up. First, if the barmaid was the first person to the table after the customers departed and dropped off the hard-on with the money to the cashier, then the waiter was pooched because the cashier (especially if it was Tina) would notice that the dummy was out of sequence with the other legitimate checks. Invariably the waiter would have to discuss this discrepancy with Medusa the next day, with his chances of being fired at about ninety percent unless he was thought of as especially valuable or handsome. And secondly, the kitchen staff kept all of the white portions of the checks so they would have an idea of how much money was owed to them at the end of the shift via tip-outs. Normally, all they cared about was the number of meals on each check, but sometimes Barry would go beyond the call of duty and put them in sequential order. If he did this, he would invariably notice the discrepancy because he was a descendent of Buddha and was omnipotent and all-knowing. Again, the waiter would have to face Medusa the next day and elucidate some preposterous story to save his ass and job, which he put in jeopardy for about $100 or so. But this is the misunderstood thing about scamming, because it obviously sounds stupid to risk your job and livelihood for $100 (or much less with other scams) if you only look at the face value of the particular scam that got you busted. However, what if a waiter pulled off many scams previously, which earned him a lot of additional money, which in turn made him a much happier employee, which in turn made him a better waiter (at least from the customer's perspective), which then actually made him more money in legitimate gratuities by the end of each shift? Then are the scams worth the risk each and every time? Some would say "Hell, yes!" because scamming can create some very enticing positive reinforcement. Let's look at a comparison of two waiters to better understand why one wouldn't be compelled to scam and why one would.

(1) Evan the Waiter: Evan is a nice guy with a wife and a toddler at home. He is putting himself through an electrician's apprenticeship and desperately needs extra money. He gets a job at a restaurant as a waiter and starts to understand the subtleties of it. He quickly decides to shun the evil social scene in order to be a good dad and husband (even though he would love to pound shots

of Jagermeister and then shag the hostess), which gets him ostracized by all the movers and shakers within the restaurant. The staff no longer invites him out or includes him within their inner circle, which hurts Evan's feelings because he was a fairly popular guy back in high school. Evan is tempted to pull a scam because he could really use the money, but being out of a job for at least a couple of weeks and having to tell his wife that he was fired for trying to scam a few bucks is a powerful disincentive. Evan chooses not to scam or to shag the hostess, which are both ethically sound decisions. However, Evan eventually becomes bitter and loathes the inevitability of having to work three nights a week because everyone seems to be making more money and having much more fun than he. This general dissatisfaction permeates the rest of his life, which is sensed by his wife, who becomes suspicious if Evan is having a few drinks after work with the cute hostess. The night manager, capitalizing on a perfect opportunity, blows plumes of smoke into Evan's anus by telling him he would make a terrific part-time manager. Evan accepts the bait, but actually makes less money than he did as a waiter. Reeling from the general turn of events, Evan decides that becoming a G.M. and making $100,000 a year is more attractive than being a tradesman. Evan then launches himself into being the quintessential management clone and swears vengeance against all the people who spurned him prior. Over time, Evan grows a little paunch and masters the skill of slowly sipping coffee in a booth while the restaurant collapses in chaotic ruin around him, but unfortunately, his career stalls at the position of night manager and his wife leaves him for a cheesy real estate agent.

(2) J.J. the Waiter: J.J. is also a nice guy, but single and planning a trip to Europe before he embarks on a chemical engineering degree. J.J. is also an opportunist and notices ways of making an extra buck at the expense of the restaurant he works at so he eagerly accepts the invitations from the staff to party with them and quickly becomes entrenched within their social scene. J.J. decides to start scamming because all of his restaurant buddies seem to be doing it. Before long, J.J. is consistently making about $30 more per shift, which makes him happy but also releases him from the stress created by being so dependent on the customers' charity for his livelihood. In fact, J.J. stops obsessing about how much his tables are tipping him because he knows he will be taking home good money at the end of the night due to his scamming. In fairly short order, J.J.'s newly relaxed attitude puts the customers at ease, which causes them to tip him better. So not only is J.J. scamming additional money and making better tips, but he is getting scheduled for the busiest shifts in the most lucrative sections

because he has partied with the powers that be and is shagging the cute hostess. In addition, J.J. is also saving money on booze because he has been granted free drinking status by the bartender. Therefore, although his fear of getting busted for scamming is omnipresent, the benefits of scamming start to far outweigh the risks in J.J.'s mind. Over time, J.J. manages to save some money, but chooses to go to Atlantic City for a week with his restaurant buddies (where he loses thousands) and puts his European trip on hold. J.J. never makes it to Europe or university and ends up getting fired for scamming, but he has much fonder memories of his waitering days. In the end, J.J. becomes a part owner of a popular lounge, grows a little paunch, and watches his staff like a hawk to prevent them from ripping him off.

From a waiter's perspective then, scamming while on shift can be likened to masturbating before a date (which is so beautifully portrayed by the Farrelly brothers in *Something About Mary*). In effect, the guy is released from obsessing about something that cannot be controlled as he takes matters into his own hands (pun intended). With the tension/stress reduced, the guy is able to have a clear head and focus on other important matters (like providing better service for his customers or actually talking to his date before trying to get into her pants). Ironically, the customer and the female often rewards the guy with what he was originally seeking (i.e., loot or booty) because his motives are not so desperately obvious.

The Blind Leading the Blind...

The truly exceptional thing about the ever-transforming Trader's staff was their diversity. There was everyone from a classical pianist who had performed in Paris, to an exotic male dancer who had stripped at Chippendale's. But regardless of their varied backgrounds, they all had to be "properly" trained as waiters. I had been a Trader's waiter all of six months before I was given the daunting task of training some unlucky bastard. Granted, I had a pretty good feel for the job and I had risen up the barmaid's rankings to number three, but I was barely eighteen, and for all intents and purposes didn't know my ass from a hole in the ground. Underlining my general neophyte disposition even further was the fact that the poor bastard I was to train was forty-two years old and was a founding member of a fairly successful rock band. His name was "Jan," and along with a couple of friends, formed a rock group that was quite popular in the early to mid '70s. I believe they even had a song that cracked the *Top Ten in Billboard* during the summer of '71, which was quite an accomplishment for a troop of local yard apes.

There was no question that Jan was a total character, which undoubtedly stemmed from his colorful lifestyle amid the backdrop of the zany '70s. He claimed he knew Elvis, Wolfman Jack, Roy Orbison, and many other notables while at the height of his fame. He lived large, blowing most of his money, but then parlayed his notoriety into a fairly prosperous real estate career after his band split up. Things were going well for him until his accountant scammed him for $225,000 which understandably pushed his life into a free fall. The loss of the money, combined with a severely depressed real estate market, landed Jan at Trader's looking to make enough money to pay his mortgage and feed his family. It was a sad story really, but Jan appeared full of bravado and never let anyone know the depths of his despair, or the motives behind his friskiness...

Jan and I hit it off quite well from the beginning. He was a fairly fascinating guy who had a thousand entertaining stories about a world that few people have the privilege (or misfortune) of traveling in. Strangely, he always remarked that my voice had "balls" and offered to give me voice lessons at a reduced rate. I never knew what to make of that. Did he see great potential in my voice and was compelled to develop it? Did he need the extra money that badly? Or did he want to jump my bones? I ask this because he seemed to get extraordinarily close to me (both emotionally and physically) in an unusually short period of time. I wasn't too concerned about the emotional part because I could usually rationalize that Jan was a passionate guy who always expressed his opinion. So when he told me how he wanted his fourteen-year-old son to turn out just like me, I was touched instead of freaked out. However, it was his physical transgressions that made me wonder. For example, he could never quite greet me without trying to grab my testicles. Seriously. I would see him approaching and hear him say something like, "Hey kid! Are you ready for another night in this bogus scene? Yeah, right on. Jesus your voice has balls, Frenchy!" then he would suddenly dive at my genitalia to punctuate his point. I just didn't care for that. It got to the point where I would talk to him at an oblique angle, effectively restricting access to my reproductive organs. In fact, I would have been totally justified wearing an athletic supporter complete with a protective plastic cup while in his company. And if he wasn't trying to examine me for testicular cancer, he would be slapping me on the back hard enough to dislocate ribs from my thoracic spine. Needless to say, being at ease was difficult around Jan.

Jan also didn't seem to have access to a car, which forced him to solicit me for a ride home on most nights. So there I was, barely eighteen and chauffeuring a forty-two-year-old ex-rockstar home in my little Volkswagen GTi, not out of reverence, but out of absolute necessity because this guy was broke, didn't drive a car, and was too proud to take public transportation. The prospects of being his age and in his position frightened me enormously. However, he taught me a valuable lesson by illustrating that anyone can come across a slippery slope and end up at rock bottom, because Jan wasn't stupid, lazy, or self destructive, but due to a certain sequence of ill-timed events, he was felled by something more powerful than any dish pit demon: plain old life. Thankfully, Jan would jump out of my car once we arrived at his place and leave me with only a punched shoulder, some tousled hair, and a casual invite in for a brandy. It turned out to be nothing too gratuitous or suspicious, just a little frisky.

After four weeks of trying to train Jan, it was apparent that the guy wasn't going to catch on to the waitering routine at Trader's. Granted, he was awesome at singing Happy Birthday to those customers who demanded we join them in celebrating their insignificant inceptions, but hopeless at virtually every other task related to food delivery. He was forgetful, easily distracted, and usually flustered. He foolishly battled with the kitchen guys, who often looked at him as if he had Tourette's syndrome. The barmaids rated him near the bottom of their lists because they all made shitty money while working with him. Most importantly, though, he came across as a bigger persona than Medusa, who couldn't tolerate being in anyone's shadow while in the confines of her little, medieval kingdom. As such, she took an instant dislike to him and quickly planned his demise. From Jan's position, he correctly identified Medusa as an inconsequential creature within this world, as somebody who was destined to never make a significant impact in any facet of life. I shared his astute assessment and admired his ability to cut to the bare essence of a situation without much prejudice. In many ways he was fearless and called a spade a spade, but unfortunately he came across the Queen of Spades who rather unceremoniously fired his ass. The last I heard of Jan, he had reunited with his old band (or a close facsimile thereof) and was performing some of his timeless classics for some very appreciative fans. I'll tell you, it was Jan who had the balls.

Chapter 6

Exiled

"And where the offence is, let the great axe fall."

- Shakspeare's *Hamlet*

A Real Trooper...

The weeks went by at Trader's as I continually tried to prove my worth. I attempted to be punctual, cognizant, and tidily attired. However, I ended up wearing the same brown knit tie for about four months without anyone either noticing or caring. Buddy had also settled into a routine within Planet Hoth and squeezed his expanding girth into the same khaki chinos shift after shift. We had become a little complacent and fatter without school or team sports in our lives. Of course, it didn't help that we gorged like a nomadic pack of savanna hyenas a couple times each week.

Like most servers who let their restaurants totally dominate their lives, Buddy, Renny, and I would eat at Trader's on all of our off days. Yes, we got a twenty-five percent discount off our food, and yes it was good food, but it really was pathetic in that we couldn't be bothered to find anywhere else to go. Typically, the three of us would sit in a server's section that we liked (as we couldn't bear tipping forty percent to some of the jackasses who worked there) and proceed to order our usuals. Not coincidentally, we would all start with the salad bar (including a bowl of Portuguese bean and sausage soup), then split a couple orders of braised shrimp, then each tackle sixteen ounces of prime rib topped with asparagus/crab meat/hollandaise sauce all nestled next to a stuffed potato and cheese toast. I stood only five ten and weighed one hundred and seventy-seven pounds at that stage, but yet I managed to cram all that food into my ridiculously distended gullet. And for an encore, we would pick at a piece of chocolate covered, coffee ice cream pie. We were total gluttons, by God! So much so that we couldn't immediately leave after we had finished masticating because we needed to unbutton our slacks and lay down for a few minutes at the table to recover (thank Jesus for booths). Sometimes our feeding frenzy actually sabotaged the rest of the evening as the enormous release of insulin from our pancreases would almost send us into comas, effectively disabling us from performing the most basic of human tasks for many hours thereafter. And as we lay at the table, belching, flatulating, and feeling a special kinship to hibernating grizzly bears, "Man" would usually walk by and give us some ill-timed and unsolicited nutritional advice such as, "Hey guys, you should eat a little slower or something, eh?"

Man was a veteran Trader's waiter who eventually became Mussolini's replacement. Most people liked him simply because he was the antithesis of Mussolini. Man was repulsed by any type of aggressive confrontation and you couldn't beat any constructive criticism out of him whatsoever. He was fairly tall and husky, and preferred to dress like a cowboy, but he was the least aggressive ruminant in the restaurant. In many ways, he was an effective manager because he didn't pretend to know your shit better than you did. Medusa loved Man because he was a complete invertebrate who hung (and quivered) on her every word. My first major involvement with Man as a manager was the day that I contracted a Taiwanese, swine derived, "B" influenza virus, or some such plague, and desperately needed to abandon my shift.

It had been a long time since I was impregnated with a serious virus. I woke up that particular morning feeling a bit odd, but was able to trudge to work and start the lunch shift without too much difficulty. However, about an hour into my shift, I started to feel nauseous and fatigued so I went downstairs to the offices and informed Man that I was obviously in some sort of trouble. He didn't seem too impressed with my self-diagnosis and offered, "Go take a quick sit on the shitter and you'll be OK." So apparently Man considered himself a certified nutritionalist as well as a gastrointestinal specialist. Alas, about fifteen minutes after that, I was fighting my old nemesis, Mr. Saliva Rush, and strongly suggested to Man that he replace me on the floor right away. Instead of any prudent action, he explained, "I'm the only person who can fill in for you and I'm too busy making next week's schedule, so tough it out big guy." About five minutes after that, I was carrying some beef stew to a customer and the smell of it pushed me over the edge. I dropped the plate off and immediately ran downstairs to the washrooms, where I opened up a stall door and literally started ejecting vomitous all over the toilet and wall. I must have puked about four or five times and was actually forced to yell while doing it because of the violence the virus was inflicting upon my body. My spewing trajectory was so powerful that it hit the wall at exactly the same vertical level as it left my mouth, not being affected by gravity in the least, which gave me new appreciation for some of the scenes in *The Exorcist*. I felt like I could have blasted some puke to the moon, for Christ's sake! After it was over, I had trace amounts of my energy left so I decided to spend it by walking next door to the offices and knocking on Man's door. He initially answered the door irritated, but looked at my dress shirt and knit tie, which were dripping with foul smelling, brown regurgitate laden with a billion viral particles from Taiwan, and quickly realized that he had better get his waiter's apron on and bust his ass upstairs to take over my full section. I managed, "Is this proof enough for you?" and he answered, "Oh yah, or that's a pretty big coffee stain on your shirt," which was about the wittiest thing I had ever heard him say. I then stumbled over to the dry storage area and started calling out, "Buddaaay!" which was eerily reminiscent of another dark moment in my life. Buddy eventually came to my rescue and brought a damp hot cloth and some ginger ale, which was thoughtful, but pretty much useless. He then drove me home in his '74 Plymouth Satellite sedan, which was brown and had a caved in driver's side from being T-boned earlier that year. As sick as I was, we still couldn't help but chuckle all the way home at the idea of Man being tossed into the chaos of a lunch shift and the fact that some poor bastard had to clean up the ungodly carnage I left behind in the men's washroom. Indeed, the entire fiasco could have been avoided if Man had paid heed to the following managerial tip:

****

MANAGERIAL TIP #2: Listen to your staff if they have uncommonly grievous complaints. Granted, there will be many con artists who attempt to bullshit you with faux claims of menstrual distress, ailing relatives, overdo assignments, unfair working conditions, and such, but it is imperative that you see through said bullshit and recognize who has integrity amongst your staff. Those who have some degree of integrity will still wage psychological warfare against you occasionally, but no one expects you to be an expert with the polygraph and have C.I.A. level training in behavioral science. In short, know who to trust for their honesty, and then simply listen to them. Hey, nobody said that being a restaurant manager is easy, just that it pays absolute peanuts.

****

My last major involvement with Man occurred the fateful night that we got slammed with about twenty tables of grade nine grads, most of whom I had to serve, just before the restaurant closed. It was clearly the worst two hours of my waitering career up until that point. I had separate checks coming out of my ass and steam coming out of my ears. My barmaid and I ran for the entire time and barely held it together, both physically and emotionally. Naturally, we made brutal money on every single table, which was like a good, stiff kick to both of our camel toes. Then, after we re-grouped and cleaned up the entire mess by ourselves, Man ambled over and inquired if I would like to join him for a beer. I thought that seemed like a nice gesture and assumed he was going to thank me for my Herculean efforts. So we sat down at a table in Planet Hoth, which had been deserted for at least an hour, and made some strained small talk until Man cleared his throat and said, "Well, big guy, this is going to sound brutal, but Medusa told me to fire you tonight."

Stiff Upper Lip...

I let fly, "You have to be fucking kidding me! I've busted my ass around here for months and just recently bought a Volkswagen and you're telling me I'm canned?!"

"My hands are tied, big guy, but I'll help you out by writing a reference letter as long as you don't tell Medusa. I'm really sorry, especially after the snafu earlier tonight," Man lamely offered. Well, he did seem genuinely upset by the situation, but it was a paltry consolation. Apparently, Medusa had told Man that most of the barmaids didn't like to work with me and that I had some customer complaints leveled at me, which was mostly bullshit. In reality, Medusa's marriage was disintegrating and she decided to pour some gasoline on the fire by having an affair with one of the perpetually horny bartenders at Trader's. This was a real classy move on her part (sarcasm intended), which caused some commotion within our family for obvious reasons. Medusa responded to the much-warranted criticisms by firing me in a sort of retaliatory maneuver. It was as simple as that. Unfortunately, Man just happened to be the messenger, which is why I didn't shoot him that night.

There was no question that I was bitter about being thrown to the lions. University was on the horizon, I had car payments to make, being fired hampered my chances of getting another job in the restaurant industry, and Medusa had momentarily gotten the better of me. It felt like there was an omnipresent black cloud overhead raining down misfortune. In addition, Buddy, Renny, and the Rabbit remained employed at Trader's, which made things rather awkward between us. For the first time, I felt the other edge of the restaurant axe: not the one that cuts through all the barriers to a jolly good time, but the one that decapitates without much (if any) warning. Being fired hurt, possibly more so than waiter's ass while taking a soapy shower, but Medusa was about to feel the great axe on her neck too. Who was going to step forward and be her hooded executioner, though?

The strangest thing happened a couple days after I got fired: someone, possibly in political protest, threw a very large rock through the windshield of Medusa's Volvo. Admittedly, the timing was highly suggestive of my direct involvement, but I fervently denied it. It did put a smile on my face, however, and made me sleep much better that night, which led to a rather bizarre dream. It went something like this:

The Bizarre Dream Sequence: It began with Buddy and I at his house for a couple of beers in order to acquire some liquid courage. After the painful gulping, the two of us then headed out in his Satellite to a rock quarry that was near Trader's. I jumped out of the car to select a choice rock; one that was big enough to penetrate the windshield of a Swedish made automobile. Once found, I heaved the medium-sized boulder into the back of Buddy's car and we drove off towards Trader's. We waited there until about midnight, which allowed most of the customers to leave the parking lot, but insured that Medusa and her new Romeo wouldn't be coming out any time soon. The minutes ticked by with anticipation. Was I really about to trash Medusa's car? Would it make me feel any better? Would I be sending a clear message that I would not be passive when confronted with such outrageous injustice? Well, the answers were all "Yes!" so we drove along side the tank-like Volvo. I wasn't weak for my age, but I struggled to hoist that boulder high above my head. As I stood near the driver's door, I soon realized that I couldn't throw the rock at an angle because the vector wouldn't be direct enough to shatter the windshield, so I had to climb onto the hood of the car. Once there, I felt pretty conspicuous standing with a rock poised above my head, but I had a mission to complete so I focused even harder. The moment was upon me, and I could hear my heart pounding and see my breath disperse in the chilly evening air. The edges of the rock were pinching and abrading my hands as I held it extended above my head, which was busy contemplating the nature of karma. I had a moment's indecision on whether it was the right thing to do, but I recounted the thousands of times that Medusa proved absolutely insufferable and made life miserable for all those around her. I soon concluded that she sincerely deserved to bare the brunt of my retribution, so with a grunt and a primal yell, I propelled the rock with all the force that one hundred and seventy-seven pounds could generate. Clearly it was sufficient, because the rock breached the windshield and banged into the steering wheel with the most savory type of crunching sound. Buddy was immediately wide eyed and offered, "Holy shit, Batman," at the sight of my destructive capabilities. It was sweet, sweet justice. Then I suddenly awoke from the eerily realistic dream, feeling somewhat refreshed, and having a strong desire to clean the fresh blood from my double-sided axe.

    Not surprisingly, all hell broke loose the next day as accounts of the "rock incident" swept through Trader's like a fart in a phone booth. Rather unexpectedly, the act seemed to polarize the restaurant, with some seeing me as a righteous hero, and others believing that I was the anti-Christ. In reality, I was probably somewhere between the two identities, but I continued to deny any involvement or wrongdoing. Naturally, Buddy, Renny, and a fair number of the serving staff sided with me because I was their comrade in arms and they all loathed the sight and sound of Medusa. I could have been Charles Manson, and they still would have supported me and probably petitioned the Pope for my Sainthood. However, the Rabbit, Yankee, Elvira, and a few others considered me public enemy number one. In fact, Elvira claimed that she saw me commit the act while she was in a secret room on the top floor of Trader's. I thought this was odd for a couple of reasons: (1) staff only went into that secret room to shag, and Yankee (Elvira's boyfriend) wasn't working that night; and (2) I simply wasn't in the parking lot when Elvira said I was. Elvira also began to spread rumors that the police were called and that they had removed my fingerprints from the rock. This was also strange because (1) my fingerprints were not on file with the police, and (2) finger prints cannot be retrieved from jagged, porous surfaces like that of rocks. But alas, no one ever accused Elvira of being virtuous or smarter than a box of tampons, so I remained calm and tried to get on with my life.

I would have gladly walked away from Trader's if they had paid me two weeks' severance pay (which equaled only $250 because gratuities were not considered part of my salary). But they were typically vindictive and refused to pay me. In turn, I refused to let them get away with another crime against humanity, so I reported them to the local labor board. A few weeks passed, but Medusa and the Vagrant's accountant ("Dilbert") didn't flinch. Finally, a sympathetic member of the labor board demanded a tête-à-tête meeting at Trader's, which was tricky because Medusa had to lift the ban that she had imposed on me because she thought I was dangerous to the people and property of the restaurant, which was a crock of well digested crudités (i.e., shit). When we eventually met, Medusa didn't quite have the fallopian tubes or the fortitude to attend, so it was just the labor board representative, Dilbert the accountant, and myself congregated in the darker dining room above the nightclub. Dilbert was prepared to stand his ground until it was pointed out that the labor board had received information regarding paying employees less than minimum wage, forcing waiters to contribute a nightly stipend to the owner, and allowing certain precocious adolescents to rampantly consume fire water as if they were displaced aboriginals on an inner city reserve. Looking suddenly pallid, but without flinching, Dilbert took out a checkbook and instantly wrote me a personal check for $250 and bid me a hasty good day. It was closure and a satisfying triumph, but one that shouldn't have surprised Medusa if she would have recalled my stubborn resolve.

Looking back, there is no question that a great axe fell, but perhaps it inadvertently cut the ties to fate, because **WAITERMAN** was finally set free and destined to find his new troop.

PART III

A NEW TROOP

"No story comes from nowhere; new stories are born from old - it is the new combinations that make them new."

- Salman Rushdie

No sooner was **WAITERMAN** starting to develop his own persona, when his growth was suddenly threatened by the falling of the great axe at Trader's. Luckily our jungle man had a tough, sinewy neck and was able to keep his head, which was fortunate because his noggin just happened to contain some wits by that time. He then proceeded to flounder through the following summer painting upscale houses on the outskirts of the city, which required negotiating sixty M.P.H. winds while perched upon a thirty-foot ladder. Occasionally the bored housewives would venture outside into the elements to inform the crew that their work was unacceptable and if they ever hoped to own $45,000 convertible BMWs like the ones parked in their driveways, then they had better pull their heads out of their asses and get serious. This abuse would have been bearable if any of the housewives had been named "Mrs. Robinson" and had an obsession for seducing young graduates, but unfortunately they were more interested in chatting to their yippy little dogs, going for three-hour pedicures, and spending quality time with their vibrative devices. Perhaps the young Dustin Hoffman just had better game, or maybe it was his red Alfa Romeo.

Without any notable seductions, the painting gig ended none too soon in early September. **WAITERMAN** then found himself sans job while the fall university session loomed on the horizon. He clearly needed a means to make some cake, and since he wasn't a small-time drug dealer like Len, his only sensible option was to find something more orthodox. Naturally, then, the restaurant jungle beckoned again because of the flexible evening hours, relatively good money (about $15 per hour including tips), and number of hot "Janes." Since our vine swinger had a flattering reference letter from Man, he was confident that he would find a waitering position in due time. That time just happened to be the first day of classes as he swung by a restaurant while enroute to the university. It was called "Duke's Place," and it had a rather interesting reputation.

Duke's originated on the west coast in the early 1980s, but spread inland to become a chain of about thirty-five restaurants by the late '80s. It was a unique concept at that time because it combined fresh food at reasonable prices in a trendy "California cafe" type of atmosphere. It seems commonplace now, but not many restaurants at that time had a plethora of "finger foods" on the menu that encouraged people to share and nibble. It allowed people of all ages to enjoy the dining-out experience without forcing them to over-indulge, either financially or gastronomically. In fact, one of Duke's mottos was "Eat a little, eat a ton," although it usually proved to be the former. They were the first restaurants in the city to popularize modern day staples such as nachos and chicken fingers. In many ways, Duke's was the antithesis of Trader's, which was one of the reasons why I was drawn to it.

Another reason why Duke's jumped out at me that fateful morning while enroute to the university was that my good friend Matt worked at a Duke's location in the south end of the city. He started there as a busser at about the same time that Buddy was settling in at Trader's as its new salad boy. From Matt's continuous tales of adventure, Duke's sounded more like a hip situational comedy, whereas Trader's was much more like a tired, old soap opera. The people at Duke's were substantially younger, with nobody (except the G.M.s) being older than thirty years of age. Most of the people also seemed to have some ambitions, whether it was attending university, traveling the world, or opening their own restaurant. Nobody seemed intent on tethering themselves to anybody and bringing them down (or so it seemed from the initial reports). Duke's just seemed like a better fit for me.

The Duke's dynasty was overseen by a colorful family that lived on the west coast. Their patriarch was a crusty old bastard named "Russ," who sired three sons before becoming moderately successful as a restaurateur in the '60s and '70s. His early restaurants were burger joints and greasy spoons, which suited his demeanor perfectly. Then, sometime in the late '70s or so, the Duke's concept dawned on him so he sold his burger joints to get capital and started to convert his greasy spoons into what became known as Duke's. Most, if not all, initial Duke's had a green and white color scheme for reasons that I couldn't even guess at. Paper mâché exotic birds hung from the roofs by the dozens. Bizarre prints of various beasts dressed as humans adorned the walls. A few of the restaurants had fake palm trees on display. All locations were exceptionally loud because of the extensive use of windows, tiled floors, metal tables and chairs, and trendy rock music that screeched from cheap speakers bolted to the walls. Nonetheless, kids and teenagers loved going to Duke's and insisted on celebrating all their birthdays there. It was also the quintessential place to go for a first date if you were young and wanted to come across as a real hipster without exhausting the bank account.

As Duke's became established, old Russ put his eldest son, "Stag," at the helm. Stag was a reputed playboy who was considered one of the more eligible bachelors on the west coast for the better part of a decade. In fact, he dated Pamela Lee Anderson before she moved to L.A. and contracted a timely case of breastitis. It was rare that Russ and Stag descended from the heavens to survey their little Adams and Eves, but when they did it was an event to behold. I remember the first time I encountered Russ. It was during the spring of '88 and he was wearing this enormous fur coat made from beaver pelts. He walked by us commoners without even a nod, looking totally ridiculous in his oversized eyeglasses and his ostentatious full-length fur. He strode directly into the kitchen and right onto the line and began peppering some of the grease weasels with questions. As they were stammering their rote replies, the incongruence dawned on me: here was the owner of the chain, a guy who implemented all the rules, including the one that demanded that all kitchen staff wear "hair nets" in order to keep their greasy hair out of the food, and there was old man Russ hovering on the line cocooned in six-inch long beaver hair! In my mind, I thanked the craggy old S.O.B. for setting such a good example.

Although I didn't yet appreciate all of Duke's inconsistencies and hypocrisies, it felt safe and familiar because I had foraged there on numerous occasions and had listened to a thousand of Matt's stories. It seemed to be a place that I could make some good money, meet some new friends, and experience some perilous adventures, plus it was conveniently close to the university, so I threw caution to the wind and stopped by to fill out an application. I didn't realize it on that fine day, but **WAITERMAN** was inadvertently back on track to becoming Lord of the Jungle and on the verge of witnessing many new stories being born from the old ones. He just had to heed the new troop's rules of engagement.

Chapter 7

Rules of Engagement

"If you pay peanuts, you get monkeys."

- Mid 20th century saying

Boot Camp...

I was a little apprehensive walking into that particular Duke's because I had been rebuked at the south location on a couple of different occasions. For some unknown reason, the dorky little assistant night manager at the south location (who insisted on rolling up the sleeves on all of his sweaters and blazers) refused to unite Matt and I at the same restaurant. So imagine my surprise when I was able to fill out an application, get interviewed, and then get eagerly hired all within forty-five minutes at the north location. Fair enough, I thought, and asked, "So when do I get on the floor?" The rather obtuse management clone thought a few moments and replied, "Well, after the orientation meeting, the G.M.'s wine seminar, successful completion of your food, bar, and philosophy tests, then a couple of weeks or so of bussing shifts, you should be waitering in about a month."

Duke's was known for its exhaustive training program (and was, in fact, an industry leader in that area), but I had no idea the amount of bullshit that one had to go through to get paid minimum wage and sling nachos and beer. Alas, this was the brilliance of Duke's: they cloned their concept from the restaurant scene in southern California, then developed an elaborate training regime that acted as a smoke screen to blur the fact that they needed slave labor in order to thrive. Let's look at each stage of the training program in an effort to tease out the conflicting agendas between the grand poobahs and the insignificant plebes:

THE FIRST STAGE - Orientation

Theoretically, the purpose of the orientation was to introduce the new employees to the Duke's family generally, and to the restaurant specifically. Much smoke would be directed up the colons of these young prospects by the management team in efforts to make them feel as if they had been hand picked for a glorious and prosperous career. The managers would go on at length about how Duke's was vastly superior to the various local restaurants that were such obviously poor impostors. "We at Duke's use only the finest, freshest ingredients, not any of that frozen crap, or shredded lettuce garbage," they would proudly proclaim. "We offer nightly fresh food features, not stale 'food specials' like they do down the street," they would point out as if the distinction was anything more than just semantics. The new recruits would soak up all this propaganda and be distracted from the fact that they weren't receiving a penny from Duke's for any segment of their lengthy training program.

In reality, the orientation served two purposes. First, it was a way for the junior managers to impress the senior managers and the G.M. with all the insignificant information they had absorbed and how sincere they could appear while toeing the party line (which should sound familiar to anyone who has attended a Party meeting within the Kremlin). A kind of, "Hey Comrade, look at me, I'm regurgitating Marxism all by myself! Can I get a new posting out of Siberia now?" And second, it was basically a Farmer's Market for the veteran waiters. While the orientation meeting was taking place in the back of the restaurant, the senior waiters would literally take dibs on the cute trainees and become ridiculously territorial if other alpha-male wannabes tried to move in on their prized stock. And it didn't seem to matter if the cute trainees were engaged to their high school sweethearts; most of them would invariably succumb to the powerful game exhibited by the unscrupulous waiters. This doesn't say much for human tendencies, but it's easy to see why they were tempted. Simply said, in the restaurant industry, nothing is as it seems; deception dominates substance. All veteran servers appear cool because they are the masters of their mini universes: they know all the trendy lingo, they seem popular and gregarious, they have hip nicknames, they have hundreds of debauchery riddled stories, they always have money in their pockets, they are always ready to party at the slightest suggestion, and they shower the cute trainees with constant attention as in, "Hey Candace, are you coming over to Blake's place to watch *Slapshot* and pound back Long Island ice teas? What?! No way, the night's young still and Blake told me to round up as many hot chicks as possible, so naturally I started with you. No, your boyfriend wouldn't mind. Is he that insecure for Christ's sake? Look, you're the only reason why I'd consider going. What?! No way, you look awesome in your Duke's shirt; I can barely see those coffee stains. Besides, Blake has a hot tub..." And it would continue until the trainee's defenses crumbled. Most were just lonely and couldn't resist all the adoration and flattery. It was like taking candy from a baby.

Couplings due to infatuation are commonplace within the industry because the stress of working in a busy restaurant brings out the best and worst in its employees; one can observe servers laugh uproariously, then curse the heavens in a wild rage, then become frantic and pale from being tossed into the weeds. I think when people are thrown together in such an environment and experience such a wide range of emotions alongside one another, they erroneously come to believe they know the depths of each other's souls. This can be intoxicating (pun intended). And much like the urgent and desperate atmosphere created during wartime, ill fated relationships burn bright within restaurants, then quickly fizzle out once sobriety is attained and reality kicks them in the ass. Believe me, seeing a cocktail waitress without her push-up bra or any makeup on at six in the morning is like sniffing some freshly crystallized ammonia salts. In other words, it's a pretty harsh wake-up call.

As a testament to my gullibility at that time, I was fairly impressed with all the rhetoric presented to me at my orientation meeting. Duke's came across as much more organized and integrated than Trader's (although, this wasn't much of a feat). I remember thinking I was fortunate to be part of an enthusiastic Duke's troop, and working alongside primates who were my age and seemed to have some energy and ambition. There also seemed to be a fair bit of information to learn, but "Bobo," the assistant night manager who hired me, assured me that if I worked hard and kept my nose clean, I would be serving tables within a month. I was satisfied with that time frame, so I pushed on and marveled at the number of attractive Janes who seemed to be gagging for it.

THE SECOND STAGE - G.M.'s Seminar

The G.M.'s wine seminar was, without a doubt, the biggest heap of steaming elephant shit in the entire training schedule. The age of the new recruits ranged from about sixteen to twenty-three years of age, yet the pompous G.M. would drone on ad nauseam about which of the Merlots had the most compelling bouquet and would complement the hickory smoked baby back ribs the best (although a cold beer always seemed like the natural accompaniment

The Adventures of Waiterman

to me). It's as if the G.M. was born into French aristocracy, having descended from an unblemished pedigree, and raised alongside the Grimaldis in Monte Carlo where they brushed their teeth and gargled with vintage Cabernets. Without question, all of the G.M.s at the various Duke's thought they knew far more about vino than they actually did. In reality, they probably weren't that far removed from twisting the caps off their bottles of wine and swigging it, but making $100,000 a year and having virtually nothing to do will force people into excessive behavior in order to justify their affluent existence. Therefore, the real purpose of the seminar was not to educate naive adolescents on the merits of combining mediocre wine with fairly ordinary food, but rather to: (1) justify the G.M.'s cushy position and his recent trip to an Argentinean vineyard that was paid for by Duke's head office; and (2) to introduce the concept of upselling higher-end items, which is obviously very lucrative for a restaurant and adds considerably to the G.M.'s year-end bonus.

Sitting through the wine seminar at the age of nineteen put an unwarranted scare into me. Keep in mind that I dealt only with food at Trader's, so aside from knowledge obtained from personal consumption, I knew virtually nothing about potable spirits. I also had no interest in wine at that stage - not to swish it in my mouth and savor its full body and woody aftertaste, nor to comment on its "long legs" and quantity of sedimentation. To my immature palate, wine was pungent, bitter, and caused heartburn and headaches, but yet the G.M. of Duke's had us believing that we had to know more about wine than the average Swiss wine steward in order to satisfy the inquisitive minds of Duke's cultured and discerning customers. Of course, months later I discovered that this premise was undiluted bullshit as Duke's typically uncouth patrons preferred draught beer and highballs on the order of about fifty to one over wine, so my practical wine knowledge got pared down to the absolute essentials. This brings us to our first and only wine-related serving tip:

****

SERVING TIP #3: If you are a "professional" server who works in a posh restaurant that carries a wine list so extensive that it is bound in hardcover and published in five languages, then by all means spend the time and effort learning about the intricacies of our planet's wine industry because it will pay off handsomely in the end. But, if you are a server who works in a mainstream establishment that serves a fairly broad spectrum of the population, then save yourself a formidable headache by following these simple principles. (1) If the customer actually needs your advice on selecting the color and dryness of the wine, then assume that same customer would not notice if you brought him Welch's grape juice. Consequently, state that the house wine is well above average and would be an excellent choice, and then simply bring him/her the red if they are eating beef, game, or pasta in a tomato based sauce, or the white if they are eating chicken, fish, or pasta in a cream sauce. Keep it basic. (2) If the customer is well beyond the wine's color and dryness, but is grappling with a type of grape, or a particular region, then clearly you are in over your head if a discussion ensues. Consequently, if a wine connoisseur is looking for guidance, recommend the most expensive Californian Chardonnay if he/she desires white wine, or the most expensive Californian Cabernet Sauvignon if he/she desires red wine, because both types of grapes have met with tremendous success in that region, are quite consistent due to mass production, and are easy to like, but difficult to offend. As such, they are very defensible choices and the price of the wine will inflate the check, which should inflate your tip.

****

THE THIRD STAGE - Written Tests

To say that the food, beverage, and philosophy tests were slight overkill would be like saying that seeing your girlfriend's turd floating in an unflushed toilet is a mild turn-off. There were pages and pages of questions on the most obscure of details. Was it imperative that we knew all ten ingredients within the guacamole? Did we have to know that a medium rare top sirloin has the same feel as the thenar area of your hand while your thumb is touching your index finger? Did it matter that the potatoes were from the State of Idaho and Blue Ribbon award winners? No, I don't think so on all counts, but if a trainee did not attain eighty percent or higher on their tests within a couple of attempts then they were bid adieu, without any compensation to show for all their futile efforts. Realistically, if Duke's ever let veteran servers create questions that they thought were absolutely essential to be able to answer in order to survive on the floor, they might read something like this. "(1) For five marks, explain to the famished customer why the fettuccini Alfredo is embarrassingly under-portioned and plated on a huge black concave plate that only serves to underline this fact. (2) For three marks, justify to the indignant customer why his four ounces of red wine is poured into a nine ounce wine glass, making it look ridiculously under-poured.

(3) For two marks, explain to the cost-conscious customer why the exact same chicken wings are less than half the price at a restaurant just down the street. (4) For one mark each, answer yes or no to the following inane questions: Will the mushroom burger fill me up? Is your decaf coffee any good? If I give you $5 can I put this bottle of wine in my purse?" These are the real questions that a server must face and respond to while battling in the jungle, but the written tests at Duke's didn't reflect this reality at all.

I acknowledge that memorizing all the portions, ingredients, and cooking times of the menu items can be helpful, but these details can be found out from the grease weasels or the bartender in fairly short order if any customers absolutely insist on the information. What I regard as much more important, though, is the ability to display professionalism when one doesn't have a bloody clue what the customer is asking for, or when one has clearly fucked-up but refuses to admit it for fear of compromising their tip. This brings us to our next serving tip:

****

SERVING TIP #4: There will be many occasions during your serving career when you will be forced to choose between two very different types of responses to your customers. Because regardless of whether you must produce an answer to an impossible question, or are pressed to explain why you screwed-up, you have the option of choosing the "apologetic / bend over backwards / brown nosing / pussy" style of response, or the "infallible / pass the buck / indignant / smart-ass" style of response. As long as you take pride in your responses, it doesn't really matter which path you choose, but being **WAITERMAN**, I instinctively chose the smart-ass path. For example, if a customer stated, "Waiter, I asked for fries with my teriyaki chicken and there's a house salad on my plate instead," and revealed my mistake in doing so, I replied, "Yes, that's obvious and correct sir. Naturally I assumed you would prefer piping hot fries, so I insisted that the kitchen prepare some fresh ones immediately, and I thought you might appreciate our house salad in the mean time. Was I wrong in this assumption, sir?" Invariably, the customer would actually thank me for being so thoughtful and wait patiently while I sprinted back to the grease weasels in a panic and begged for a side plate of fries. Or if the customer asked, "Waiter, is there any cumin in the guacamole?" and exposed my ignorance in doing so, I responded, "In the original recipe, yes. But the kitchen is experimenting with a more authentic Mexican recipe and I'm not sure if they replaced the cumin with fresh cilantro. Allow me to check for you." I would then dash off to the kitchen and frantically check the recipe book, but the customer was none the wiser to my lack of guacamole knowledge.

Be warned, though, because if you choose the flippant, smart-ass path, you are essentially (1) never admitting that you are at fault (blaming the kitchen works beautifully in this regard), and (2) never admitting that you are not all knowing. In the unlikely event that a customer calls you on your bullshit, a good back-up line like, "Yes, sorry sir, you're absolutely right. I was just being a silly twit," will most likely rescue your precious gratuity. Of course, one could always go down the path of the pussy, but if the customer doesn't pity your pathetic song and dance routine and leaves you a shitty tip as proof of their displeasure, the resulting kick in the camel toe feels that much more penetrating.

****

The most surreptitious part of the written tests was the philosophical questions. With these questions the managers at Duke's were able to determine which recruits were willing to abandon their own identities and consider drinking grape punch at a Jonestown reunion party, and which ones were willing to actually consult their cerebral cortexes before relaying electrical impulses to their pen wielding fingers. Duke's claimed that they wanted honest, unique, and well thought out answers, but they really wanted to know who the "square pegs" were so they could quickly weed them out and alert the F.B.I. If they were more honest about their intentions, they would have asked something like, "Do you consider yourself a mindless drone who would set aside your principles to act as a food and beverage trafficker capable of excessive servility and whoring in the name of profitability? If your answer is yes, then bend over and assume the submissive position so we can test the extendibility of your anal passageway."

Generally speaking, chain restaurants spend a large amount of money on streamlining and homogenizing their operations, and this includes certain philosophies and scripted responses for the front house staff. Consequently, an efficient management team will not spend additional time and money on training individuals who aren't willing to blindly spew forth carefully manipulated dialogue. The irony is that a growing percentage of the population is becoming cynical of big business tactics and are often offended at being treated like a pixel on a demographic pie chart. For these people, antiseptic expressions like, "B-bye now, have a nice day" or "It was a pleasure serving you, please come again," are merely reminders that they are interacting with lobotomized drones who regard them solely as faceless consumers, not as discerning individuals. Personally, I'd rather hear, "The owner of this establishment thanks you because he is closer to completing the west wing of his estate in the Bahamas. I, on the other hand, will continue to curse the bastard because I'm tired of being exploited for minimum wage, so piss off," because it would be much closer to the truth.

It must have taken me about two hours to complete the written tests and I felt that if I would have had access to a thesaurus and been able to come up with two dozen words synonymous with "fresh" and "delicious," then I would have had a serious chance at scoring one hundred percent (the record was ninety-five percent at that point in time). But alas, I scored only eighty-five percent because my vocabulary was obviously less than the average Harvard Ph.D.'s, and because I lost partial functioning of my right hand due to the cramping that resulted from writing so furiously. Most of the questions caused my eyes to roll back into my skull and vow to never regurgitate the sought after descriptions in their entirety. For example, I never thought, not even for a second, that I would describe the apple cobbler as, "A truly original and delicious recipe consisting of fresh, tart Granny Smith apples from Australia lightly baked with sweet brown sugar and honey in a moist, homemade shortbread filling, then topped with fresh rolled oats and warmed until golden brown," because it was time consuming and sounded too contrived. Instead, I ended up saying, "The cobbler is absolutely stellar and I guarantee you'll like it. If you don't, then I'll take it off your check." It was a bold guarantee, but it always worked because I was being honest which, I assume, was refreshing to most people's ears. As a result, I very rarely had to beg a manager to promo an apple cobbler due to a customer's dislike of it, which was good because most managers' promo budgets were already grossly inflated from doling out a shameful quantity of consumable items in hopes of balling a cute staff member.

THE FOURTH STAGE - Bussing Trials

For the fifteen-, sixteen-, and seventeen-year-old recruits, the job of bussing was their final destination. They were primarily hired as bussers (or hostesses if they were winsome and busty enough), so there wasn't any humiliation or shame in doing the job. But, for those hired to be servers, and especially if they were servers previously at other restaurants, having to bus tables for weeks on end was almost unbearable (both financially and psychologically). According to the Duke's training manual, the purpose of forcing would-be servers to bus tables was to have them learn the sections, the table numbers, and the general whereabouts of things in a quicker and more thorough fashion. In addition, one supposedly learned to better appreciate the workings of the restaurant from other perspectives, at least in theory. In reality, Duke's management seemed to use the position of bussing as a type of purgatory in order to determine who had the fortitude to survive it and rise above, thus demonstrating their relentless desire to become servers. The problem with this penal system was threefold. (1) Making proud servers bus tables was simply cruel, and consequently forced the servers to manifest feelings of bitterness, revenge, and vindictiveness, which invariably got channeled into the act of scamming the restaurant if they survived the bussing trial. (2) Only verbal agreements existed (which were largely unrecorded) between the junior managers and the "transitional bussers" regarding the duration of their bussing trials. Therefore, when junior managers quit, got fired, or got transferred to another Duke's location (all of which were very common), the transitional bussers were basically abandoned and fell through the cracks of the system, where they remained for months with their expired promises and broken dreams. As a result, some ended up behaving and sounding like the infamous *Papillon*, who went wacko trying to escape from the work camps in French Guiana for so many years. And (3) having people languishing in the gallows as bussers often befouled their social status, and usually branded them as "inferior" servers in the eyes of the veterans if they ever made it out. Once branded, it was tough to be regarded as an equal or as part of the "in-group." The only real chance a server who bussed too long had was if there was a massive turnover of staff, which essentially allowed the server to make a fresh start without the shackles of prejudice.

    I had never been a busser prior to working at Duke's. This was because I was strictly a salad boy at Trader's and never had the misfortune of being a desk help there (which was Trader's equivalent of a busser). In reality, there was probably a substantial amount I could have learned by being a busser at Duke's if I would have accepted my situation, but I felt that it was below me because I had been a venerable Trader's Inn waiter and was accustomed to the money and respect that that position commanded. Bobo, the assistant night manager who hired me, assured me that I would spend no more than a month bussing tables and claimed it was necessary for two reasons: (1) I had never worked at a Duke's restaurant before, so he thought I needed the time to understand how everything functioned; and (2) there were a fair number of veteran servers working there at that time which meant there weren't many extra waitering shifts to pick up. It was this latter reason that played a much bigger role in determining when one got promoted to the rank of server.

    I had only been bussing for a couple of weeks when Bobo transferred to another Duke's location to become their sniveling day manager. I recognized this as not a good thing immediately because Bobo was my lifeline out of the bussing realm. Bobo's replacement was a sphinctorial little dork that we nicknamed "the Kiwi," because he was from New Zealand. He dressed very conservatively, had a heavy "Down Under" accent, and was the pettiest little prick in the entire restaurant. He never tired of carefully monitoring the times by which people arrived for their shifts so he could bust their asses for being late. This was a controversial issue for the staff because Duke's required everyone to be at work fifteen minutes before their shifts began (which Duke's refused to pay the staff for) in order to prepare themselves for the impending shift. Why Duke's couldn't have scheduled everyone fifteen minutes earlier and actually paid them for it was beyond me. Undoubtedly, one of the reasons was to give people a time cushion in case they were running behind, or traffic was bad, etc. Fair enough, but the shit would hit the fan when the Kiwi busted people's asses for arriving only ten minutes before their shifts, which he considered five minutes late! He would literally stand by the front door when the majority of the staff were due, looking at his cheap plastic wrist watch (which could have been a few minutes fast), and chastise everyone who was tardy. So imagine my frustrating situation: in class at the university the entire day and feeling lucky just to have gotten an occasional seat on the perimeter within the overcrowded amphitheaters, then driving like a "lane jockey" down the busy highway that Duke's was located on to get to work, then sprinting into Duke's feeling somewhat harried, but motivated to work my ass off so I could be liberated from busboy purgatory and salvage my self-worth, and then being castigated for not being early enough by some little colonial cocksucker who probably sprouted a modest erection at the thought of wielding dominion over the near mutinous staff. Needless to say, this was not good for staff morale, and as such, warrants a managerial tip:

****

MANAGERIAL TIP #3: Do not be a petty little prick to your staff by busting their balls or crushing their ovaries over comparatively unimportant matters. I call it "crying wolf" because a manager's job is to crack the whip in order to keep things operating smoothly, but if the manager is always bitching and nit-picking people, then the staff will lose all respect for that manager and drown him/her out whenever he/she opens his/her mouth, regardless if it has merit or not. This is counterproductive because everyone needs to hear and internalize constructive criticism to improve. So as a manager, pick your spots carefully and remember that a pat on the back goes much further than a slap on the wrist. In addition, if someone does need a chastising, do it in private and after work, because otherwise you risk deflating them in front of others and rendering them useless for the duration of their shift.

****

THE FIFTH STAGE - Shadowing

Once the transitional bussers were rescued from busboy purgatory and were supposedly laden with insights on the workings of the restaurant, they became ready to play the role of shadow. Shadowing doesn't have to be an exercise in futility if the would-be server is actually in need of additional serving skills, and is paired with a competent, more veteran server who takes the time and has the inclination to impart some wisdom. However, what usually ended up happening was that the shadow was paired with someone who was actually less talented in the art of serving, but who absolutely excelled at demonstrating a squalid variety of bad habits and attitudes. These inadvertent lessons in incompetence and cynicism didn't make a dent in the armor of the hardened trainees who served at other restaurants previously, but the last thing that young, impressionable rookies needed was to be taken under the wings of tainted, crusty curmudgeons who had more interest in scamming the restaurant and shagging the hostess, or worse, forcefully shagging their new shadows.

Shadows were called such because they had to follow their assigned veteran servers around like bloodhounds, trying to pick up scraps of valuable information whenever they could. Sniffing at the server's heels, the shadows were, in more descriptive terms, like fifteenth century manservants or valets.

They were simply at the beck and call of their masters for the entire shift. For example, if a veteran server felt he/she was unable to properly wipe his/her ass after a mid-shift dump, the shadow could always be called upon to complete the task without much protest. Or if a veteran server was depleted of post-shift ale, the shadow could always be dispatched to the nearest barkeep or tavern for replenishment. Shadowing would continue for at least one entire shift, and sometimes two or three shifts if the trainee had virtually no experience in any service industry whatsoever, or had an I.Q. that hovered below one hundred. The entire concept of shadowing was very subjective and could be considered good, bad, or ineffective depending on one's vantage point.

From the veteran server's perspective, having a shadow was both beneficial and annoying. It was beneficial because one essentially had an eager slave to complete all the manual tasks. Thus, the shadow often ran all the food, cleared all the dirty plates from the tables, and finished all of the onerous closing duties. In addition, being assigned a shadow afforded one a certain amount of prestige because it inferred that one was regarded as competent, consistent, and trustworthy (never mind that it was the alpha-male waiters who usually trained the shadows). On the other hand, having a shadow tripping on one's heels for hours at a time was annoying and similar to having a stainless steel ball and chain attached to your ankle. One always had to introduce them to tables, explain everything at least twice to them, and verbalize all thoughts that were meant to be kept as such. Therefore, in a way, it was like going out with a new girlfriend, but without the sex (although some of the alpha-males managed this nicely).

From the shadow's vantage point, shadowing was simply embarrassing and a total waste of time, especially for those who had previously served tables at other restaurants. Although I learned a fair bit when I originally shadowed at Trader's, the single shift that I had to shadow at Duke's was tough to bear, and it was all I could do to stop from commenting on the long list of waitering faux pas' that I witnessed. Naturally, I was paired with a rather robust alpha-male (although he wasn't the silverback of the restaurant) who prided himself on prying telephone numbers from his young female customers, even if he had to illegally serve strawberry daiquiris to the underagers in order to distort their judgment so he could get them. The only tangible benefit that I received from shadowing at Duke's was having an opportunity to practice serving beverages and working that into my waitering routine, because at Trader's the barmaid had dealt with all the customer's liquid needs. Overall, though, it was an interesting evening and one that I patiently tolerated because it represented my much-anticipated departure from the world of bussing tables. Without Bobo doing my bidding, though, it had taken me over three months to become a Duke's server.

Finally, the managers were rather indifferent to shadowing because although they had more staff at their disposal to accomplish more work around the restaurant, they had to pay the shadows for their time (albeit minimum wage). Consequently, the labor costs would rise and possibly draw the G.M.'s ire. This could prove unsettling because the lazy G.M. would have to cut his hibernation short and emerge from his cave (i.e., booth) to grunt at his underlings and show his general displeasure, as if he was an incontinent grizzly bear awakened in the dead of winter. This show of authority could be perilous for anyone who got between the territorial G.M. and his cub (i.e., cup of coffee). Meanwhile, high above from head office, the standard response was that shadowing concluded the training period with a sort of mini apprenticeship, which was thought to be an opportunity to sort out any existing deficiencies before the trainees officially became Duke's servers. In all honesty though, following a jaded alpha-male waiter around for a shift probably did more harm than good.

THE SIXTH and FINAL STAGE - Half Sections

When I first started at Duke's, each section consisted of six tables (usually four four-tops and two deuces). This seemed like child's play to me because the sections at Trader's consisted of eight tables, most of which were four-tops. Consequently, a half section at Duke's was a whopping three tables which was pretty lackadaisical, but paradoxically, it often proved challenging to experienced servers because there was a tendency to provide too much service and irritate the customers.

I eventually came to realize that five-table sections were ideal, as long as the restaurant was busy and the tables turned over at least five times. This allowed a server to be perpetually busy and develop a rhythm, to provide attentive yet efficient service, to make enough money to be worth his/her time, and to be insulated against being totally slammed. Of course, it's all dependent on the genre of the restaurant. If the restaurant's menu is more upscale, then the tables needn't be turned over as much in order to make some good cake. For example, the average guest check at Trader's was about $27, which meant that a table of four would ring up a tab of about $108 and tip us an additional $15-25. Therefore, for each of us to take home $100 in tips at Trader's, we needed to serve about seventeen tables over the course of a shift. However, Duke's menu consisted of less expensive items, such as burgers and finger foods. As a result, the average guest check at Duke's was about $10, which meant a much larger volume of people had to be pushed through a section in order to make good money. So in contrast to Trader's, we had to serve about thirty tables or so to take home $100 in tips at Duke's. Not surprisingly then, the $100 barrier was not broken very often at Duke's because we just couldn't push the checks up any higher due to the fact the clientele were largely from the university down the highway or the technical college across the street. I soon came to realize that the "starving student" adage was not entirely accurate, because the students who I served rarely looked hungry or gaunt due to their tendency to spend the majority of my expected tip on extraneous nutrients such as cheesecake and special coffees. These patsies clearly didn't resemble the malnourished, pot-bellied "Biafrans" my Mom once spoke of in order to harbor guilt and deter me from wasting precious brussel sprouts as a child.

As my training session drew to a close and the specific rules of engagement were ingrained, it finally dawned on me what was so odious about Duke's approach to their human resources. A major theme of our training was "Your Section is Your Stage," and by this they implied that they wanted talented entertainers (i.e., high energy, unique individuals) to write, choreograph, and perform their one person shows (i.e., to serve people) each night within the confines of a sold out theatre (i.e., at Duke's) to much acclaim and riches (i.e., for good tips). As a result, this became a very convenient justification to freeze every server's wage at the absolute minimum, because they contended that as servers became more experienced, they would flourish and develop an appreciative following who would tip them more. Consequently, according to the propagandists at Duke's, the hardest working veteran servers, regardless of gender, would always make the most money in tips. Well, this just didn't happen for reasons mentioned in Chapter One (remember the tipping hierarchy?), and because Duke's didn't actually tolerate people "running their own business" or acting "outside the box." In fact, after working at Duke's for five years I made slightly less money in tips compared to when I first started (legitimate tips that is) because I was less of a keener and could no longer rely on sympathy tips for being a dufus. Regardless, the absurd training period was complete and I was about to reach the canopy of the Duke's rain forest, where I was hoping it would rain down some serious jack on my head.

Chapter 8

The Rain Forest

"He that would eat fruit must climb the tree."

- Ancient Proverb

Expedite This...

It had taken me three mercilessly long months, but I had finally reached the lush rain forest and become an esteemed Duke's waiter. This accomplishment was not entirely without recognition as a Duke's waiter was considered a fairly hip thing to be at that age, during that era, and within the circles that I mingled. One could almost proclaim the fact that one worked there in public and not feel unbearable shame, or fear being pummeled about the head with rotten tomatoes. Of course, we (my training cohort and I) were low men on the ladder within the Duke's serving hierarchy and were very much made to feel that way. To a man, the established alpha-male waiters put us through the gears and ground us on a nightly basis, with their attacks often transcending into the personal realm. They quite simply resented our attempts at assimilation and most of them really enjoyed seeing the look of misery painted on our faces. This mask of misery was especially common when we, as new waiters, had to work the odd expediting shift.

Expediting was a foreign concept to me initially. At Trader's, the waiters were one hundred percent responsible for running all of their tables' food. If the waiter was having a cigarette, or was slammed, or just plain forgot, the food would sit under the heat lamps indefinitely with no other waiter even fleetingly entertaining the thoughts of running it. Of course, Muppet Lou would explode with expletive Cantonese after about fifteen minutes of seeing the food wither, but all the waiters in the vicinity would mind their own business and thank their pagan gods for not being in the weeds themselves, or being addicted to nicotine so badly that they spent more time puffing on their fags next to the garbage dumpster in the alley than looking for their table's food in the pass-thru. But this situation rarely occurred because we were trained to be good time managers and to respect the fact that people primarily came to Trader's for its food. As a result, we took the food aspect of the dining experience very seriously. Bringing more wine, refilling the water glasses, even emptying the ashtrays were all secondary to making sure the meals were prepared well and delivered on time. Granted, this was easier to accomplish at Trader's because we had barmaids who focused on the other aspects of the dining experience, but even solo servers must assume total responsibility for satisfying their customer's hunger (gastronomical hunger, that is).

Duke's was a different jungle, though, because it was a chain restaurant and primarily concerned with self-preservation through maximizing profits and marching as many people through the doors as logistically possible. Consequently, they tried to push altruistic food running on their employees and thinly disguised it as providing good service to the customers. But, from the customer's perspective, having a particular individual state that he/she is your server, then having a plethora of individuals drop off your beverage, appetizer, main course, and dessert could be considered competent and time efficient, but should never be confused with good service because it's impersonal and disjointed. There is simply no flow to the dining experience because nothing is coordinated; the apathetic food runner who drops off the guacamole nachos doesn't care why the margaritas are delayed, or if extra napkins are needed, or when the main courses are going to be ordered. In short, the food runner is inflicted with the old, "Why work harder and make less cake?" selfishness that was discussed in Chapter Two. Of course, none of this would have been an issue if Duke's had made attempts to hire quality servers who were capable of fulfilling the job's primary role (i.e., bringing hungry people food), but instead they tried to acquire the most amount of T & A for the least amount of wages and were consequently left with individuals who were great eye candy, but largely incompetent. As a result, the job of expediter was created and the concept of food running was launched out of absolute necessity.

Duke's management teams preached the benefits of altruistic food running and claimed the customer didn't give a rat's ass as long as they received their grub on time, because management's primary mission was to get the customer in and out quickly, then have them return and spend more money the next time. I disagree with this assertion because I think customers appreciate knowing who to ask for certain things, appreciate being asked how something is before it's half eaten, and feel at ease knowing that their server is timing their dining experience so they won't be late for a movie. Consequently, I would argue that customers feel less satisfied with their dining experience and tip less in situations where they are unsure who their primary server is. Psychologically this makes sense because customers do not have a chance to identify and bond with their server. Thus, it is easier to inadequately tip an anonymous, faceless server who has failed to establish a personal connection because the social pressure to do so is less. Some servers erroneously believe that greeting customers with, "Hi, my name is Bambi and I'll be your server tonight," and flashing some stellar cleavage is enough to establish that personal connection, but it's not. Personal erection maybe, but no connection. Therefore, conscientious servers would be remiss not to strive for some sort of connection so that all the psychological impediments vanish and their customers feel justified (nay, compelled) in loosening their purse strings and slapping down some decent jack for a tip, whether it's truly warranted or not.

So there I was, working my first shift as an expediter and trying to figure out why everyone was so incompetent at running their own food, but enjoying all the T & A bouncing around me nonetheless. Servers were flying by each other in the pass-thru while running each other's food. It was total madness, but I had been put in charge of orchestrating it. Not everyone was physically incapable of running their own table's food, mind you. On the contrary, most people chose not to run certain food orders for a variety of reasons. For example, sometimes the plates were considered too hot to handle, sometimes too heavy to carry, sometimes the waitresses didn't want to soil their outfits, sometimes the waiters preferred to shmooze with their female customers, and sometimes servers had no real reason other than they just didn't give a shit and couldn't be bothered because they knew the food would eventually get to the table via someone else's sweat equity. As a result, working as an expediter provided me with an excellent opportunity to assess who was a competent server and who was brutally inept and inclined towards sloth. In my mind, I set up an unofficial balance sheet for running food and came up with the following statistics (I've included the situation at Trader's for reference):

TRADER'S:

	% of own food ran	% of other server's food ran
waiters............	100%	0%
barmaids.........	0%	0%

DUKE'S:

	% of own food ran	% of other server's food ran
waiters............	60-90%	0-20%
waitresses.........	40-90%	0-10%

From the above numbers then, one can see that some waitresses at Duke's ran less than half of their own food and none for anyone else. Therefore, these pooch humpers were rated at a minus sixty percent, meaning that they relied on the food running juggernaut to do sixty percent of their work. In essence, they were heavily "overdrawn" and acted as a drain on the entire system. In contrast, some conscientious waiters ran ninety percent of their own food (it was impossible to run all of it, unless you physically threatened the expediter with a beating to the temple) and twenty percent of other server's food, which meant they had a rating of plus ten percent. Unfortunately, many more servers were in the negative than the positive side of the ledger, so the overworked little bussers were often grabbed to run the balance of the food because the expediter was strictly forbidden to leave the pass-thru.

At this point, one could ask, "Why is it so damn important to run your own food?" Well, in my opinion, there are only certain situations in which servers should approach tables for the purpose of asking questions and doing their business, otherwise they risk intruding on the customer's cherished dining experience. Specifically, there are six main opportunities to approach a table, and they are:

(1) The Greeting

This is the customary, "Hi folks, how is everyone tonight?" During this initial approach, customers are informed of the features/specials, asked what they would like to drink, and allowed to state if they are in a hurry or if more people are joining them. This initial approach is entirely expected by the customer and should take place within about three minutes, otherwise anxious feelings of abandonment begin to take hold. Upselling can be initiated in this stage, but common sense would hopefully restrain the eager server from trying to push a jumbo pitcher of Long Island ice teas on a young Mormon family. In addition, customers requesting water at this stage does not necessitate bringing them $4 bottles of "sparkling" water and zealously adding it to their check; ordinary tap water usually suffices. As a waiter, I eventually got over my fear of approaching tables and greeting them when I realized it wasn't analogous to "cold sales" calls, because the customers were already in my section and virtually guaranteed to purchase something. They didn't need to be solicited; rather, they just needed me to guide them through the process and deliver the desired product to them. It was more like "inside sales," and I didn't mind it so much. Approaching and greeting tables reminds me of another important serving tip:

****

SERVING TIP #5: Do not be an oblivious, repetitive drone who is stuck on automatic pilot while greeting your customers. Obviously, a witty, original greeting for every table is impossible but, depending on the size of the restaurant and the space between the tables, have three greetings in your repertoire so that all the tables in your section do not hear you say exactly the same thing to everybody, thus making you appear like an airline flight attendant. The three I used in rotation were: (1) "Good evening, how is everyone here tonight?" which is pretty boring, but it was most appropriate for older, more mature tables; (2) "Hi guys, how's it going?" which was most appropriate for younger people within my cohort; and (3) "Well hello there, how have things been?" which was most appropriate for regulars, or people who I was familiar with but had not seen in a while. It may be largely subconscious, but your customers will appreciate not being treated like they are on an assembly line, Henry Ford be damned.

****

The Adventures of Waiterman

(2) The Drink Drop-off

This is obviously when the server drops off the desired beverages, assuming that he/she has not made the fatal error of ordering too many blended drinks or cappuccinos, in which case the bartender might choose to punish the server with a baneful look and an impossibly long wait. Again, the drink drop-off is totally expected and allowed by the customer, even appreciated if accomplished within five minutes. Once the beverages are safely on the table, the server can then seamlessly launch into the food order, inquiring as to what is wanted to eat. However, wise servers do not habitually lay their hands on customers of the opposite sex during this ordering process. Upselling is traditionally practiced at this time too, but resisting the urge to suggest "super-sizing" everything is prudent. Keep in mind that there is a fine line between letting the customers know their dining options and obnoxiously assaulting them with a thinly veiled attempt at squeezing more money out of them. If a server considers him/herself a mastermind with the memory of an African elephant and is intent on impressing the entire table (which only occasionally increases the gratuity), then there is no need to write any of the order down, but my experience dictates that all orders should be written down because having to skulk back to the table to reconfirm an order makes one look like a retard, or a cocky asshole if the table originally queried, "Aren't you going to write any of this down?" If a server insists on being cool though, he/she can always use cryptic abbreviations that few others will understand while recording the order, such as, "H2O X2, g-nach, mush w/ff, BBQ w/alf," meaning: two waters, guacamole nachos to start, then followed by a mushroom burger with fries and barbecue chicken with fettuccini Alfredo.

(3) The Food Delivery

The food delivery, be it an appetizer or the main course, is a crucial stage because of all the confirmations that are required and all the tasks that can be accomplished. Firstly, it must be established that the food was ordered correctly (but not necessarily prepared correctly, as this should have been done by the grease weasels and affirmed by the expediter). If the desired item is incorrect, then one's talents in the art of professionalism are robustly tested. If the items are as ordered, then the server should inquire as to the status of the beverages (including if tap water is wanted), if extra napkins are needed, or if any side plates are required. Thankfully, brown-nosing bussers are dully qualified to fetch such items if any are requested and are only a shout and a crack of the whip away. Finally, the server concludes this stage with something along the lines of, "Super then, enjoy your meals," before he/she can scamper off to flirt with the staff for a couple of minutes before having to return for the quality check.

(4) The Quality Check

The quality check on the food should be done within the first half dozen bites, which allows the customer to taste his/her meal and render a judgment, but also leaves enough food on the plate to show the manager or kitchen staff if the food is considered inedible. Unfortunately, some customers believe that restaurants have access to DNA testing facilities and, therefore, only need a few molecules of their meal to determine that it is substandard. This is clearly not the case and these customers should be challenged with a suspicious stare-down. If, on the other hand, the item in question is less than half finished and does seem poorly prepared, or if the customer can produce the offending hair, insect, shard of glass, or band-aid for inspection, then immediately blame the incompetent grease weasels and offer to replace the item with a flawless duplicate. If the customer is not interested in such a settlement, then immediately find the most secluded booth and drag the ruminating manager away from his/her precious coffee and prompt him/her to do what they were supposedly trained for. Finally, stand back and hope that the resulting arrangement makes the customer deliriously happy so that your sacred gratuity is not adversely affected.

(5) The Clearing of the Plates

The plates should be cleared when the customer is finished eating the food that was presented on them, not when the server is bored and has nothing better to do. Trying to pry an unfinished plate away from a customer can be a dangerous miscalculation; servers have lost fingers for attempting such foolishness. As a rule, customers will place their cutlery on their plates when they are finished, so this is the cue to remove them quickly as customers don't like to be reminded of how much food they wasted, or what gluttons they were. If a customer asks to take leftovers home, then focus on making the "doggy bag" structurally sound and leak proof, as opposed to making it look like a genetic abomination with ears. And if the doggy bag is forgotten on the table, resist the temptation to take it to the back and rip through it like an inner city raccoon. The plate clearing stage is also when desserts and coffees are offered. But be careful if the customers are starving students, because they will gladly spend your entire tip, no matter how well deserved, on such superfluous items and then stealthily slip out the door while you are preoccupied with your footing in the dish pit.

(6) The Check Delivery

Aside from the initial greeting, delivering the check is the most time sensitive. Customers will wait an extra few minutes for their meals, but they will not tolerate waiting for the check or their change once they are ready to leave. Your service may have been exemplary, but your tip will drop quicker than the *Nasdaq Index* if you are not mercuric during this final stage. I found it convenient to print a copy of the customer's check immediately after they ordered coffee and/or dessert and I kept it in my apron pocket so I could hand it directly to them once they asked for it and before they started to look around impatiently. This saves some precious time, especially if they have their credit cards ready to give to you. If the customer pays the check with cash instead of a credit card, then there are a few things to keep in mind:

****

SERVING TIP #6: Believe it or not, the way in which you make change influences your gratuity to a greater extent than does the service you provide. For example, if the check total is $27 and the customer lays down $40, do not bring him/her a ten dollar bill and three ones because you will most likely receive a $3 tip (which is an eleven percent gratuity). A wiser move is to bring back two five dollar bills and three ones, which will probably land you a fiver (which is an eighteen and a half percent gratuity). Related to this is the art of manipulating the final total of the check to your advantage. In short, wait to add the coffees and the sodas (or any item which is at your discretion to ring in) to the check until the last possible moment because some totals are more desirable than others. Since most bank machines exclusively dispense twenty-dollar bills, customers will usually pay in increments of twenty if not using their credit card. For example, if the check totals $54 and the customer is in a hurry, he/she will most likely leave $60 (which is an eleven percent gratuity), but if you "forget" to add a couple of coffees then the check drops to $52 and the customer will most likely still leave $60 (which is a fifteen percent tip), especially if they notice you've given them two free coffees. Yes, this is scamming, technically, but your ethics are your own problem.

****

Once the change or credit card slip is dropped off at the table, resist the overwhelming impulse to collect your gratuity before the customer leaves. I think this comes across as uncouth and greedy, but maybe I'm just being too "old school" about it. Admittedly, one problem with not immediately collecting your gratuity is not knowing the degree of appreciation that should be conveyed to the customers as they leave. Nothing is worse than saying, "Thanks so much folks, have a great night and I hope to see you again real soon," then walking back to the table and finding a pittance worth of small change left as a tip. Once again, this feels like a swift kick to an engorged camel toe. To insulate yourself against such a degrading faux pas, don't commit to such exorbitant gratitude; instead, stick to a more neutral response like, "OK, bye now folks, we'll see you again," because a customer's poor tipping behavior should never be positively reinforced.

In summary then, a server should only approach a table at certain times, unless a customer specifically summons him. While at the table during those times, it is imperative that the server accomplishes as many essential tasks as possible. Unfortunately, systematic food running inhibits the primary servers from approaching their tables at the most opportune times, and forces them to interrupt the dining experience more than would otherwise be necessary. Food running also erodes the skills of servers because they tend to become far too reliant on it. Consequently, it is easy for servers to lose touch with their customers' needs, which is the real key to providing good service and earning decent tips.

So even though I was opposed to the concepts of food running and expediting, I was glad to be doing it because it was much better than bussing tables; the money was superior and the work was physically less demanding. Emotionally, though, it was possibly more ravaging because I had to consistently deal with overwhelmed servers who were on the verge of massive seizures and infarcts. In addition, some of the alpha-male waiters refused to run any of their food just to fuck with me and test my ability to cope with a pass-thru full of smoldering food. Those bastards would just smile as I scrambled to load the bussers up with as many plates as their pubescent bodies could haul, as if they were transport mules scaling the slopes of Mt. Kilimanjaro. I guess, as kids, their appetite for cruelty was not entirely satiated by burning ants with magnifying glasses.

While working as an expediter, I experienced first hand just how petty and controlling Duke's could be. One night in particular, I was coming from the university and in a hurry. When I arrived at the restaurant (exactly fifteen minutes early), I cursed myself when I realized that I had forgotten my shirt and tie that were mandatory for all male front house staff. Fortunately, I had a very presentable turtleneck in my possession that looked rather rakish with my chinos (so suave, in fact, that I took considerable ribbing for looking like the perpetually debonair Robert Wagner). But, the Kiwi was aghast at my blatant disregard for the dress code and immediately informed "Piggy," who was our G.M. at the time. Piggy was short, balding, and obese, but desperate to appear like an upper crust prep school graduate. He boasted that he could shift gears in his BMW without using the clutch. He wore large horn rimmed eyeglasses that were always sliding down his sweaty, pug nose. He was one of the few people who could look totally disheveled in Ralph Lauren attire. When he wasn't sitting on his expansive ass in the office sipping coffee, he was waddling around the restaurant with his Napoleon's Syndrome on full display and looking for situations to ignite with his malicious manner. No one had any respect for Piggy because he was a repugnant little prick, but we all feared him because: (1) he was the almighty G.M., (2) he seemed to revel in the roles of interrogator and executioner when he fired people, and (3) his family had connections to Duke's ownership (i.e., Russ and Stag). As such, he was an untouchable little general who waged war and fought battles entirely on his own accord. So there I was, standing on the battlefield wearing my turtle-neck within full view of General Piggy, who was safely stationed at the far end of the pass-thru sitting on his faithful white stallion, hand tucked into his tunic, and looking through his field glasses at me. It didn't seem to matter that I looked presentable, or that no customer could possibly see me expediting within the pass-thru, or that we were ridiculously busy that night, or that I lived a half hour away by car, because the little general insisted I "looked like a shit bag and had better run my stupid ass home to change." Needless to say, I felt shame, embarrassment, and a little rage, but I dutifully drove home and came back with a shirt and tie on about an hour later. Piggy and the Kiwi never knew how close I was to going AWOL that night by saying, "Piss on it" and staying home to watch the hockey game, but an observant few might have noticed my subtle protest upon return: I chose to wear my tacky Porky Pig necktie.

Day vs. Night Staff...

While at Trader's, there was no distinction between day and night staff because we wore the hats of both. All of us worked split shifts to some degree, so there were very few people who exclusively worked days or nights. At Duke's, though, there was a very clear demarcation between the two, with the night staff being regarded as superior in most aspects (by everyone, that is, except the day managers who vigorously defended the largely merited reputations of their lame staff and became enraged at the mere mention of the term day turd). Generally speaking, day shifts were a training ground for becoming night servers because they were less demanding and required lesser skills and knowledge. Granted, there were always people who chose to work the day shift because they had commitments in the evening, but most of the day servers would have preferred to be working at night because of the better money (in terms of higher ring-outs, better tips, and more hours on their paychecks).

Day serving was seen as less challenging for a number of reasons, mainly: (1) the shifts were much shorter in duration, usually lasting only three to four hours; (2) most customers ordered the lunch features or items like burgers, so the server didn't have to worry about timing appetizers or having extensive knowledge of the menu; (3) lunch customers rarely ordered wine or liquor, so knowledge in this area wasn't a priority either; and (4) day waiters rarely suffered from waiter's ass. However, working a lunch shift was challenging in that you were guaranteed to be slammed with about five tables right around noon, and with people who were in a major hurry. The usual scenario was: a table of two tightly budgeted office drones who wanted two coffees, two sandwiches, and two doggy bags containing the meager remains of said sandwiches, and who needed to be walking out the door forty-five minutes later. Yes, it was an unreasonable request in most cases, especially when the check totaled about $18 and they left only $20, but such was the fate of the day server.

By not yet being an alpha-male night waiter at that stage, I was forced to pick up the occasional brunch shift on Sunday mornings when I wasn't scheduled to work the previous Saturday night. Simply put, brunch shifts were painful to work because most of the staff was hung-over from a night of going hard, and most of the customers were aged geriatrics on a day pass from some long-term care facility. Now don't get me wrong, I truly enjoy the company of the elderly, and as customers I generally found them impeccably polite and genuinely friendly, but I worked as a waiter out of financial necessity and, therefore, loathed serving people who were naive to the ways of tipping. Perhaps volunteering one's time as a doctor is noble, but working as a server and not trying to maximize your tips is woefully misplaced kindness. Unfortunately, the elderly at Duke's used tipping guidelines that were last applicable when Johnny

Weissmuller played *Tarzan the Ape Man* in theatres, and we all know how much inflation has eroded the value of a twenty-five-cent piece since. Making matters worse was that the vast majority of people who survive until that age are female, usually widowed, in some stage of dementia, and without a clue on how to tip even during their more lucid moments. And try as I did to place the check in front of someone from a younger generation, it always found its way into Grandma's arthritic, knobby hands, who then shuffled through her purse amongst her prescription bottles and produced crisp fifties that were numbered in the corners (isn't that illegal?). This little show of affluence may have impressed a rookie server, but I knew I would be hard pressed to be tipped something made of paper. Granted, it was touching that Grandma wanted to take her progeny out for brunch and foot the bill, but I just didn't want it transpiring in my section. Ever.

  The day shift was certainly not without its fair share of characters. A good case in point was "Biff" the bartender, who worked the day shift and the occasional Sunday brunch before an opening became available on the night shift. Although some might have considered Biff an exceptionally pretentious asshole, I liked him from the onset. He was a little taller than average, with a barrel chest, dimpled chin, receding side-parted chestnut hair, and soft eyes to match. He had one of those impossibly small mouths, even though his mandible was prominent and jutted forward. He was raised in a small town, then moved to the city as a teenager at which time he became convinced he was living in a vintage Ralph Lauren advertisement. Not surprisingly, he became a massive "clothes horse" and purchased high-end luxury items usually reserved for the very affluent. For example, imagine a day bartender owning an alligator skin wallet and $500 wing tips!? Biff could also be quite fussy and a little anal, as evidenced by his aversion to wearing seat belts because they creased his fresh linen shirts. But, we enjoyed mimicking "Thurston Howell III" from *Gilligan's Island* together, and he could often be heard saying, "Lovey, lovey come hither" as if he were a Harvard alumnus beckoning from his yacht. He did have decent talent as a writer (he idolized F. Scott Fitzgerald and no doubt envied the lifestyle of *The Great Gatsby*) and as a jewellery artisan (which he took training in), but he was the type to be sabotaged by his own insatiable appetite for opulence and grandeur. For example, a few years later when Biff and I were good friends, he decided to get out of the restaurant industry and open his own jewellery store. This idea was applauded by his friends, but he claimed he needed a trip to Europe to get motivated and to ease his right of passage, so he worked hard, saved his money, and embarked to continental Europe with his antique clothes trunk filled with fine garments and toiletries. All was going well until he wandered into a watch shop in Geneva and found an impeccable timepiece on sale. Without much hesitation or consternation, Biff shelled out well over $2,000 for a Cartier watch, which was a must have for any young man without a pot to piss in. But, Biff marched on like a trooper, refusing to compromise his posh hotels or his penchant for fine food and drink. In short order, credit cards were maxed out and his return ticket was cashed in to support the relative lavishness, so he made his way to Greece and landed a bartending job at the infamous "Blue Palace."

The Blue Palace was a party haven for young tourists from around the world who fancied unbridled debauchery. It was also a destination for travelers who needed money, because the Blue Palace had a policy of hiring almost anyone who agreed to their terms and conditions. In essence, an employee had to sign on for an entire season (in Biff's case it was the summer months) and work six long shifts a week for about $12 per day, while living in one of the establishment's "pensions," which crammed three or four people into a ridiculously small area. At the end of the contract, the employee received a lump sum payment of roughly a couple thousand dollars (which Biff desperately needed to get home). I'm sure the irony was not lost on Biff: he had left a relatively cushy job as a service bartender in a First World country, to be a club bartender making peanuts in obscene conditions within an essentially Third World country. He literally worked his fingers to the bone, which were constantly sticky from pouring shots of Ouzo, and stood behind the bar in slop that rotted his fine shoes for ten hours or more at a time. It must have been educational for Biff in his pension, watching mould grow on his clothes, and listening to his transient roommates lay the nuts to an interchangeable assortment of party girls. But alas, Biff survived his Greek tragedy and returned home to immediately work within the restaurant industry again because he was penniless and his creditors were lining up. So much for the jewellery shop.

The day shift was also the domain of "Nine Fingers," the assistant day manager at the time (the Kiwi was promoted to day manager by that stage, but was within a few months of being fired and sent back Down Under; so much for being a human time-punch card). We called him such because he lost an index finger while water skiing at a younger age. Apparently, the rope wrapped around his finger as the boat was accelerating and literally ripped his finger clean off his hand, providing an unexpected mid-day snack for various fresh water fish. This undoubtedly hurt like a son-of-a-bitch and warranted much sympathy at the time, but as a Duke's manager years later, it didn't cut him any additional slack and, in fact, provided us with a wealth of comic material. The truly unfortunate thing about Nine Fingers, aside from his refusal to accept his male pattern baldness, was the glaring fact that he did not get into management because of his superior people skills and compelling leadership qualities. On the contrary, Nine Fingers was flawless in his ineptitude as a waiter and perfectly defined the term "day turd." Nonetheless, plumes of smoke were eventually directed up his anus by management regarding the enormous potential they claimed he had within the organization. Nine Fingers took the lure, and in doing so became a great example of how Duke's strung their managers along and used them as the scapegoats when it was convenient for them to do so.

Nine Fingers displayed all of the maddening managerial habits I have been harping about from the beginning of this book. Namely, he spent too much time sipping coffee in booths, too many evenings eating his dinner at inopportune times, too much energy on busting our asses on minor dress code violations, and too little time on showing appreciation to key employees. But sadly, he wasn't unusual in any of his behaviors, and as such garnered as much respect from the staff as most other managers did: in other words, bloody little. Regardless, Nine Fingers was steadily promoted up the managerial ladder and ended up as a G.M. at a brand new store in the northwest quadrant of the city. By that time, he certainly must have known the subtleties of running a Duke's restaurant, so I suspect he was as proficient as any other G.M. who came before him. However, because of the location of the restaurant, and/or the newness of it, and/or typical staff problems, and/or initial training issues, Nine Fingers' store was not turning much of a profit. In addition, rumor had it the regional manager and director of operations (who was now the insufferable General Piggy) didn't get along very well with Nine Fingers. As a result, it could be said the "writing was on the wall" for Nine Fingers and he was essentially doomed. Having said that, not too many months into his tenure had passed when some young, careless grease weasel (pardon the redundancy) forgot to extinguish the embers in the forno oven (a ceramic oven used to cook pizzas), which caused part of the restaurant to catch fire and burn down. Not surprisingly, Nine Fingers was blamed for the tragedy because he was ultimately responsible, even though he had worked the day shift and was at home probably dreaming of a new hair follicle regeneration therapy at the time of the mishap. So, after spending well over a decade busting his hump (or at least humping a bust while sipping coffee in a booth), Nine Fingers may have had only nine digits, but he sure didn't have nine lives at Duke's because he was canned quicker than you can say, "Here's an apple and a road map, now bugger off." The truly sad part was that

Nine Fingers struggled for a little while afterwards and had to subsist largely on cheap Ichiban noodles, the salt from which must have really stung the corners of his mouth, which were still stretched from having had dutifully felated Duke's upper management for so many years.

The A-Team...

Within a couple of months of proving myself as a competent expediter, I became a full fledged member of the night crew and commanded three waitering shifts each week while attending university. Typically, I would work Wednesday (which was busy because of the ten cent wings that were offered), Friday, and Saturday nights. Consequently, I was in a position to eschew working Sunday brunch ("call display" would have made the avoidance much easier when the day manager was short staffed and trying to drag me in, but the technology was in its infancy at that time), which allowed me to sleep in and recover from the varied adventures from the nights prior. This recovery was needed because the most lucrative shifts to work were Friday and Saturday nights and the main characters of the night crew consistently worked those nights, which became the backdrop for most of our shenanigans. Unfortunately, Duke's was open until two in the morning on the weekend, which meant the "games" didn't begin until quite late, or at least later than I was accustomed to at Trader's. But that didn't seem to infringe on the good times in the least because that original night crew at Duke's was a colorful collection of hearty, diehard shit disturbers. In essence, they were a cross between the "brat pack" from *Less Than Zero* and the "sweat hogs" from *Welcome Back Kotter*. And without question, the three most significant people from that period, aside from Jeff, Randy, and Biff, were "Missionary Man," "White Man," and "Scameron" because of the friendships that were eventually forged between us all.

Missionary Man was hired at Duke's at the same time as I and was subsequently within my training group to be a waiter. He was a tall kid with poor posture who had jet black hair styled in a fashion reminiscent of the band *Depeche Mode*. He looked quite a bit like the actor Robbie Benson, but didn't like the clean-cut image he projected. Missionary Man was edgy and considered himself counterculture, but was exposed as a fraud by playing volleyball and foosball as if he was a typical, middle class suburbanite. He was difficult to get to know initially because he was so caustic and bitter to everyone, but that was before I found out both his parents died of cancer only a handful of years earlier, so I tried to cut him some slack. His quick, biting sense of humor bordered on cruel, as he would fixate on your most self-conscious physical feature for hours on end. For example, he would relentlessly antagonize you about a particularly inflamed pimple, or an especially small set of breasts, or an outfit that wasn't considered overtly trendy. To be honest, he was a certified bastard most of the time, especially to the females who worked at Duke's. It wasn't unusual for a hostess or a waitress to be awash in tears because of Missionary Man's perpetual sexual harassment and disrespect, which usually took the forms of intense verbal abuse, bra snapping (or undoing), and underwear hoisting. At first, I thought his lewd behavior towards the girls was due to some latent anger he felt from his Mom's death (I was taking a psychology course at the time and was eager to apply some of my new found psycho-babble), but I later learned differently. Much differently.

Missionary Man's nickname came to be because we eventually copulated with the same waitress at Duke's. And since I was her second mount, I was privy to some interesting information about him and let me state unequivocally, obtaining detailed carnal knowledge of a friend, even vicariously, is disturbing, but endlessly fascinating. As it turned out, Missionary Man's sexual preferences were surprisingly conventional, and bordered on being compulsively non-experimental. It was as if he had never chanced upon anything pornographic, or tuned in to watch the baboons frantically pump each other from behind on *Wild Kingdom*. I didn't quite know what to make of his behaviors at the time, but I was glad to find a moniker that so enraged him (and he knew exactly what I meant by it) because he would quit harassing me about anything immediately at the mere whisper of it. In essence, it was his kryptonite and I had stumbled upon it.

It wasn't until the autumn of '93 that Missionary Man's mysterious behaviors were solved. I was teaching English in Japan by that time and reading a letter from a friend, when I came across a gossip laden paragraph referring to Missionary Man officially "coming out of the closet" and quitting Duke's to work at a local gay bar that featured drag queens doing stand-up comedy and singing torch songs every Sunday night. Of course! It must have been his feelings of denial, frustration, shame, fear, or whatever he struggled with that caused him to act the way he did during those formative years. I had no problem with his sexual orientation as it made sense and explained a multitude of things on many different levels. In fact, I was glad he was able to finally express his true identity, but unfortunately, I was never able to experience his newer, softer disposition within a restaurant setting because I had essentially moved on by that time and never worked with him again. In fact, I must admit that I still brace myself when I run into him around the city and realize my complexion is looking a little ruddy, or my breasts a tad small.

At the other end of the spectrum, White Man was about as gregarious as they come and a real sight to behold. He was over six feet tall, had a pinkish complexion under receding, straw colored, wispy hair, and carried considerable weight on his frame. I'll refrain from calling him obese because he wasn't uniformly fat; his legs and arms were fairly muscular and lean, but he was exceptionally thick in the middle. He made repeated efforts to be physical and lose weight, but he always kept that cannonball in his mid-section, often referring to it as his "Molson's muscle" because he loved to consume beer and potable spirits. He also liked to consume food, especially brutally hot wings late at night after his cash out was completed. I'll always be able to recall White Man sitting down in front of me with his plate of thirty or so wings, drenched in a thick red cayenne pepper sauce, and with a half pitcher of beer and a cocktail balanced in his other hand. The beverages weren't paid for, but they weren't scammed either, which was partially a testament to his frugality, but also to his ability to be incredibly hearty and the most pragmatic partier I've ever come across.

White Man was a few years older than the rest of us and seemed to have much more life experience, at least in terms of doing drugs, consuming booze, and going to rock concerts. He was nearing the completion of his university degree and was the president of the biggest and wildest fraternity on campus, while the rest of us were mere wide-eyed freshmen. He was not only an alpha-male waiter (this despite his lack of athleticism), but also the restaurant's silverback when we first started, and was renowned for never missing an opportunity to cut loose, regardless of the location, time of night (or morning), commitments the next day, or his physical condition. He could have been ravaged by flesh eating bacteria, intestinal parasites, viral pneumonia, and a head splitting hangover, but he would still raise a glass of booze to his lips and bop his head to the beat of the music. Not surprisingly then, White Man was our ringleader when it came to partying. He would drag us out after our shifts on Wednesday nights to a bar that offered triple highballs for $1.49 and encourage us all to indulge copiously as he leered at all the hardcore headbangers grinding atop the floor speakers. He would also rally the troops after the weekend shifts and made sure we all got thoroughly devastated on pollutants at various clubs until we hit Denny's at dawn for steaming stacks of pancakes with blueberry syrup. That fat bastard was like our evil den mother.

White Man was only in his early to mid-twenties, but he was a veteran of the partying scene, and as such was wise to the ways of getting drunk and wasn't particularly discerning when it came to the necessary ingredients. This brings us back to the half pitcher of beer he would start his night off with: the half pitcher was actually a collection of the "run-off" from bleeding fresh kegs of beer. Typically, when a keg is changed, foam accumulates near the top of it, so the beer lines must be bled for a few seconds before a proper glass or pitcher of beer can be drawn. Bleeding a fresh keg might produce a full pitcher of foam, which will then eventually evaporate and reduce itself to a couple mouthfuls of beer. With this in mind, the White Man figured that saving all the foam from the various bleedings over the course of a shift would produce about a half pitcher of composite beer, which it did, brand loyalty or homogeneity be damned.

His cocktail concoction was obtained along the same lines because the booze that was used for it was from the "bar-rail," which is a rubber mat used to place shot glasses on while bartenders are idle. Due to gravity then, the bar-rail collects drizzles of booze all shift long, often accumulating two ounces or more of it. The problem is that it becomes a mixture of all the booze poured during that shift, which virtually guarantees it to be an appalling mixture. But the White Man reasoned that it wasn't much different from the booze mix in a Long Island ice tea, which was a combination of most of the bar's "whites" (vodka, gin, white rum, triple sec, and sometimes tequila) combined with Coke and citrus mix. To be honest, he wasn't far off the mark because his bar-rail cocktail could be kept down and almost enjoyed as long as it was mixed with Coke and some sort of juice. The key to keeping it down was avoiding the curdled globules of Baileys that would invariably float to the top of the glass. Consequently, White Man was often in his glory when he joined me after a shift because he had managed to secure a fair bit of booze without paying for it or having to scam it, plus he was about to delve into his precious hot wings.

White Man didn't consume food so much as he romanced it. It was as if he had a short-lived love affair with everything that graced his plate. He would get a frenzied look in his eyes and scan his plate looking for the best morsel to start with, as if he was Bela Lugosi in *Dracula* searching for a distended neck artery. He was also blessed with plumbing made of stainless steel, because he was able to eat things that would have made an old Billy goat puke. During the eating affairs, it wasn't possible to hold a conversation with him because he would be too distracted and in a mesmerized trance. And while in full gorging mode, he would begin to sweat from every gland and pore above his waist, especially those on his upper lip and around his eyes. He was actually forced to pause every couple of minutes in order to mop his face, which was convenient because it allowed him an opportunity to re-hydrate by drinking his run-off and bar-rail.

White Man was also the king of modifying food orders. Although any person who works at the same restaurant for an extended period of time will most likely feel dissatisfied with the menu and be tempted to modify certain things to provide some variety in their diet, White Man took it to a much higher level and made it into an exacting science. He was the first server to realize that ordering an itemized burger (i.e., hamburger patty, bun, tomato, onion, etc.) for his staff meal was substantially cheaper than ordering it directly off the menu. He was the first employee to toss the dry ribs in the hot sauce normally used for the chicken wings and then dip them in Dijon mustard. He was the first person to combine Parmesan cheese dip with absolutely every item of food on the menu, as if it was a mainstream condiment, and finally stumbled on a marvelous union with it, cheese toast, and fresh cilantro. He was also the bastard who introduced me to the dastardly "calamari sandwich" which produced an outcome that will be explored in detail in the next chapter. In short, he was a pioneer, a risk taker, and always thought outside of the box. Unfortunately, he didn't spend much time thinking outside of his very limited clothes closet.

White Man was, without any doubt at all, the worst dressed individual that Duke's had ever hired. Granted, we had some real *GQ* dandies like Biff and Missionary Man who put most of us to shame with their panache, but White Man stood out as the most fashion challenged, even to the most unbiased and objective observers, which was a tremendous feat because the restaurant also employed Nine Fingers and the Kiwi. However, perhaps White Man's most endearing quality was that he really didn't give a flying fuck about material things or aesthetics. He seemed to be immune to all the social pressures to look more successful or attractive than he actually was. This was evidenced by the fact that he drove his dead grandma's Toyota Tercel around town with aplomb, didn't own anything of any major value, and occasionally wore a baby blue short sleeved shirt with matching three quarter length cotton shorts to work (think summer leisure suit). This ridiculous ensemble brings us to the origins of his nickname: I was taking a course on South African history at the university when I came across a picture of an early, white settler in a book. The man was a tall, rotund, sunburned, balding Boer farmer who wore a khaki, short sleeved military shirt with matching three-quarter length shorts and knee high socks. It was an eerie likeness, possibly even an ancestor of our beloved silverback. In essence, they both were extraordinary sights to behold, at least in the eyes of the Duke's staff and possibly even the local Zulu tribes of that earlier era, who undoubtedly asked themselves at some stage, "Who is this goofy white man who loves to bust our balls?"

Finally, there was Scameron, who was the original night bartender. We didn't necessarily call him that because he was a prolific scammer, but he was the guy who determined who had free drinking status and undoubtedly scammed for his own profit as much as the rest of us did. Scameron was a little shorter than I was, of medium build, and had short blonde hair that was plagued with murderous cowlicks. Consequently, he could never force a side or middle part into his hair; rather, he was at its mercy and often ended up looking like he had spent considerable time with his Mom's curling iron. Golden locks aside, Scameron was a tenacious worker and always in motion. He was reminiscent of Crash from Trader's in this regard, but he had much more body awareness and, consequently, never smashed into people as if he was a short yardage running back.

Scameron wasn't exactly a dominant athlete, but he excelled at a game that he referred to as **chuck and ploy**, so he qualified as an alpha-male on the merits of that. The codes and ethics of chuck and ploy dictated a large portion of our behavior at Duke's, much like dueling might have in eighteenth century Europe. If someone insulted you, challenged you, or wronged you in any way, a chuck and ploy series was always at one's disposal. For example, if someone observed, "Hey Frenchy, nice fish lips. Do you have gills too?" I might have responded with, "That's pretty funny for a porn star, Missionary Man. Now sashay your ass over here for a chuck and ploy because the loser is staying late to clean the ice cream whore." If people knew that someone was quick to demand a chuck and ploy and risk suffering the dire consequences, then that deterred them from fucking with him/her.

For practical reasons, if there were more than three people chuck and ploying, then pairs would square off to determine losers and the losers would subsequently square off until a single loser was left standing. Surprisingly, there was more strategy to chuck and ploying than most people fathomed. Naturally, one could cheat by forming alliances with others to target a certain individual, but barring this, one had to rely on either luck or strategy. I didn't like to lose because the consequences were endless and usually involved the outlay of considerable cash or performing an undesirable task, so I developed a fairly comprehensive strategy involving three key areas: the initial hand sign, sequencing of the subsequent hand signs, and hand sign bluffs.

The initial hand sign was crucial, because it was easy to get flustered and lose the handle on your strategy once the chuck and ploy challenge started to progress. So with people who weren't especially perceptive with the game, I would always lead with the scissors sign because I came to realize that most people would change from the rock sign as they finished their three count (the rock sign was always used to start with and to count to three with before you revealed your first sign). As such, when people changed from the rock sign they either lead with the scissor or paper signs. By leading with scissors myself, the worst I would do was neutralize my opponent's opening sign. At best, I beat them immediately. This single strategy won me about sixty percent of chuck and ploy contests.

A sign sequencing strategy was important if the opening signs neutralized each other. As I said above, I would often open with scissors, but if this was matched then I would go with paper because I also came to realize that most people allow their previous sign to influence the decision of their subsequent signs. For example, if a person was to start with scissors and get matched, they had a tendency to show rock as their second sign because they subconsciously wanted to beat the previous sign. As a further example, if we neutralized each other with rock, I would assume this would influence my opponent to show paper, so I would show scissors as my second sign to counteract this tendency. As complicated as it might sound, it worked about seventy-five percent of the time.

Bluffing worked well too, especially if I was chuck and ploying with someone inexperienced and I wanted to psych them out. For example, just as we were about to chuck and ploy, I would say something along the lines of, "I don't know about you little vagitarian, but I'm going scissors," which would cause the flustered chuck and ployer to do one of two things: (1) he/she would show rock in the desperate hope that I was telling the truth and being charitable; or (2) he/she would show paper because they assumed it was a trap and wanted to vanquish me by using some reverse psychology. Knowing this, I would then show paper because at worst I would get neutralized, but at best I would win immediately. If I were neutralized initially with paper, then I would use my sequencing strategy and show rock. This worked very well with new staff and the simple minded (who were often one and the same), but it just became too elaborate with the veterans and couldn't be counted on to gain any significant advantage.

However, Scameron managed to master the various strategies and techniques of chuck and ploy as if he were an old Russian chess master. In fact, it would have been interesting seeing him chuck and ploying Garry Kasparov for double shots of Stolichnaya vodka.

Slaving Away and Serving the Masses…

In many ways it was a refreshing change of pace being a solo server at Duke's. Unlike Trader's, there was no one to continually coordinate with, or monitor for scamming cigarettes, or chastise for being a lazy dog fucker, or share the tips with at the end of the night. Initially, I felt unencumbered and free to run my own business and control my own destiny as if I was an entrepreneur. But was I really that free to thrive, or was I actually a shackled captive within the underbelly of a Duke's slave ship and under the gross misconception that I was using the restaurant as my stage? Well, let's examine the situation to find out…

To begin with, I didn't have the freedom to choose the clothes that donned my back, because if I did you can be assured that I wouldn't have worn any Duke's polyester emblazoned shirts, patio shirts, or theme outfits (gotta love a ten gallon sombrero clipping everything within a twenty foot radius during the dreaded "Mexican Days"). Granted, I was able to wear black shorts year round during the early years (which lead to a nickname of "Legs" to be bestowed upon me by a couple of committed groupies), but a rigidly enforced dress code eventually became entrenched at Duke's. It was the dastardly assistant night managers who usually enforced the dress code and made sure all of our denim jeans were not too faded, all of our white dress shirts were properly ironed, and all of our colorful ties were knotted with tight half Windsors (OK, I'm exaggerating now). But honestly, who was it within the restaurant industry that concluded the combination of jeans with a white dress shirt and necktie looked hip and was practical to wear within a restaurant setting? Maybe the ever-conspicuous Tommy Hilfiger has a brother who had clout in the industry, because this "casually professional" dress code spread to many other restaurants in addition to Duke's. By consensus, wearing a white shirt just emphasizes the various food stains that have clung to the cotton fibers, a necktie manages to dip in more things than a rippled potato chip, and denim jeans become far too hot, thus promoting the rapid formation of waiter's ass. Consequently, in this worker's opinion, the ideal outfit to wear in a casual restaurant setting would consist of a dark cotton polo shirt (stylish, comfortable, and great at hiding stains), khaki or matching walking shorts (stylish, comfortable, and slow to promote waiter's ass), and practical shoes of the server's choosing (a single pair of quality work shoes will serve one much better than an Imelda Marcos closet full of Keds). I realize that this ensemble might be too L.L. Bean for some, and the T & A quotient would be noticeably reduced, but a comfortable server not distracted by trying to shake his/her "money maker" is a focused, efficient server.

Secondly, I wasn't able to choose when my shift started, and worse, never knew when it was going to end (gotta love getting home at two in the morning, showering off the restaurant's filth, struggling through a waiter nightmare, then having to rise before seven in order to write a final exam at the university by eight). I pretty much knew week to week that I would be working Wednesday, Friday, and Saturday nights, but my starting times always varied. Sometimes I started as early as four, sometimes as late as eight. Generally speaking, the earlier I started the earlier I got cut, but there was an insane amount of jockeying that occurred over the course of a shift that always seemed to decimate any plans. For example, there was always at least one waitress complaining to the doting manager about life-threatening abdominal cramps, always one waiter unable to stay past midnight because of an intensifying hangover that mimicked a brain tumor, and always a couple of servers who had to leave early in order to cram for pivotal exams. It was as if some servers put more energy into sloughing off their shifts than actually working them. Of course, the veteran servers had preferential treatment in that they could sometimes choose which shifts and sections they worked, but veterans were also considered the most dependable and were the first to be begged by management to stay late when the panic to evacuate the restaurant began each night. This was really irritating and warrants a serving tip:

****

SERVING TIP #7: If you have important plans involving your life outside of the restaurant, book the related shifts off entirely weeks in advance because nothing pisses the other servers off more than having to scramble for an excuse as to why they can't cover your pathetic, whining ass by staying later and working harder. So unless you can produce fresh blood, vomitous, or a psychiatrist's note certifying mental illness, shut your sniveling mouth and work your shift as scheduled. Do you think for a moment that every other server couldn't produce an exhaustive litany of reasons why they should be cut early? In point of fact, every server has other things they would rather be doing, and every server experiences some form of physical discomfort during every shift, so you are not unique. If you do have the audacity to pressure other servers to stay late for you, then you had better offer some serious cash, a tangible asset, or some deviant sexual act as compensation, because the other veteran servers are not compassionate altruists who will accept your bullshit promise of "owing a favor." In short, put up or shut up because your reputation is on the line.

****

Thirdly, I wasn't really in full control of my own section because of the constant intrusion that having to run other server's food created. At times, it was difficult to pry myself away from another server's section to get back to my own. For example, typically I would be grabbed by a desperate expediter in the pass-thru and begged to run something to another server's table. I would do this swiftly and without much consternation, but before I could turn on my heels and walk away from the table, a neglected customer would invariably ask me for a list of sundry items that would have dwarfed the needs of a Mt. Everest expedition. Meanwhile, my section had digressed into the kind of chaos and ruin last seen at Pompeii. And to what end? To ensure the future return of a few disgruntled customers who might coincidentally sit in my section, remember my unselfishness, and reward me with a polite gratuity? Well big fucking deal, because by letting the level of service slip in my section, I was sacrificing certain guaranteed gratuities from at least five of my own tables. Shall I do the math? No, I didn't think so.

Lastly, I wasn't able to choose which tables got sat in my section. Granted, very few servers have any say in who garnishes their tables, but it is this uncertainty that contributes a considerable amount of anxiety to the task of being a server. And since servers must rely on customers for at least seventy percent of their income, it pays to be discerning when it comes down to who sits at their tables because not all situations are as lucrative as they may seem, and there are a limited number of sittings over the course of a shift. Given my druthers then, I would choose to avoid big tables, tables of celebrities, tables of foreigners, and patio tables.

The Bottom Feeders...

Without a doubt, serving big tables (roughly ten or more people) can be a risky venture. On the one hand, they may take up an entire section for many hours and end up stiffing their server; on the other hand, they may be an extraneous table who are in a hurry and make a server's night with their overt generosity. But as a rule, gratuities from big tables rarely hit fifteen percent because of the "big table mentality." Big table mentality is a phenomena that influences the minds of all the people at a big table when only one check is presented to them and forces everyone to be honest about how much they owe. In this situation, there are three types of people who emerge from the group. (1) The opportunistic customer who realizes that he/she can save money by tossing in far less than they owe in hopes the gratuities left by everyone else covers the difference. These degenerates are usually the last to contribute money, but the first to stand up from the impending ruckus and attempt to leave. (2) The totally stupid customer who honestly underestimates how much he/she has consumed and forgets to factor in any service tax or gratuity. These people sometimes realize their idiocy when it's discovered that the check is short of being covered by about $100, but usually don't because they are in their own oblivious world. And (3), the conscientious customer who ends up being the "collector" and is aghast at the money shortage, so throws in twice what he/she owes in hopes that the server is satisfied and doesn't think of him/her as cheap and ungrateful. Bless the souls of these latter day saints, but unfortunately, they are far outnumbered by the other two types. Due to this inequitable dynamic then, servers are lucky to receive much over a twelve percent gratuity from big tables. Accordingly, to help insulate yourself from such a snafu, heed the following serving tip:

****

SERVING TIP #8: If one person emerges from a big table as the sugar daddy and wants to pay the entire check with a credit card then that's very fortuitous, but this is typically not the case. A much more common scenario is a wild group of people frantically tabulating what they owe and then waving twenty dollar bills in the air in hopes of depleting you of all your change. To save yourself some grief and to ensure a higher gratuity, mentally divide the big table into smaller groupings (based on married couples, families, or seemingly close friends, for example) and give them separate checks. Granted, this strategy will require slightly more organizational ability to accomplish, but your overall gratuity will be significantly higher than if you just present one check for everybody to decipher.

****

      Big tables weren't as perilous at old Trader's Inn because they instigated a policy that forced tables of over ten people to tip at least fifteen percent. This arrangement was amicable to the servers and always provided an opportunity for customer befuddlement. The perfect example was a table of about fifteen commercial bankers who came to Trader's to celebrate their Christmas holidays one evening. The vast majority of the table consisted of female tellers, although there were a couple of female manager types too. They were a frugal bunch as everyone chose cheaper items on the menu and many looked perplexed at the suggestion of fermented grains or fruits (i.e., booze) with their food. After an exhaustive explanation of what celebrating and having a good time entailed, it was as if the giant black monolith from *2001: A Space Odyssey* suddenly fell from the sky, landing behind their table to the sound of some austere music, and sparked the momentous realization that food and alcoholic beverages can be combined into a complimentary duo. Then, hardly able to control their excitement of having discovered something so profound, some of the more audacious ladies indulged in a cocktail or a glass a wine. Believe me, it was an exciting moment to be alive and bear witness to something so historically significant.

      Overall though, things went smoothly and everyone was pleasant and seemed to enjoy themselves. I wasn't concerned about getting stiffed because we were guaranteed a fifteen percent tip, which was clearly labeled on the check when I presented it to them after they finished their decaf coffees. Within ten seconds of placing the check on the table, about ten calculators were pulled out of various purses. I kid you not. And as bankers are known to do, fingers were flying and things were being tabulated for the better part of twenty minutes. At one stage, seven of them were tightly huddled over the check, conferring as if they were fiendishly deciding on which mutual funds to push on their wealthier clients. Finally, they ended up leaving the restaurant and as I approached the table to count the tidy stack of cash, I realized they had tipped us fifteen percent (to the penny) on the total amount of the check, which had included the mandatory fifteen percent gratuity. In essence then, the tight fisted female bankers unknowingly tipped us about thirty-two percent on the original total. How deliciously ironic it was. Too bad they've never over-inflated my savings account that way.

Big tables usually grow big for good reason. If it's due to a corporate function, then there can be some rejoicing because "the boss" will most likely pay the check by credit card and reward the server justly. However, more often than not, big tables assemble to celebrate someone's insignificant inception and are expecting the server to round up all the other servers in order to bellow out an obnoxious song in an attempt to unduly embarrass the poor soul. Being a server, just imagine the hassle of having to beg and cajole enough fellow servers to join in rhapsody so that the shear loudness of your combined voices distract from the obvious lack of melody and harmony. And unless there are some who have spent their entire youth in choral clubs, the vast majority will bristle and balk at the suggestion of singing in front of total strangers while stone cold sober, although those very same servers may be totally pixilated if it's a Friday or Saturday night. Be that as it may, it's always been a mystery to me as to why some customers think they can demand such performances from their servers without paying an additional fee, because without question, having to sing the birthday song is the bane of all servers' existences and deserves some sort of additional compensation. Simply said, it's tough bloody work that nobody relishes. In summary then, big tables tip poorly and exponentially increase the odds of having to yodel like *Gomer Pile*, so unless servers are independently wealthy and have someone like Jan the Rockstar in their midst, they should avoid them at all costs.

Big tables aside, serving celebrities was not much of a treat either. During my waitering career, the most famous celebrities to have graced my section included: Mario Lemieux (N.H.L. hockey player), Brett "The Hitman" Hart (W.W.F. wrestler), Mike Love (lead singer for the *Beach Boys*), Dr. Ruth Westheimer (sex therapist), and David Copperfield (magician). From a personal standpoint, they all managed to disappoint my expectations and dispel the positive images I had of them. Mario chain-smoked as if he was auditioning for the role of Marlboro Man, Brett stuffed various menu items into his mouth like a boorish glutton, Mike solicited then tried to lure a sixteen-year-old hostess back to his hotel room with a promise of a limo ride, Dr. Ruth was like a tacky little yard gnome, and David was a total megalomaniac who insisted on roaming the restaurant and interrupting people's dinners with cheesy card tricks (despite just having performed an elaborate magic show in the local auditorium). But from a server's standpoint, they were all pains in the ass primarily because they made me feel like some invisible servant. There never seemed to be a good time to approach their tables, it was nearly impossible to force intelligible verbal responses out of them, and none of them tipped especially well. Therefore, being a jungle celebrity myself, I didn't have much use for any of them and neither should anyone else.

Although I've always loved to travel to foreign countries and interact with "the locals," I didn't enjoy serving said locals within my own country. They couldn't be directly blamed for problems that arose out of cultural differences or language barriers, but they could have been more understanding and tolerant than old "Archie Bunker" from *All in the Family* for Christ's sake. People from the United Kingdom lamented that our beer was too cold and fizzy and that we didn't have any decent "brown sauce," East Indians didn't appreciate any ice in their drinks and thought our curries were too bland and tasteless, Italians were up in arms over our watery espresso and lack of quality Chiantis, and the Chinese were overwhelmed by the shear quantity and decadence of virtually everything related to our food and beverage industry. I could endure the questions, comments, and complaints from my tables of foreigners, but I could not tolerate being stiffed and disrespected by them. The worst peoples for refusing to recognize our tipping protocols were the Australians and New Zealanders. I'll admit that they were generally fun people to serve, but they were the cheapest bastards on the planet when it came to digging into their pockets and leaving a little some-thing-something for their server. And frankly, I don't give a rat's ass if they are not accustomed to tipping in their own country, because when in Rome one acts Roman, or is at least concerned enough to inquire about the local customs and practices. It got to the point that when I heard, "G'day mate" from a table, I immediately forfeited any hope of a tip, then instinctively bent over and prepared to take an turgid probe about six inches up my hoop. Fortunately, though, my anal membrane could no longer be torn as the scar tissue that initially formed within my ass while working at Trader's took on the consistency of something tough and unrippable. Perhaps soccer ball leather.

About the only exception to my aversion to serving foreigners was serving indigenous Japanese people because they often over-tipped, if such a thing is possible. I'm not sure if it stemmed from their obsessive desire to be well thought of and respected around the globe (in which case their inflated tips were a classic case of bribery), or if it was because our woefully devalued dollar was like *Monopoly* money to them (in which case their inflated tips were due to sympathy and charity), or if it was an attempt to gloss over the fact that they were fiendishly purchasing the planet's prime real estate (in which case their inflated tips were a rebate). Regardless, I gladly took fists full of Yen from the Land of the Rising Sun. Domo arigato, Mr. Roboto.

The Rain Forest

It is no secret that most people enjoy the idea of consuming good food and beverage while sitting on a patio surrounded by all the glory that Mother Nature can bestow. Unfortunately, the romanticized ideal of being on an outdoor patio often fails to account for common climatic conditions such as wind, rain, and hail, and fails to realize that "nature" infers the presence of other creatures such as aphids, wasps, and birds that occasionally must defecate. As a result of these inconveniences, most people become quickly disenchanted with sitting on a patio and ask (nay, demand) to sit inside because they are not nearly hardy enough to deal with the full force that Mother Nature can inflict on its inhabitants. Making matters worse is the fact that some area's weather patterns are extremely variable, which makes patio dining especially unpredictable. The jungle that I waitered in actually had a tremendous number of sunny days throughout the year, but it was also vulnerable to constant wind, precipitation, and stray beasts because of its proximity to the mountains. However, these issues did not deter Duke's management from tirelessly promoting the endless pleasures to be had by frolicking and debauching on their patios. Admittedly, on rare evenings when it was warm, calm, and free of any precipitation, the patio truly was a fabulous place to enjoy some wine, dinner, and lattes, but this is speaking strictly from a customer's perspective. From a server's perspective, customers either linger too long on the patio in an attempt to prolong their nearly perfect outdoor experience (which is displeasing because servers must turn over all the tables in their section at least five times every shift in order to make good money), or they are soundly defeated by the elements and bemoan that a cheeky little aphid has dive bombed their pasta, or an impudent pine needle has fouled their margarita, or an audacious gull has crapped near their table, or the wind has turned their hair into a tossed salad, so they demand to be moved into the sanctuary of the restaurant (which is also displeasing because it's a hassle moving a table inside and transferring their check to another server). In my opinion then, only mountain guides (or goats), veteran roofers, and bikers from Hell's Angels should be entrusted to sit on patios because only they exhibit the necessary hardiness.

Now, getting back to the question of whether I was an entrepreneurial server or a slave while at Duke's, let's consider the conditions that "Kunta Kinte" from *Roots* had to endure: Kunta certainly didn't get to choose his attire, and although he was lucky to get hold of a rancid loincloth (which may have led to many serious bouts of waiter's ass), he didn't have to wear a shirt and tie with jeans either; Kunta also didn't get to choose when he started his shift, but he could have been almost assured it was from sunrise to sunset; Kunta definitely didn't get to choose who he "served" and, in fact, often got horse whipped by those he did; Kunta no doubt loathed and feared all big groups, celebrities, and foreigners equally, but had to kowtow to them nonetheless (which may have led to a few waiter nightmares); Kunta got paid the most minimal of minimum wage (i.e., nothing) and often worked while chained to something or someone; finally, Kunta rarely got laid by any of his co-workers and never had the pleasure of experiencing cheese toast with fresh cilantro and Parmesan dip.

In conclusion then, it can be said I had it quite a bit better than Kunta Kinte did, but it was still a far cry from freedom and job security. In reality, I had made it to the canopy of the rain forest and sat perched there, better able to see danger coming and to shit on those below me, but the canopy at Duke's was my "stage" to the same extent as a tree stump in Coney Island is a stage to an accordion playing, cigar smoking rhesus monkey trapped and exploited in a second-rate, traveling carnival. In other words, it's still a cage and the leash is still pretty short. However, having said that, the tyranny of the restaurant didn't rob us of our innate enthusiasm or our primal urge to carry on like cheeky monkeys and swing from the vines at every opportunity.

Chapter 9

Swinging from the Vines

"All men are liable to error; and most men are in many points, by passion or interest, under temptation to it."

- John Locke

Always a Shit Show...

My waitering routine at Duke's wasn't as all encompassing as it was at Trader's (primarily because I was only working three night shifts while attending university), but the magnetic force trying to draw me into the restaurant lifestyle was still a constant. It didn't seem to matter that most of the people had ambitions beyond that of being servers, because Duke's managed to destroy most of the motivation to accomplish things outside of the restaurant. But Duke's wasn't unusual in this regard as slothfulness is simply an unsavory by-product of the industry as a whole.

It can be said the restaurant lifestyle is probably most comparable to the lifestyle of rockstars. While rockstars perform their craft, party under the influence of something hallucinogenic, get laid by groupies, then sleep the entire next day away, so do many restaurant servers. At Trader's, we definitely partook in some debauchery as servers, but we were still thought of as "those little salad boys" and, as such, were shielded from the hard core drugs and evil element by the older staff members who presumably thought we had some potential worth safeguarding. It wasn't until I left Trader's that I became aware of the rampant drug use there, with cocaine being the stimulant of choice. In fact, Dilbert (the anal little K-car driving accountant who cut me the check for $250) turned out to be a major drug dealer for the Hell's Angels. Who knew? On the flip side, Duke's was much tamer, primarily because the majority of the staff was young and not yet so hardened. Although, it would be a mistake for Baby Boomers to think their Caucasian, middle class kids who work in the industry are all wholesome and residue free. On the contrary, almost all of the WASPish Generation Xers whom I worked with dabbled in marijuana, hashish, and "magic" mushrooms, but admittedly, very few did cocaine, acid, or heroin. In addition, everyone drank copious volumes of booze during multiple binges throughout the week. It was as if we were anticipating and preparing for another Prohibition, or maybe Armageddon. Were we alcoholics? Most of us probably weren't because we didn't drink alone, nor did we drink first thing in the morning in order to function, but the Duke's lifestyle undoubtedly led some addictive personalities down the path of substance abuse. For example, I remember occasionally meeting Matt and his co-workers (from the south Duke's location) at a downtown club after our weekend shifts had ended. We would get there just prior to "last call" and immediately order a tray of Sambuca shooters and a tray of double Jack Daniels and Cokes. I'll never forget the sight of Matt and his buddy "Ginger" feverishly scooping the ice out of their highballs so they could gulp them down more efficiently, then tossing in their fists to chuck and ploy the tray of Sambuca away. They would literally consume about fifteen ounces of alcohol within about fifteen minutes, and then look to each other to see who was going to start the shit show. Ginger was usually the instigator of said show because as an orange haired pencil dick who induced images of Ichabod Crane, he was the most desperate to impress his cohort. He was the south Duke's equivalent of Missionary Man, but much more cruel in nature and with far fewer redeeming qualities. He had a wide range of physical shortcomings (think multigenerational inbreeding in Arkansas), but he counted on the fact that precious few of his combatants had the callousness to make mention of them. And while Ginger was rapier sharp and exceptionally quick with his cut-downs and denunciations, he was a lame athlete and a total anti-mack with the ladies; it was as if he wore chick repellent for deodorant on most nights. Accordingly, he was the rare example of a Duke's waiter who became an alpha-male entirely on intimidation and the merits of his audacious shenanigans.

 It was the escalating craziness of the shenanigans that fuelled the entire process at Duke's: the booze and/or drugs eliminated all inhibitions, the lack of inhibition led to thoughts of "raping, burning, and pillaging" small villages, the resulting debauchery then led to uproarious stories, said stories eventually desensitized those who waited with baited breath to hear them and, therefore, created the need for more sensational stories which could only be accomplished under the influence of additional booze or other stimulants. As a friend of mine at the time was fond of saying, "It's all about the stories and the opportunity to be the champ." And really it was, as pointless as that sounds.

The social pressures that propagate within restaurants can be very compelling because there is tremendous influence created from shear numbers, which leads to a type of "herd mentality." Also, the greater the number of people who are getting wasted, doing stupid things, and foolishly reprioritizing their outside lives, the easier it is to justify that behavior to oneself. Consequently, the ringleaders within restaurants continually try to rally the troops and mobilize the intoxicants in order to create an influential mob that builds momentum and provides soothing distraction to all those under its hypnotic umbrella. So instead of having a little devil on your shoulder whispering temptations, there's an entire flock of satanic servers loudly goading you into staying late and drinking, which often derails you from heading home and being productive. This continual congregating in order to drink, snort, smoke, laugh, cry, bitch, confess, challenge, fight, deify, and fornicate causes an unusually strong bond to develop amongst participating members, which flatters the new staff members who are "lucky" enough to get invited into it, but it also pressures the veterans into continuing with the charade because it has become their adopted family and they fear being exiled from it. This largely explains why restaurant staff show up at work on their off days, drop out of school in order to work as full-time employees, completely forget about essential tasks that must be performed in the outside world, and cheat on their significant others by rabidly humping fellow staff members. As I wrote earlier, the restaurant jungle mixes all types of young people in a big black cauldron and then seasons the broth with money, booze, stress, and opportunity. Add to this a fear of being rejected, and the resulting soup becomes absolutely irresistible.

A good case in point, and one that illustrates the irresistible magnetism that a restaurant can have on an impressionable worker, is the fateful morning of Matt and I's much anticipated Caribbean holiday departure. We had planned this holiday to the Dominican Republic for months. We obsessed over the details, trying to make it the quintessential two-week getaway, one that would have made the most promiscuous of twenty year olds molt with envy. We planned to take no prisoners, zero bullshit, or any attitude from any chickie with anything less than absolutely stellar T & A and a supermodel's penchant for pouting and going braless. But then, on the night before departure, a long, penetrating tentacle from the restaurant jungle violated poor Matt without Vaseline and filled him with strange needs and desires. He felt it more important to embrace the dark side of anarchy and debauchery while holding hands with Ginger and the other descendants of Beelzebub.

Matt actually was a fairly conscientious young man. We were best friends almost from the moment we met in grade ten. And he had good intentions and really wanted to embark on our Caribbean odyssey. However, he just couldn't resist a lurid solicitation from the silverback of his frenzied troop. His need not only to be accepted, but also celebrated, clouded his better judgment and put our meticulous plans in jeopardy. My Mom and I didn't appreciate the extent of his vulnerability as we sat outside of his parent's house at nine in the morning and lightly honked the horn. We were pressed for time, so I approached the house and rang the doorbell. No response. His parents were away for the weekend, so maybe he slept in and was running a few minutes behind, I thought. I then knocked repeatedly on the door with the brass knocker. Again, no response. I walked around to the back deck and beckoned him to appear at his second story window as if I was an impatient Romeo and he was a rather butch and balding Juliet. Nothing. No sign of my travel partner. As this was before cellular phones, my Mom and I were about to frantically drive to a pay phone when I saw the front door open a crack and reveal a beckoning hand. He must need help with his luggage, I thought as I approached, but it wasn't his gear he was struggling with, it was his central nervous system.

I was confused as I saw a vaguely familiar silhouette in the doorway. It was dressed in a pair of tight, white Jockeys and propped up against the door frame; its sparse long hair was greasy and matted, it had trouble focusing on me because it couldn't hold its head up properly, it had something that looked like oatmeal on its chin, and it had some odd discoloration across its nose and around its eyes. Who the fuck is this heroin addict and what has he done with my buddy, I asked myself. Speak vampire speak, I demanded, but silence hung in the morning air. At the risk of infestation and permanent disability to my organs of smell, I moved closer and confirmed that it was indeed Matt, albeit postmortem and on the verge of decomposition if it wasn't for the pickling effects of the various alcohol based fluids cursing through his vessels, which were all clearly visible through his transparent, mealy skin. In fact, the discoloration on his nose, cheeks, and in the whites of his eyes was due to thousands of broken blood vessels, presumably from puking so hard and so often, which Matt had a reputation for when he overindulged. And I can tell you, that wasn't oatmeal on his chin, unless he thought himself a bovine and got a little sloppy chewing his breakfast cud. All I could do was sigh and resign myself to the fact that I wasn't getting laid in the Dominican with this emaciated albino as a wingman.

Not only was Matt in an alarming state of disrepair mere minutes before we had to blast to the airport, but he had failed to pack the night before so as not to miss the opening credits to the much heralded Friday night shit show at Duke's. Heaven forbid falling behind the level of inebriation and degree of brain atrophy of his fellow Luddites. Consequently, I had all of ten minutes to pack, wash, and berate Matt for being a sheep and partying with the wolves. As such, packing consisted of randomly grabbing things that looked summery and stuffing them into a gym bag; washing consisted of dragging a damp face cloth over the fetid remains on his chin; and berating consisted of several coarse barbs of displeasure and a sinister threat to reveal to the restaurant community at large his circumcision at the ripe age of seventeen.

As zombie-boy started to regain his faculties, the vile details of his misadventures started to pour out. Suffice it to say that many potable spirits were consumed via shots, countless rounds of chuck and ploying, and quite possibly through intravenous. And as the boys became utter piss tanks and started to raise the hackles of patrons around them, the manager (who was whacked on magic mushrooms) suggested they take their shit show on the road to the "Spanish Maid," which was a seedy strip club of gravely ill repute. After the activities ground to a halt at the "ballet," a taxi dropped the gang off at Matt's house. Unfortunately, Matt didn't recall the ride home or the Pakistani driver he slumped upon, as he was absolutely blotto to the point of comatose. Once inside, Ginger and the others stripped Matt naked, wrote, "Thanks for the lovely felching. Call me," in black ink on his ass, then tossed him into his bed along with a dozen frozen tofu wieners. Matt eventually awoke from his cryogenic state and stumbled into the bathroom where he quickly commenced the destruction of his subdermal blood vessels. He then lay prone on the cold, ceramic tiles until my beckoning from the outside deck startled him out of his coma. In the end, we made it to the Dominican Republic, but were within a whisker of a total snafu. Why Matt risked his health, our much-anticipated holiday, and ultimately our friendship is a strong testament to the lure of the industry's promise of unbridled debauchery.

Unbridled Debauchery...

Saturday nights were the big nights at Duke's, both in terms of the number of customers who packed the place, and the number of drinks that were consumed by the staff. Unlike the downtown and south Duke's, we didn't drink all that much booze while on shift, but we kept pace with every other restaurant on Earth once we were all cashed out and the front doors were locked. Typically, there would be an energizing buzz in the air, which was accentuated by the likes of White Man and Scameron for the purpose of getting the staff all lathered up in anticipation of what was to come. Sometimes we would take the shit show on the road if someone had the courage to offer up his or her humble abode; if not, we stayed at the restaurant and tested its structural integrity. There were nights we cleared a wide swath on the tiled floor, then dumped soapy water on it and used it to conduct belly surfing regattas (followed by wet T-shirt contests, naturally), or pushed the tables aside and played full-contact floor hockey, or stacked all the chairs and tables outside and configured our own Euro-trash discotheque. Other nights, however, we respected our surroundings a little more and suppressed the urges to redecorate like an overzealous Martha Stewart (pardon the redundancy). Unfortunately, on those particular nights we didn't show the same respect to our cirrhotic livers.

☹ WARNING: THE FOLLOWING PASSAGES REVEAL ANOTHER GRAPHIC PUKE STORY

It started out like most other Saturday nights. The restaurant was hopping and we had a solid crew working. I was an established alpha-male by that time, so I was fortunate enough to have secured the much sought after "four-to-eight" shift. There were two such shifts on Saturday nights and they were relished by all of us because they allowed a server to make about $50-60 in legitimate tips, and then catch a movie or properly prepare for a night of partying depending on one's mood. By the time I had settled with my final tables, completed my closing duties, and then cashed out, it was after nine o'clock, so I thought I would have some dinner and drinks and wait for my comrades to join me. My intentions were very innocent at that point and I had no idea what was in store for me.

I had picked a secluded deuce in the back of the restaurant, sat down, and agonized over a menu I had perused about a thousand times before in vain. While I was waiting for divine intervention, most of the staff trickled towards my outpost to recite questions and comments that they had compulsively uttered thousands of times before, as if they all suffered from Asperger's autism. And mainly it was to: tell me what a lucky bastard I was to be off so early on a Saturday night; inquire about my ring-out as if it had any relevance to anything whatsoever; feel out my mood regarding the night's festivities; give me advice on what to have for dinner in hopes they could nibble at it while on shift; and groom my gel-laden head for lice, which is also practiced in chimpanzee society when an alpha-male is separated from the group and looking pensive. Anyway, White Man eventually made an appearance at my table and strongly suggested I try his latest modified concoction: a calamari sandwich, which consisted of deep fried squid tentacles, tsatsiki sauce, and a cheddar cheese slice all between a sesame seed bun. It sounds atrocious, but I enjoyed Duke's calamari and went with his suggestion out of pure curiosity. But before my dinner arrived, Biff (who had replaced Scameron as the night bartender) dutifully acknowledged my free drinking status and sent over a generously poured lime margarita thickly rimmed with salt and a half pitcher of draught that was drawn in "error." As it turned out, the calamari sandwich was quite tasty and it was complimented wonderfully by the gratis lager. Once I had finished my dinner and drinks (which included two additional margaritas made with Cuervo Gold tequila and Grand Marnier) it was about eleven o'clock and my table had grown to include White Man, Missionary Man, and the infamous "Death Chick."

Death Chick was fascinated by the whole goth culture long before it was truly en vogue. Not surprisingly then, she dressed entirely in black, wore dark, dramatic make-up, and had a shock of spiky, peroxided hair which all made her look as if she had died and was prepared by some talentless mortician. She wasn't necessarily a homely girl, nor was she in poor shape, but she was the most annoying person in the restaurant and, consequently, never got the slightest sniff of "trouser snake" from any of the waiters, alpha-male or otherwise. If she wasn't asking us if we thought she was fat, she was proposing the most bizarre scenarios to us. One of her classics was, "Would you rather be an chocolate sundae that has to be eaten, digested, and pooped out, or a strawberry margarita that has to be blended, drank, and peed out?" Our replies were often along the lines of, "Actually, I'd rather be the creature from *Alien* so I could attach to your face and shut you up, but also implant an offspring into your intestines so it bursts out and kills you. Now piss off and quit talking stupid shit." She was a good sport and remained unfazed by the abuse, though, because she desperately wanted to be accepted, included, and quite probably tagged.

Another irritating habit she had was developing psychotic crushes on the alpha-male waiters. Unfortunately, her puppy love at that time was directed entirely towards me. She obsessed I looked exactly like one of the singers from the band, *New Kids on the Block*, which I didn't according to most rational human beings with functioning optic nerves, but when she brought in a plastic figurine of one of the "kids" I was speechless. The rather generic looking blonde doll looked exactly like me, much more so than the kid that it was supposedly based upon, but believe me, not in any good way. She must have paraded that thing around for weeks, as if it were a voodoo doll she was casting a love spell on. It clearly didn't work, and I was the brunt of an endless variety of jokes week after week. Needless to say, I didn't savor the idea of a big-time stalker sitting across the table from me at that particular moment.

As more and more people started joining us and getting settled in, it became obvious the party was going to burn bright then fizzle out within the confines of the restaurant. Our table had reached about ten people by two in the morning and everybody scrambled to order drinks from Biff so he could lock up the bar. Beer just seemed to be the most convenient, so we ordered about six pitchers and saw about a dozen arrive. This disregard for bar costs wasn't unusual when "Zeus," the assistant night manager, worked the weekend closing shifts.

Zeus was like a little bulldog; he was about five foot seven and weighed one hundred and forty-five pounds, and had a bark louder than most beasts' bites. He was about twenty-six years of age, had a "mullet" haircut to rival Billy Ray Cyrus's, was virtually untrained in anything valued by society at large, lived at home with his parents, and absolutely loved his adult toys. His net salary was about $1500/month, but the cost of his '72 Oldsmobile (with a nitrous oxide kit), his three-quarter ton truck, his water-skiing boat, his motorcycle, and his two dogs totaled about $1450/month. Therefore, he literally had $50/month to spend on food, booze, clothes, and entertainment. Not surprisingly then, he was a notoriously brutal dresser, his girlfriend had to pay for any movies they rented, and he relied on Duke's to provide all the food and booze beyond which he could liberate from his gullible parents. Yes, Zeus the manager scammed the restaurant just as much, if not more, than the rest of us.

Zeus was an infectiously funny guy and quick with a laugh. He adored everything about Clint Eastwood and Las Vegas. His favorite sayings were, "You gotta ask yourself punk, are you feelin' lucky today?" and "Double down and let it ride cowboy." He wasn't quite the natural ringleader White Man was, but he could always be counted on for good stories, torrid controversy, and a supply of free booze courtesy of Duke's. As a result, the A-team servers loved Zeus and were very loyal to him. In fact, most of those servers would vote him their favorite all-time manager because he had a great ability to be their friend foremost, and their boss secondarily. As a manager, one could argue that Zeus fucked the dog shift after shift (or at least "Rona," an assistant female manager, doggy style in the office), but he had an innate understanding of when to leave well enough alone. In all honesty, we had a very capable crew during Zeus's reign, and we didn't need him meddling in our affairs or busting our balls for petty bullshit. All we really needed him for was his plastic manager's card in order to correct our mistakes on the computer, which he often had the courtesy to tack onto a board in the pass-thru while he was in the office playing computer games, reading an *Auto Trader*, or shagging Rona from all fours. In fact, Zeus's managerial style was so effective it warrants a tip:

****

MANAGERIAL TIP #4: Resist the urge to reinvent the wheel if you have the tremendous fortune of becoming some sort of restaurant manager. There is no need to put your personal stamp on everything by implementing a bunch of new, ill-conceived rules and policies. Keep in mind that the restaurant existed and probably thrived long before you became part of the team; therefore, don't throw a wrench into the engine just for the sake of change. If you are struggling with the idea of being labeled a dog fucker, relax, because the servers will respect you more for not pretending to be busier or more important than you actually are. The key to being a successful manager is assembling a hard working, fun loving, cohesive crew, then heading off to the nearest booth to sip coffee and leave well enough alone. And if you're smart, you will consult with the more respected veteran servers about what changes should be made. Finally, remember that a couple pitchers of free beer after a busy shift will make your crew more loyal than a purebred Beagle.

****

So there I sat at two o'clock in the morning with four double margaritas, two Tanqueray and tonics, a pitcher of beer, and a calamari sandwich corroding my gullet, while contemplating the role the fresh pitchers of beer were going to play. But, we were having a riot so I didn't much care. Hilarious stories were being told, U2 was blaring from the cheap speakers, and people were dancing in that random way people do when they have reached a state of nirvana. However, it didn't take long for White Man to want to separate the wheat from the chaff, so he got everyone chuck and ploying for booze and added a new wrinkle known as "hold the phone."

Holding the phone was a beer drinking crime that meant holding a beer glass with a right hand while drinking from it. Therefore, if you saw someone drinking their beer with their right hand, you had the right to point and yell, "Hold the phone!" in which case the offender had to drink the remainder of their beer in one continuous swig. The cruel part of holding the phone was that the drunker people became, the more they instinctively drank with their right hands, which meant they got busted and drank even more. Missionary Man was the hawk at our table and never missed a drinking infraction. At one stage, he called back-to-back infractions on Death Chick and almost sent her to her grave for real. She literally coughed as if she was choking for about ten minutes. It got to the point that I thought I'd have to give her the Heimlich maneuver, or worse, mouth to mouth resuscitation to revive her, but then I thought of that haunting "Boy Band" doll and decided to remain still. It was Zeus who was the first to jump up to assist her by giving her a long drag on his hand rolled cigarette which, ironically, resolved her coughing fit almost immediately. With Death Chick revived and properly ventilated, we were able to refocus on our drinking.

By about three o'clock in the morning, all of the beer had been consumed due to our feverishly paced bouts of chuck and ploying. But before any of us could develop the shakes from withdrawal, Zeus summoned me to the bar area. His criminal minded plan was to break into the bar and pull out whatever bottles he could. This wasn't an easy task because Biff, like any other night, had turned off all the beer taps, pad locked the bar fridge, and chained up a giant sheet of particle board across the shelves that contained the bottles of liquor, then had dropped all of the keys into the office safe. In essence, we were totally locked out, but Zeus, being as cunning as he was, reasoned if I pulled back the particle board as hard as I could, he could slide his skinny forearm through the opening and liberate a bottle of booze. With a little brawn and ingenuity, we accomplished our mission and he ended up pulling out a cheap bottle of dry gin, to almost everyone's disappointment. It wouldn't have been all bad if we had had access to tonic water, but Duke's served tonic water from cans, which were also locked in the bar fridge. Not to be deterred, we placidly accepted our fate and decided to chuck and ploy for shots of pure gin, medical claims of blindness be damned.

By about four o'clock in the morning, the situation had digressed into an absolute fubar. Some people had excused themselves to go to the toilet and were never heard from again. A corpse, looking suspiciously like Death Chick, was passed out on top of a table and swimming in what looked like her own bile, but it was actually just drool tainted black from her gothic lipstick. By sheer elimination of viable chuck and ploying bodies, I had started to lose more and more challenges. I didn't know it at the time, obviously, but Missionary Man and Biff had plotted my demise by agreeing to show nothing but the rock sign. Therefore, every time I showed the scissors sign I lost and had to drink a shot of cheap gin. The last round of chuck and ploying I remember partaking in, I battled hard with a combination of clever strategies, but I inevitably lost and was given a shot of gin to slam back for my efforts, which I did, but with my right hand. Naturally my transgression was noticed by the man who resolutely preferred the missionary position during vaginal intercourse, so I was given another shot of gin which I habitually pounded back with my evil right hand again, which was also caught, and so on. Consequently, I consumed four ounces of gin within about thirty seconds, which added to the fifteen ounces of liquor, and two pitchers of beer already polluting my body. All I could think of was, "Why is my mouth filling up with saliva?"

Mr. Saliva Rush had once again dropped by for an unwanted visit, as if he were an alien returning to abduct me for some horrifying experimentation (although I would have welcomed a stomach pump and a liver transplant that night). With great effort, I managed to pull myself up from the table, deliver a baneful look towards Missionary Man, and stumble off in the general direction of my car. I had no trouble spotting my gold '78 Honda Civic, but I had trouble convincing my ethanol paralyzed musculoskeletal system to get me there. I wasn't entertaining the idea of driving drunk, but I needed somewhere to sleep and regain my faculties. As I lurched closer and closer towards my chariot, my black shorts and white T-shirt failed miserably to insulate my body from the crisp October morning and forced my dilated flesh to shiver uncontrollably. It was a small victory just to reach my destination, then to actually unlock the door and fall into the vinyl driver's seat. I was still shivering, but was physically and/or mentally unable to grab the wool blanket from the back seat, so I remained frigid. I was desperate for sleep, but the spartan interior of the Civic would not stop spinning, which caused my stomach to protest loudly. "God no," was all I could think as a botched attempt at a belch precipitated the eruption of my stomach's contents up through my mouth and nose.

I retched at least four times, some of which sprayed the interior of the car, but most of which landed on my chest, groin, and legs. Believe it or not, I was thankful for the warmth my vomit provided, and the sleep state that was brought on by the exhaustive action of regurgitation. I slept happily in my own puke until about seven o'clock in the morning, at which time hypothermia rocked me awake. Having regained most of my faculties, I looked around and tried to assess my situation. This is what I saw: there was partially frozen puke on the windshield and driver's side window, partially congealed puke on my arms, legs, shirt, shorts, shoes, carpet, instrument cluster, and steering wheel, and an undisturbed puddle of puke at the base of my gear shift. But it wasn't benign watery puke, it was of the more viscous variety and had a million little half-digested pieces of baby squid that were pink in color, making it look much more heinous. It was as if a grenade had detonated within the belly of some rubbery creature. Simply put, the sight and scent was enough to have made a maggot gag.

"Sweet mother of God," was all I could croak and my immediate instinct became a need to escape and get home so I could incinerate my clothes, scour my body under a hot shower, remove pieces of squid from my nasal cavities, then fall into a deep sleep within the warmth and seclusion of my lumpy futon. But could I transport myself home?

I was one of the few alpha-male waiters who didn't think I drove better while drunk, so it concerned me how I was going to get home. Consequently, I went through a ridiculous series of motor coordination tests, and then tried to recall the previous five World Series Champions to prove to myself, and any M.A.D.D. members who may have been in the vicinity, that I was capable of safely operating my econo-box from Nippon. I passed my self-imposed test with flying colors so I fired up the Honda, but much to my horror, realized I didn't have enough gasoline to get home. And although there was a gas station directly across the street from the restaurant, I dreaded the idea of anyone seeing me in such an appalling state. Realistically though, the people who worked the graveyard shift at that gas station had routinely witnessed the darker side of our debauchery. They had seen us streaking down the highway absolutely naked, belly surfing through the restaurant in our skivvies, passed out on the patio amongst an orchard of empty Corona bottles, "chicken fighting" with topless waitresses upon our shoulders on the front lawn, and clumsily petting or humping each other in the backs of Volkswagens, but nothing would have prepared the cashier for the sight of my pathetic condition.

After putting $5 worth of gasoline into the tank of the Civic, I skulked towards the cashier's window feeling weary and rather conspicuous in my soiled attire. The cashier grew wide-eyed at the sight of the carnage, which was highlighted beautifully by my stark white T-shirt, as I approached his booth. I felt bad for drawing him into my nightmare, but I felt much worse for myself, so I quickly pulled out a five-dollar bill and placed it on the counter. But before I could pull my eyes away and escape back to the anonymity of my car, I noticed the five-dollar bill had not escaped the shrapnel from the exploding squid because it was clearly saturated with the fetid remains of my ill-fated dinner. Our eyes only locked for a fraction of a second, but it was long enough to see utter contempt and to decipher his nonverbal communication as, "You have to be fucking kidding if you expect me to touch that." Unfortunately I wasn't, so I abandoned the soggy legal tender on the counter and slinked away. Needless to say, I lived to drink away many more nights (albeit vomitless ones) at Duke's, but I never did return to that gas station where I committed perhaps my most atrocious crime against the working poor.

Incidently, that Honda Civic was originally purchased new by my Mom, but given to me shortly after high school graduation. It was a tremendously tough little car and virtually bullet proof. I had been lured away from it by sportier Volkswagen products for a handful of years, but faithfully returned behind the wheel of the Civic during my heyday at Duke's. It served me well while I was serving the masses, but it nearly became my coffin early one Saturday morning.

Six-Million-Dollar Idiot...

The official story is that I had pulled an "all-nighter" the previous Thursday night trying to study the intricacies of cellular biology, then wrote a ridiculously detailed exam at the university late on the Friday afternoon, then went immediately to Duke's to work a closing shift, then was baited over to someone's house for a Long Island ice tea party at about three in the morning. Although I had a few drinks as I was cashing out, I didn't really indulge in the spiked ice teas and, in fact, snuck out of the premises prematurely when it became obvious that my wannabe concubine had dried up on me. But still, I had been awake for about forty-five hours experiencing a variety of highs and lows and was utterly exhausted. As I pointed the Civic in the direction of home, I hoped my entry level commuter had been installed with an automatic pilot option by mistake, but it hadn't, so I rolled my window down and blasted the monotone AM radio in efforts to fend off slumber.

I was doing well amongst the sparse morning traffic and managed to appear energetic as I lip-synched to the likes of *The Beatles* and *Steely Dan*. As I approached the desolate highway, though, my eyelids were gaining weight faster than Elizabeth Taylor after the *Academy Awards*. The long straight-aways were mesmerizing and my blinks were getting slower and slower. This was occurring despite the fact it was treacherously snowy and my window was entirely rolled down to let in the cold. My body was refusing to acknowledge the frostbite on my left ear; instead, it was preparing itself for deep delta wave slumber. It progressed to the point where my chin began to bounce off my chest, but I was less than seven miles from home so I continued to navigate the Civic at a cautious fifty miles per hour. Normally, this rate of speed would have been entirely appropriate given the conditions, but my eyes were taking in progressively less visual stimuli between blinks. I barely remembered veering off to the right in order to follow an exit sign before falling dead asleep. Now I was probably only asleep for about two seconds, but something in my subconscious screamed, "You are driving a vehicle down a snowy highway, NOW WAKE UP CRACKER HEAD!" so I obeyed immediately, but in a total panic, and in so doing inadvertently jerked the steering wheel to the right, which sent the front-wheel drive Civic into a slow spin.

After a series of miscalculations and over-corrections, the Civic was headed backwards toward a steep embankment. I was vaguely aware there were lamp posts every fifty yards, but I was at the mercy of Newton's Laws, so I just gripped the wheel and prepared for the worst. Having spent years training to be a lord of the jungle instead of an astronaut, I was not familiar with the awesome fury that re-entering the atmosphere in a fiery shuttle entails, but flying down that embankment while backwards and on my side, and traveling at over fifty miles per hour, had to have been somewhat analogous. I knew it was about as close as I would ever get to being the resident test chimp at N.A.S.A. I remember seeing the driver's side mirror snap off like a dry twig, then the road disappear from view as my shuttle plunged into the depths of a snow filled gully. I felt like "Steve Austin" from *The Bionic Man* and wanted to call out, "Oscar, I'm breaking up, I'm breaking up," but it would have fallen on deaf ears. The little Civic was shaking and groaning from the g-forces, but it managed to keep from exploding into a ball of flames as it performed a double half-gainer and landed right side up within about two feet of virgin snow at the bottom of the uninhabited gully. After a few minutes of thanking Saint Christopher, I climbed out of my pod to survey the barren landscape and the damage to the Civic. In doing so, I left deep tracks in the snow with my woefully inadequate penny loafers and thought, "One small step for **WAITERMAN**, one giant leap for an absolute idiot."

While stuck in the snow, I noticed the front tires had popped off their steel rims and I considered just leaving the Civic there as proof of human exploration, but reconsidered and speculated it would be more economical to tax payers if I reclaimed it and used it for other space missions. In the meantime, however, I was without terrestrial transportation and forced to jog the approximately five miles to my base. Luckily, I was wearing chinos and a light jacket which provided some warmth, but I was handicapped by my penny loafers that began to freeze and crack in the subzero temperatures. Incredibly, it only took about an hour or so to jog, walk, and limp the distance, but the frozen leather of my loafers had dug into my left big toe and caused it to bleed like a stuck pig on blood thinners. When I finally arrived home, I was about as haggard as I had ever been, but alive nonetheless. I had been awake for forty-eight hours straight, sodomised by a university exam, repeatedly sodomized during a long shift at Duke's, refused sodomy by a prospective concubine at a house party, directed by N.A.S.A. to fall out of orbit and re-enter the atmosphere in a '78 Honda Civic, subsequently crash landed without a co-pilot, stumbled across five miles of frozen tundra, and in the end, only managed to sustain a lacerated toe that had saturated my sock with cherry-red blood. If there was any doubt as to me being the authentic Lord of the Jungle, it was obliterated that night.

I eventually sold that indestructible little Civic, which had sustained a slightly bent frame, a twisted driver's seat, and a dented rear quarter panel due to my disastrous attempt at an emergency landing that fateful morning. And although I owned a succession of vehicles after the sale, I was between cars for a short period of time and had to borrow my Mom's red Honda Prelude in order to join the boys in celebrating a fellow waiter's stag party many months later. His name was simply "Hog."

He Shoots, He Doesn't Score...

Hog was also an alpha-male waiter at Duke's and roughly the same age as I was. He was about five feet eleven, a husky one hundred and ninety pounds, with wavy, short dark hair, and the ability to flash a killer smile at will. He was an English major at the university and planned to follow in the footsteps of his parents, who were both schoolteachers. From that brief description, you might think his nickname was coined out of irony or because he liked Harley Davidsons, but believe me, he lived up to its piggish connotations on a nightly basis as he farted, belched, scratched his genitals, and marginalized women with the most repugnant members of his gender. You see, Hog played major junior hockey away from home during his impressionable teen years, and was essentially raised by apathetic billets and the team's twenty-year-old veterans while on the road. Said veterans provided an excellent education with regards to whoring, circle jerking, surviving eighteen-hour bus rides, lighting farts on fire, and consuming entire flats of beer in a single sitting, but social graces, tolerance, and sensitivity were usually swept under the Zamboni. Due to this five-year hockey odyssey then, Hog developed into a true hybrid: half brooding intellectual, half brooding mountain gorilla.

As with most Duke's related stag parties, we ended up at the downtrodden Spanish Maid. And although Hog's boozing endurance was already legendary, he was putting on an especially remarkable exhibition of poison tolerance that night. After a plethora of vomit inducing concoctions (Eye of Newt, Jack Daniels and milk, Rusty Nails), Hog was air tight and standing, even cognitive and full of entertaining sarcasm. Except for the panties, bra, and striped "Grinch" hat that adorned his exterior, you wouldn't have known it was his stag. He was even well behaved while at the strip club, although he hit a dancer in the boob with some coins (but Hog would have done that while sober). It wasn't until we began to patrol the "red light district" to do some shopping that Hog started to look a little pale. You see, Scameron and Missionary Man were intent on renting Hog a hooker, a pro, a swinger, a streetwalker, anything really. Most of us were morally against it, but the bastards that had fallen prey to the dark side took Hog hostage in their truck. Because I was the most sober (yes, it's all relative), I ended up driving the only other vehicle and was responsible for negotiating with the street urchins. So there I was in my Mom's car with White Man and Biff, talking the talk with some pretty rough characters while being scrutinized by the omnipresent coppers, who were probably running a search on the license plate and creating a file of my Mom under the heading, "Lesbian Pedophiles." The young girl we eventually chose was actually very nice and understanding of the circumstances; almost relieved we weren't residents of skid row. Her only concerns were: (1) if Hog had been puking, and (2) if we could pick him up after the adulterous deed was done. He hadn't and we could, so the logistics were worked out and the non-negotiable fee of $100 was agreed upon. After reporting back to the conspicuous "investors" in their truck, they had the audacity to question my bartering abilities. As if being eyed by a dozen drooling guys at three in the morning, while bitterly cold, wasn't demeaning enough for her. Finally everything was set (she agreed to our non-negotiable counteroffer of $90) and her private taxi was on standby when she approached Hog for the first time and said, "Hi, my name is Angel. Are you ready for a good time tonight?" Hog thought for a moment and, after a wet fart, replied, "Well, I am tempted, but I think I'm comfortable right here in this truck. Sorry, senorita." However, Hog's unexpected act of morality allowed for another pathetic alpha-male to enter Angel's private taxi and consummate the dirty deed in an old mobile trailer, which then actually turned into a disastrous three month relationship with her! Zany, yes I realize.

To Hog's credit, he survived the ultimate test, which was compelling evidence of him really being in love. I later heard that the hoard had continued to feed Hog alcohol until the wee hours of the morning (or mourning, as it should have been thought of). He eventually passed out in Scameron's kitchen, probably due more to exhaustion than inebriation. In the final analysis, I think Hog was born five hundred years too late. He would have felt right at home in Medieval / Renaissance Europe. Armed with a big flagon of grog, a thick leg of boar, and a hockey stick, he could have debauched with the peasants and highwaymen, and then expressed Hog-esq philosophies with the genteel nobility. In hindsight, Hog may have felt more comfortable farting, belching, scratching, and marginalizing within the jungles of Trader's Inn. Maybe the New Jersey bar slut would have taken a shine to him.

South Side Stories...

The shenanigans we pulled at our particular Duke's were different in nature than what occurred at the south location, which was the home of Matt, Ginger, and the various other lecherous bastards. Whereas we were much less physically intrusive (with the exception of the occasional **waiter sandwich** and Missionary Man trying to unlatch every bra that made an appearance in the pass-thru) and didn't involve our customers to any great extent, the south store relished physically assaulting their own staff and customers at every opportunity. Truth be stated, it was a dangerous place to work or eat at.

From a busboy's perspective, working at the south Duke's was like being sent to prison as a child molester: every inmate (i.e., waiter) wanted a pound of your flesh and a piece of your ass. For pure blood sport and/or initiation, busboys were routinely tackled in the dish pit by a group of bull waiters and thrown into a cauldron of cold water while entirely clothed. Imagine being a sixteen-year-old busser and getting dressed up in wool slacks, a nice shirt that you got for Christmas, and your Dad's paisley silk necktie, then becoming giddy from the anticipation of working at a place as dynamic as Duke's. You then find yourself running about, cleaning tables, gossiping with the cute hostess, and generally feeling pretty good about your lot in life, until you head back to the dish pit and get surrounded by a pack of rogue alpha-males (led by Ginger) intent on exerting their dominance. You laugh nervously in a high-pitched way, and try to get back to the dining room, but the waiters close in on you and grab you by the arms and legs. You begin to struggle and beg for leniency, but the waiters have whipped themselves into a frenzy and disregard your pleas. They are forced to half carry and half drag you towards a greasy cauldron normally used for making stock and soups, but filled instead with cold water for the occasion at hand. You realize the intent of their mission and become frantic as the waiters forcefully stuff you into the cauldron ass first. You can feel the cold water permeate your wool pants and your reflexive thrashing inadvertently soaks your Dad's silk tie. The waiters then run off howling like hyenas and leave you to ponder how you will complete the rest of your shift while completely soaked and explain to your Dad that his splendid silk tie is ruined. You sheepishly walk back into the dining room with your head down and feeling deeply violated. Your face is red and burning due to a variety of unpleasant emotions that have caused an assortment of hormones to course through your body. With your drenched hindquarters on full display, you look up and notice the cute hostess smiling at you, but more out of pity than admiration or amusement. The shame of it all is simply unbearable. You want revenge desperately, but that's not a possibility. In fact, you have no recourse whatsoever because you learn that even the managers were conspirators in your assault.

It was common practice for the managers to be intimately involved with the shenanigans at the south Duke's, much to everyone's detriment. Perhaps the best example is the night that "Hammer" had a few drinks and went on a shooting rampage. Hammer was a slick, veteran alpha-male who was a little older and less inhibited than the rest of us. He was a little taller than average, very lean, and wore his brown hair to his shoulders, which made him look slightly androgynous. His incredibly narrow waist and tiny ass also didn't do much to promote his masculinity, so he overcompensated for it by being a total mack with the ladies. He was renowned for getting involved in ménage et trois and talking the most prudish females into sexual situations previously reserved only for hardcore porn stars nearing the end of their careers. His game with the ladies was silky smooth, which matched his voice and luxurious hair. He was stylish, cultured, sensitive, and even good-looking; his impossibly dimpled chin would have made Kirk Douglas envious. In short, Hammer led a charmed life and was the type of guy who found laughter around every corner, a stiff cocktail on every bar top, and labia minora and majora in every pass-thru. But, on some nights, he needed all of his lucky charms just to remain employed.

The night of the shooting rampage started out like any other Friday shift: the restaurant was full of middle class families and the servers were entrenched in chaos. Hammer was acting as the assistant manager that night, which was something he did on a part-time basis. But disregarding any attempt at setting a good example for the staff, Hammer endorsed the idea of having a few drinks while on shift. So sometime after the dinner rush was over, Hammer et al started boozing, which they often did to loosen themselves up and make the shifts pass a little quicker. They usually hid their alcoholic beverages in metal milkshake containers and placed them within the busser's station to avoid being busted, but there was no need for wariness that night, obviously. I can't recall what happened to motivate Hammer (a lost round of chuck and ploy perhaps?), but he eventually went into the office, stripped totally naked, donned a long, white kitchen apron, then filled up a squirt gun and emerged from the office ready to stir the shit. He then proceeded to run around the dining room with his bare ass exposed for all to see and squirt the staff and various customers with a squirt gun that was in the shape of an erect human penis and filled with skim milk. He was hitting people in the arms, asses, even faces, with long streams of fluid that looked eerily like fresh man's milk. From a customer's point of view, they witnessed some drunken freak running around half naked and pretending to ejaculate all over the unexpecting. Most customers would have been pissed off by having milk accidentally spilt on their clothes by some clumsy server, let alone having it squirted on them from an erect, ten-inch penis that was wielded by some cocky manager (pun intended). Needless to report, many people were absolutely enraged and phoned in the following day to complain about Hammer's lewd conduct. But, Hammer must have eaten his lucky charms for breakfast that morning, because upper management only mustered up enough courage to confiscate his "squirting member" and slap him on the bare wrist (although, I'm sure he would have preferred it on his bare ass). In point of fact, the G.M. was actually in the restaurant during Hammer's escapade, but he was busy doing a few lines of white powder in a toilet stall, then sucking helium from a tank in the lounge (that was being used to fill balloons for some special promotion) until he lost consciousness and plunged into the bar's countertop with his mouth, then slumped to the floor where he remained bleeding for a few minutes until someone dragged him off to his sports car to sleep it off. Entirely bizarre, but true.

Sexually themed shenanigans were popular at the south Duke's for reasons that can only be ascertained using Freudian theories. I remember Matt relating a story about a night that he had to cover a hostess's shift. Accordingly, Matt worked the door and was responsible for greeting customers and showing them the venerable fresh food display (which was usually related to the evening's features) while en route to their tables. The features that night included some type of fish, so the display was filled with ice, raw fish, and the various fresh ingredients used to compliment the fish. It looked quite presentable, as it did on most nights, because creating the fresh food display was the responsibility of the hostesses, who were often starved for mental stimulation and believed they had some innate creative flair. So while Matt was seating a table, Ginger thought he would add a little something controversial to the hostess's creation. What he added was a male masturbatory device called a "Blowfish." The Blowfish was a blue/green parody of a fish that was made of plastic and about the size and shape of a small "Nerf" football. It had a disproportionately sized hole for a mouth, which was meant to envelop the male sexual organ and then vibrate it briskly. From all accounts (most notably Ginger's), it accomplished these tasks very well indeed.

Matt was initially surprised at the sight of the peculiar plastic fish that had invaded the fresh food display, but after many minutes of being doubled over with hyena-like shrieks of laughter, he decided to incorporate it into his routine with the customers. Again, imagine being an innocent customer and walking into a family restaurant, being greeted by a slightly cheeky host, then being paraded past a fresh food display that contained a blatantly obvious sex toy. Matt would say something along the lines of, "Folks, tonight's features include a local Chinook salmon and a lovely Blowfish from Japan. It would be your server's carnal pleasure to explain the details ...," which went straight over most people's heads, but quite a few looked incredulously at the Blowfish then back to Matt, who merely shrugged as if it was just a regular night at Duke's. And the scary thing is, shenanigans like that were a fairly regular occurrence.

The Adventures of Waiterman

The outlandish shenanigans didn't come to a stop when the core group of servers transferred to a new downtown Duke's during the late '80s. In fact, if anything, they intensified. For a lengthy period of time, that downtown location had the reputation of providing the worst service in the city, mostly because of the gross apathy displayed by the arrogant servers who worked there. It was fairly common to wait thirty minutes for a beverage, or twenty minutes just to get a "hello." It was truly ludicrous, but customers blindly shuffled in as if they were gluttons for punishment. The primary cause of the customer directed apathy was the servers' preoccupations with getting drunk and creating a script for the nightly shit show. The best example of their total disregard was the infamous, "Jack Dash," which was mostly a weekend ritual that entailed running down the street to another bar for a shot(s) of Jack Daniels whisky before returning to Duke's somewhat shit faced. Anywhere from two to five staff members would dash out of the restaurant during the middle of their shifts and abandon their customers for up to twenty minutes at a time. In most cases, the little bussers were relied upon to "hold the fort" and were directed to inform the managers (the ones who didn't fully endorse the Jack Dash, that is) that a noble gang of conscientious servers were busy risking life and limb by chasing a deadbeat table down the street who were attempting to dine and dash without paying their check. Upon return, the tipsy waiters were far from repentant and, in fact, were often quite flippant and gave their customer's looks that implied, "Hey, you're really cramping my style asshole. Can't you see I'm in the middle of a fabulous shit show performance, one that might actually land me that cute hostess later tonight?" The nerve of the customer to think the server was there to deliver food and beverage, instead of delivering pick-up lines to the hostess. In Matt's case, when an irate customer launched into a complaint like, "Waiter, it's been twenty minutes for Christ's sake, where the hell is my side of steamed vegetables?!," he would literally reply in all honesty, "I have no idea sir, I was enjoying a stiff Jack Daniels down the street."

Survival of the Fittest...

Charles Darwin's *Theory of Evolution* included the notion that there are more individuals that can possibly survive in a given environment, therefore, there is a fierce struggle for existence and those with favorable variation in size, strength, running ability, or whatever characteristics are necessary for survival, will possess an advantage over others. Those that possess the advantages will then thrive due to natural selection, or in other words, they will survive because they are the most "fit" from nature's perspective. This struggle was especially evident at Duke's, as the waiters often digressed back to the laws of the jungle and behaved like they were alpha-males jostling for rank and competing for females within a turbulent chimpanzee society. In fact, Darwin must have been an observant little busboy before he set sail on the *Beagle*, because he noticed, "Man with all his noble qualities still bears in his bodily frame the indelible stamp of his lowly origin." And by God, it was tough to get any lower than the primitive primates who worked as Duke's waiters.

It seems whenever a bunch of alpha-males (regardless of species) accumulate in a particular area, some form of competition always erupts. At Duke's, we competed for the best shifts, most lucrative sections, most generous customers, cutest mates, and for the highest levels of distinction. As proof, I remember cozying up to the managers when they were making the schedules and offering subtle bribes to secure the prime shifts. I remember occasionally arriving at the restaurant an hour before my shift started to ensure getting the most lucrative section. I remember greeting valued regulars (pardon the oxymoron) at the door when the hostess was distracted and shuttling them into my section. I remember sitting down at a table after a shift with four other waiters and collectively coming to the realization we had all inseminated a particular waitress within a span of eight months (as if we were a rogue group of blue balled chimps), then debating who had serviced her needs most proficiently. The debate hastily ended and a clear winner was declared once one of us shamelessly admitted to performing cunnilingus while sucking on a eucalyptus lozenge (disturbing visual, I know). Apparently she tingled and convulsed for hours afterward. And finally, I remember fighting for distinction on the various battlefields that we alpha-males waged war on; in particular, on the vast woodlands that we used to play "capture the flag" with guns powered by carbon dioxide and filled with paint balls.

Over the course of the nearly six years that I worked at the north Duke's, I dawned battle fatigues and played capture the flag about ten times. Each time we would gather at the restaurant on a Sunday morning, with most of us being parched and stinky from a night of going hard, and then depart within a convoy headed towards the mountains. The playing fields weren't actually in the mountains; they were nestled within the foothills on property owned by a retired pro football player whom we knew as "Kilgore." He had a modest house that was dwarfed by a huge satellite system, some rickety barns that contained a few swaybacked mares, and about six playing fields spread out over many acres. Some of the playing fields were a couple hundred yards long and contained diverse terrain: tall conifers, grassy plains, creeks, swamps, and burned out trucks. Other fields were about the size of a football field and more densely packed with deciduous trees and forest undergrowth, which always compelled me to draw comparisons to the fighting conditions in Vietnam during the late '60s. For added realism, I would call out to the troops, "Hey GI, you so cute. Long time no boom-boom, eh? Five bucks for some fucky-sucky, eh GI?" Sadly, I never had any takers.

The rules to capture the flag were straightforward: two teams congregated at either ends of a playing field with guns that spat out marble-sized paint pellets in efforts to shoot and eliminate as many members of the other team as possible in order to steal their flag amidst the least amount of resistance. Typically, there would be about eight to ten people on each team with at least eighty percent of the warriors being male, which was no doubt directly related to the production of testosterone. We would all be decked out in Kilgore's well-used camouflaged polyester jumpsuits, plastic goggles, facemasks, and semi-automatic weapons. Some of us had never fired a weapon before, so Kilgore always gave us the same presentation and demonstration the moment we arrived at his ranch. About the only things we couldn't open fire on for target practice were Kilgore, his family, his house, his truck, and his mares; everything else was fair game. Technically, headshots were against the rules and cause for eviction from a particular game, but we alpha-males reveled in such methods of elimination. In fact, we would have cut the ears off our kills for trophies had Kilgore allowed it.

At either end of the playing fields were fortresses of some sort. On some fields it was rusty, old campers, on others it was wooden tree houses, but there was always some enclosed dwelling to hide the team's precious flag. In close proximity to the flags were air horns, which were blown when a member of one team returned to his/her fortress with the other team's flag. The piercing sound of the air horn signaled the end of that particular game. A game could last anywhere from fifteen minutes to one hour, depending on the number of participants, the size of the field, and whether or not "killed" players could return to action. Conditioning was obviously a big factor too, as we were essentially running around in the woods for hours at a time as if we were filming our own version of *Deliverance*. And although no one squealed like a pig or worried about the prospects of violent sodomy, being hit with a paint pellet traveling at a couple hundred miles per hour never actually felt pleasant. In fact, if a pellet hit you in an exposed area, it could literally tear your flesh and draw blood. Hog still has a jagged scar on his neck from an "errant" shot by Missionary Man over a decade ago.

One particular Sunday afternoon at Kilgore's ranch in late August was especially memorable. I was in a foul mood because people had used my new car for target practice as I was pulling up to the property. I was quite anal about people fucking with my stuff back then, so I had a hate on for all the bastards who marked the pristine black paint of my car with red and yellow paint splats. The villains on that day just happened to be Missionary Man, Zeus, and "Meat," who was a night waiter and a buddy of Zeus's. He also had dark, curly hair that was longish in the back, but he was taller than Zeus and had much more muscle mass. He wasn't a bloated steroid monkey though, he was more like Michelangelo's *David*. As such, he was considered attractive, almost irresistible to female customers and staff alike and got more ass than a toilet seat. In many ways, Meat was the quintessential bad boy: he was tall, dark, handsome, rode a "crotch rocket" motorcycle, studied martial arts, aspired to be a sleazy private investigator, consumed pot by the kilo, and humped everything that had an appropriately sized orifice. He wasn't stupid so much as he never considered the repercussions of his actions. And if he did appear to be pondering something, it was surely with his head below his waist. A prime example was the time he shamelessly cuckolded and stole Hog's first serious girlfriend.

Hog was in love with this little blonde waif whom he met at the university and eventually worked alongside at Duke's. Hog would've gone to the far corners of the Earth for this girl, but the rest of us weren't especially impressed with her omnipresent "my shit doesn't stink" attitude. Consequently, I called her "Queenie" and gave her the royal wave whenever I saw her. Regardless, Queenie and Hog appeared to be a confirmed couple, that is until she fell for Meat's cheesy lines late one night after work and followed him home to rock his world. Needless to say, Hog was devastated by the sudden turn of events and it became extremely uncomfortable when the three of them had the misfortune of working the same shifts. Observing Queenie patiently waiting for Meat to cash out, then walking out with him to his motorcycle and zooming off to his rented house to undoubtedly experience various forms of carnal pleasure was totally uncouth in its nature and absolutely unbearable to watch in Hog's presence. However, about a month into their new fling, Meat became more interested in a pair of hard bodied, seventeen-year-old twins who were also friends of Zeus's. We were all familiar with the crass twosome because they came into Duke's all the time in their bohemian leather coats to smoke cigarettes, drink coffee, eat raw avocados, and trash talk the hunky alpha-males. "Pocahontas," the only available member of the duo at that time, was experienced beyond her years and made it clear she wanted to add Meat to her growing list of body counts. Naturally, Meat was up for it (pun intended) and romantically whisked her off to the back of her flatbed truck where he promptly laid the nuts to her while rush hour traffic crept by a mere ten feet away. Meat and Pocahontas carried on their "secret," torrid affair for many weeks until they became bored with one another and went their separate ways, but not before Queenie cornered Pocahontas in the washroom at Duke's one night and demanded to know if she was the slut who had been covertly riding her boyfriend. The blunt Pocahontas must have bristled at Queenie and said something like, "You have got to be bloody joking me, you hypocritical little cow. Trust me, that daft meathead is exactly what you deserve." which all of us, especially Hog, would have instantly echoed. As a couple, Meat and Queenie didn't last much beyond that confrontation and both of them eventually faded away from the Duke's scene. The last I heard of Meat, he had to actually fire a very bitter Zeus for being an incurable alcoholic (whom he owned a small restaurant with many years later), and had used his modest entrepreneurial success to attract none other than a lonely Pocahontas, who had gone on to become a semi-manic psychologist searching for an allusive self-diagnosis. No, I'm really not making any of this up. Before I continue with my capture the flag story, though, recalling Meat's deeds has precipitated another serving tip:

****

SERVING TIP #9: I know it's incredibly tempting and it may actually be the reason you got involved with the restaurant industry, but try to avoid being promiscuous with large numbers of the staff, either concurrently or sequentially. While zoos have signs that read, "Please don't feed the animals," the staff rooms within restaurants should have signs posted that read, "Please don't fuck the staff." The reasons for showing sexual restraint should be obvious, but never underestimate the extent to which the rumor/gossip mill can utterly destroy your reputation. Having various staff members shooting you icy glares and plotting your demise does not create a healthy work environment for you. Masturbation is certainly a viable alternative and should be practiced more often due to its calming effect and its ability to dissolve a horny disposition. And remember, the good things about masturbation are that you don't have to dress up for it or purchase a lot of strawberry daiquiris. But, if you absolutely must sew your oats with gullible members of the opposite sex on a regular basis, then do so with the customers who are considered groupies. Just remember to practice safe sex because adding a venereal disease to your waiter's ass will render you practically crippled.

****

Getting back to the story, there were definitely some hard feelings that day which superseded the usual tension associated with playing capture the flag: Hog loathed Meat for sticking his genitalia in his precious Queenie, Missionary man resented me for finding and using his sexual kryptonite against him, Scameron was cross with Missionary Man for not settling a debt within a reasonable amount of time, Jeff was pissed off at planet Earth because his girlfriend was grinding his gears instead of his midsection, Zeus felt threatened by White Man for undermining his power within the restaurant, I was tired of being continually pushed to the limits of my tolerance for being fucked with, and we were all out for revenge against some of the grease weasels who had tagged along and were secretly drinking our cold beer. Therefore, to a greater or lesser extent, everyone had chips on their shoulders regarding something or someone.

The teams ended up consisting of Missionary Man, Nine Fingers, Zeus, Meat, Jeff, and a handful of waitresses, grease weasels, and strangers from some bastard's stag party, versus White Man, Scameron, Hog, the Kiwi, myself, and a different handful of waitresses, grease weasels, and said stag guys. To make a long afternoon short, the final and deciding battle pitted Missionary Man and

Meat against Scameron and I. The rest of the troops had been retired or eliminated for reasons entirely consistent with their personalities: White Man was too cheap to spend any money on additional paint balls, Zeus sat out because he had no money for anything but managed to eat and drink very well that day nonetheless, Nine Fingers had trouble pulling the trigger of his weapon when ambushed by a stealthy waitress and was subsequently shot in his paunch (although his matching love handles remained unscathed), the Kiwi sprained his ankle earlier in the day and was rendered useless because he was an uncoordinated pussy, Jeff was too reckless and was shot in the back as he ran by an undetected trap, Hog had become irrational and charged Meat who quickly cut him down with a gallon of paint from his upgraded Uzi submachine gun, the waitresses had largely lost interest and were tanning themselves on Kilgore's deck, the majority of the grease weasels believed they were the Vietcong and were shot in the asses while shimmying up trees and trying to dig elaborate tunnels, and the stag guys became too drunk and provided easy target practice for all those who relished preying on the feeble.

Scameron and I had Missionary Man and Meat pinned down at their fortress, which was a flimsy wooden structure on stilts. Their flag was in front of the fortress in plain view, but being carefully monitored by Missionary Man, who was inside the fortress, and Meat, who was about fifteen yards away, nestled in the bushes. They were daring us to make a move for their flag. We also had to keep an eye on Meat in case he made a run for our flag that was about eighty yards away and potentially being guarded by a stoned grease weasel who had begun to hallucinate as if he were in *Apocalypse Now*. Or maybe he had buggered off to drop acid with Martin Sheen, we had no way of knowing for sure. So there Scameron and I remained, about ten yards from one another, lying on our stomachs in the underbrush and trying to hatch a plan worthy of the D-Day Invasion. I was tired and sweaty from spending the day running around and dodging enemy fire, and had a mild headache from pounding beer between games. We realized we were at a disadvantage because we had opted for the standard issue semi-automatic pistols, whereas both Missionary Man and Meat had upgraded weapons that were fully automatic and had better range. In fact, Meat so enjoyed playing capture the flag he had outright purchased his Uzi months earlier. The down side to having those weapons was that they expelled a tremendous number of paint balls with each squeeze of the trigger. I was obviously interested in kicking some ass that day, but I wasn't into spending over $100 on ammunition.

However, I soon regretted that type of frugal ideology.

Meat eventually got impatient, probably because he knew the girls were sun tanning in their bras and panties on Kilgore's deck and might offer him a tight orifice, so he decided to jump up and expose his position. In so doing, I could see Meat's blurred image start to run in the direction of our fortress where our flag most likely stood unguarded. With his bandana around his skull and his exposed, hairless chest, he looked like Sylvester Stallone in *Rambo* darting through the woods. Scameron leaped up to intercept him, but had to dive behind a pine tree when a staccato burst came from Meat's Uzi. From the ground, and amidst red paint vapor, Scameron carefully took aim and, unbelievably, hit Meat in the groin from about twenty yards away as he was hurdling a stump. The impact to Meat's camel toe (which was wonderfully showcased by the polyester jumpsuit) was enough to fell him immediately. And after a few tumbles on the forest floor, he became still, but continued to groan softly. The showdown between Scameron and Meat had greatly distracted me, so I didn't notice that Missionary Man had vacated his fortress and was kneeling beneath a tree about ten yards directly in front of me. Startled, but seeing his shoulder exposed, I pulled the trigger of my lame gun and heard the last of the carbon dioxide try to expel a single volley. The pellet hit him in the forearm, but not with enough force to explode and leave proof. I expected Missionary Man to confirm the hit like a gentleman, but instead, he solidified his reputation as a complete and shameless cheat by denying it. And just as I opened my mouth in protest, Missionary Man unflinchingly shot me in the chin. The yellow paint pellet exploded and found its way into my mouth. Before I could spit enough of it out, my taste buds quickly affirmed my theory that it was a vile, petroleum-based product. I started to gag, and was oblivious to the fact that Scameron was subsequently hit in the forehead mere moments after me. Technically, Missionary Man was disqualified because of the headshots, which meant we became the victors by default, but it was a small consolation with me on the verge of getting my stomach pumped and Scameron looking like his forehead had been ripped a new asshole. Vindicated at least in his own mind, Missionary Man couldn't wait to return to Kilgore's fire pit in order to relate his stories of grandeur as if he were William the Conqueror. However, Missionary Man may be the only alpha-male on record who became a King for a day and didn't use it to his advantage to get laid; or perhaps he did, but as a Queen instead.

Capture the flag was a perfect metaphor for working at a restaurant: various alpha-males battling each other tooth and nail to attain some measure of distinction. Although to be accurate, alpha-males (regardless of the species) do not compete merely for distinction; rather, they prefer to briefly bask in the glory of victory, but then use it to attract their true target: chicks. Yes, it all comes down to impressing members of the fairer gender and getting laid. I called it "six degrees of getting laid" because no matter what a Duke's alpha-male waiter did, it could be traced back to increasing the odds of laying his nuts. For example, something as obscure as never deviating from the type of pen used at work allowed one to seamlessly alter the gratuity after the customer had signed the credit card slip, which allowed one to scam an extra $15-20 a shift, which then could be used to buy a nicer vehicle, which invariably impressed the cute, young hostesses, which would ultimately increase one's odds of getting laid (but not before letting the assistant manager eagerly promo her a bunch of strawberry daiquiris). Therefore, with no mention of Kevin Bacon whatsoever, one could identify a seemingly random action performed by an alpha-male and connect it, in six steps or less, to increasing his odds of notching another body count. Regardless of the complex pathway, though, it always involved some form of scamming, which led to a continual game of "cat and mouse" with the hapless managers.

Cat and Mouse...

Cat and mouse is an age-old game that has been played since the positions of employee and employer were first established. For example, in Neanderthal times, the disgruntled Woolly Mammoth hunter undoubtedly cut a few extra pounds of meat off the carcass for himself without telling the tyrannical tribal chief. This is the way it has always been between hominids who are in a power struggle and feel disrespected, under appreciated, and/or taken for granted; they find a way to seek retribution. The restaurant jungle is clearly not immune from this type of social phenomena, as demonstrated by the dummy scam at Trader's and the various acts of scamming that were performed at Duke's. But why do restaurant employees scam to the extent that they do? Is it because the industry almost exclusively attracts thieves and grifters with unethical tendencies? Probably not. I think the answer lies in the central premise of social psychology: bad things are not always done by bad people. In other words, social circumstances dictate the majority of people's actions. For example, without being too macabre or controversial, I think it would be naive to think the entire German population during the World Wars was evil to the bone. Most were wonderful, ethical people, but as horrific agendas percolated down the ranks, otherwise good people performed very bad acts. They were simply swept up in the propaganda, acting out of fear for their own lives, and/or seeking retribution for some perceived injustice. At Duke's, we certainly weren't swastika-wearing Nazis, but we perceived much injustice nonetheless.

Looking back, most of our indignation can be traced to a single conversation with "Little Pharaoh," who had ascended to the position of assistant night manager after toiling away as a waiter for a couple of years. Little Pharaoh was so monikered because his actual name was similar to an ancient Egyptian King's, and because he was about as ruthless when it came to abusing his authority and treating his staff like Hebrew slaves. He was of Asian/Scottish ancestry, walked with his chest puffed out, and had a nervous habit of vigorously scratching his nose. Unquestionably, he was a very clever guy, but full of contradictions on a multitude of levels. He could appear gregarious, charming, and loyal, but also self-centered, malicious, and deceitful. He was a classic paradox, but someone whom you felt compelled to trust before you learned to deeply regret it. For example, although not many people were aware of it, he was the dirtiest dog of the Duke's litter as he continually cheated on his long-time girlfriend in the most sordid of ways. Perhaps the worst time was when he had a fling with the kitchen manager's wife. She was tall, had short blonde spiky hair, a big mouth with fantastically large teeth, and a ruddy complexion. Overall, she was quite hideous, but for some reason Little Pharaoh felt he had to add her to his growing list of conquests. Consequently, he reveled in meeting her behind the restaurant during his shift for some frantic fellatio while in the front seat of her little sport utility vehicle. Undoubtedly, he smiled to himself as she bobbed up and down in his lap, knowing her husband was less than fifty feet away and handling tube steak of a different nature. With these diabolical episodes in mind, we were a little leery of what he might be capable of when he jumped ship and became a manager. On most nights, our biggest fears were fully realized.

Anyway, a handful of alpha-males approached Little Pharaoh when he became a manager and appealed for a token twenty-five-cent per hour wage increase on the basis that they were reliable, loyal, hard working waiters who went beyond the call of duty by consistently towing the party line, training new servers, and organizing extracurricular activities. What they wanted was some form of recognition that they were worth more than minimum wage to Duke's management. Again, it was only twenty-five cents for Christ's sake. Unfortunately for everybody involved, Little Pharaoh indignantly rattled off the standard reply that if they were truly such good waiters, it would be reflected in their inflated tips from their dazzled customers. Well, that wasn't really the point or the case (primarily because we didn't have inflated boobs), so the alpha-males became bitter, vengeful, and began to seek retribution because they felt disrespected, under appreciated, and taken for granted, which are all excellent motivators to push one into the act of scamming. So from that point forth, the scamming began on a larger scale with the manipulation of their promo abilities on the new computer system.

For the era, Duke's used a fairly sophisticated computer system that was referred to as the "Gopher" for reasons that remain unknown. The Gopher consisted primarily of a touch sensitive computer screen that was used to order food and beverages, but it had to be activated by a plastic card first. Therefore, every server and manager had their own programmed cards that gave them access to various functions depending on their position in the hierarchy. For example, the managers could delete items from any table at any time or switch items to other tables; they had the freedom to play God on that bloody Gopher. On the other hand, the servers were restricted from performing these tasks for obvious reasons, but some of the more trusted alpha-males had the ability to promo items at their discretion. However, after the mood at the restaurant changed from ass kissing to ass fucking, said alpha-males began to abuse the system to shameless proportions. So instead of offering legitimate promos to valued customers, the waiters would wait until the customers paid their checks, then they would retroactively promo food items before they closed out their tables. In essence, it appeared as if the waiters were buying something for their customers, but in reality they were pocketing the money. This type of "promo scam" netted the waiters an additional $15-30 per shift and saved them from the rage that ensued when customers didn't respond with appropriate gratitude to the legitimately promo-ed items.

The promo scam was eventually shut down by the managers, because most of them had used it while they were servers and were familiar with what to look for. Consequently, all promo items had to be verified by the managers before the server could proceed with the altruistic act, which essentially defeated the purpose of the entire idea, so servers eventually lost the privilege of being able to promo any food or drink items for their customers. But, the alpha-males, being the devious bastards that they were, realized the Gopher could be activated by a four digit code in addition to the plastic cards (which they discovered when a manager had to come to the rescue of a server who had lost her plastic card while in the middle of her shift and needed to gain access to her tables). The alpha-males reasoned that if the servers had their own four digit codes that correlated with their cards, then the managers must have had codes as well. They did, and the codes were listed in a binder and hidden in the office, which was quickly found late one night while Zeus was preoccupied with vigorously shagging Rona in the bottle shed that was behind Duke's in the back alley. Soon thereafter, about a half dozen servers knew most of the manager's codes, which they immediately used to delete a plethora of items from the Gopher on a nightly basis. This "code scam" netted the servers an additional $25-50 per shift.

Eventually, one of the more flagrant alpha-males became far too greedy and overzealous. He was caught feverishly deleting items as Zeus silently watched from over his shoulder. Needless to say, said idiot was fired and Little Pharaoh became inspired to program the office computer to track all of the deleted items over the course of a shift. He would then emerge from the office after each shift with a printout of the night's deletions in his hand and interrogate the most suspicious servers. It was McCarthyism at its finest. Accordingly, a few more greedy mice were caught by the lazy cats before the code scam had to be retired. However, there was a key difference in the way that Zeus and Little Pharaoh went about the chase: Zeus never actively tried to persecute his friends; instead, he only took action when the offender was so blatant in his/her actions that ignoring it would have threatened his managerial job. Little Pharaoh, on the other hand, savored the cat and mouse game from an intellectual standpoint and he didn't give a shit who he made an example of because he needed the balance of power to be continually on his side. This was morally wrong (can you believe my audacity?) because Little Pharaoh began using his managerial privileges to scam Duke's as much as anybody else did! Simply said, he was a temperamental, hypocritical turncoat who had no allegiance and didn't have the decency to be honest to those in his intimate circle. As such, Little Pharaoh was arguably the

The Adventures of Waiterman

least liked, admired, or respected manager of that era. In fact, his shabby conduct warrants a managerial tip:

****

MANAGERIAL TIP #5: When you jump ship to become a manager, put things into the proper perspective. It's been established that everyone scams, so don't be a hypocrite by trying to cleanse the restaurant of the "bad element." You were once an eager participant within the bad element, so pull your head out of your tight ass and realize you are not a descendant of J. Edgar Hoover. Your job is to assemble a solid crew and make them happy so they can operate like a well-oiled, low maintenance machine. In order to make them happy and minimize the degree of scamming, show them more respect and pay them more money (either directly per hour or through incentives). In essence, if you can make them feel guilty about scamming such a generous restaurant, they won't scam as much. I call it the "pay now or pay later principle," because if you don't provide for your staff, they will find a way to even the perceived disparity ten fold. Remember the old adage, "An ounce of prevention is worth a pound of cure."

****

The promo and code scams may have been rendered obsolete, but the alpha-males could always rely on altering the customers' credit card slips for some extra cash. Yes, this was fraud and probably punishable by a short jail term, but the alpha-males were fairly cavalier in this regard. The customers made themselves vulnerable to such fraud by not filling in all the necessary spaces on the merchant's copy. In particular, the most foolish thing a customer could do was sign the slip without filling in the tip or the final total portions. The feeble-minded customers who committed this moronic act usually paid the check with a credit card, but preferred to leave cash for a tip. Little did they know their server was taking the liberty of adding a very generous tip for him/herself on the credit card slip in addition to the cash gratuity. Some slightly more intelligent customers filled in the final total portion, but not the tip portion, which made it pretty easy to alter the numbers if one had access to a pen with similar colored ink. For example, a three could become an eight with a flick of a wrist, thus putting an extra $5 in one's pocket. These types of credit card scams were inherently more risky because the alpha-males relied on the customer's indifference to matching their credit card slips with their monthly statements from their banks, but it could net a restrained server between $5-20 during most shifts.

A final scam that could be attempted by the servers relied more on being opportunistic, and was known as the "cash bag scam." Cash bags were purse sized, zippered bags that the servers used to deposit all their receipts, cash, coinage, and credit card slips at the end of each shift. On busy nights, some cash bags could contain upwards of $800 in hard currency. After a server finished cashing out and tipping out, a manager would have to be dragged from a booth to the office and observe the server dropping their cash bag into the safe and signing a piece of paper verifying that they had indeed dropped the cash bag. However, sometimes the cash bags were so stuffed with money that they didn't completely fall into the safe and could be felt by the subsequent dropee. The essence of the scam was to somehow distract the manager (like claiming there was a tight gibbon at the door with perky boobs), pull out the previously dropped cash bag, hide it somewhere on your person, then drop your cash bag in the safe and get the hell out of Dodge. Surprisingly, this scam was successfully pulled off every five or six months, but the server whose cash bag was stolen, and the server who subsequently dropped their cash bag, would both come under great suspicion and scrutiny from panic-stricken managers and office "cash girls." However, those who had the fortitude to pull it off and withstand the intense interrogation usually walked away with about $400-500 in small, unmarked bills.

Perhaps the greatest scam that occurred at Duke's during my tenure was the time $25,000 was stolen from the office safe in the middle of the night. The office cash girl, who also doubled as the Director of Fun, was not able to deposit a weekend's worth of cash and receipts for some reason, so it accumulated within the office safe. However, when the prep cooks arrived at the restaurant on the following Monday morning, they noticed a window next to the patio door had been broken, the patio door was ajar, the office door had been forced open, and the office safe was empty. The official Duke's response was, "What a coincidence that some random thief broke the only window that was not connected to the alarm system and then robbed the office safe when it just happened to have

$25,000 in it." And then the cash girl was promptly fired for being a negligent bonehead. A bunch of us alpha-males said "bullocks," to that explanation, but it wasn't until many months later that I learned the true identity of the thief: it was a senior kitchen manager (no, not the same one whose wife was fond of smoking adulterous pole). Apparently, said kitchen manager had walked in the back door, disabled the alarm system (which he knew didn't record the times it was deactivated or reactivated), opened the patio door and smashed a small window from the outside (which he knew wasn't wired to the alarm), pried open the office door with a crowbar for the sake of authenticity, opened the safe somehow, and stole the $25,000 in small bills that he knew had accumulated there (the rest of us had no idea that much money was in there or else an alpha-male would have surely attempted some sort of heist). Finally, he walked out the back door with fists full of dollars and reactivated the alarm system. From our standpoint, it was a brilliantly executed diversion that warranted a standing ovation. No doubt the G.M. found the whole situation very suspicious, but the evidence supporting the theory of an "inside job" was largely circumstantial. Perhaps foolishly (after all, he was a variety of grease weasel), the kitchen manager purchased a sports car from Biff about a month after the incident, and then he promptly quit in order to work for one of Duke's competitors. In the final analysis, it was a great example of how even the big cats can be motivated by the atmosphere within a restaurant to steal the cheese from the mousetrap instead of solely by the alpha-male mice.

SOME SOBER LAST WORDS

"The good critic is he who relates the adventures of his soul in the midst of masterpieces."

- Anatole France

Well, **WAITERMAN** continued on at the north Duke's location until he graduated from university and took a teaching position in Japan (see *The Adventures of WAITERMAN - Green Gaijin of Japan*), at which time he was forced to relearn the ancient art of putting quill to parchment in order to have any contact whatsoever with the Western world. With the patient guidance of Jeff and Randy, he succeeded at this task, which eventually motivated him to trade in his hunting knife for a thesaurus. But before he entirely shed his jungle paraphernalia, he came home from Japan (albeit twenty pounds lighter) and was forced to return to the restaurant industry because he was planning on going back to school for many more years and was in need of tuition monies. He initially chose a different restaurant chain to make his comeback at, one that was renowned for its connection to rock and roll. In a word, it was arduous. Four table sections, mandatory altruistic food running up and down endless flights of stairs, highly questionable cuisine, and the appalling noise were but a few of the scourges our ape-man faced on a nightly basis. If there was huge money to have been made he could have endured it, but the cake was well below expectations. In addition, he seemed to spend an inordinate amount of time giving impromptu tours of the cheesy memorabilia plastered all over the walls. So feeling exploited and underutilized, he promptly quit.

Eventually though, our Lord of the Jungle returned to the Duke's troop and resumed his adventures over two consecutive summers while he was between semesters at post-graduate school. It was a new Duke's location in the southwest part of the city. In reality, the southwest Duke's proved pretty bearable in many ways. The legitimate gratuities were acceptable ($50-90 a shift) due in part to the volume of people created by the theatres nearby, but mainly due to the upscale clientele who lived in the surrounding hills and patronized the restaurant on a regular basis. Compared to the mudslide **WAITERMAN** usually dealt with at the north location, the southwest location might well have been a testing ground for a new species of hominid: a specimen capable of patience, empathy, appreciation, and of rewarding for services rendered. In short, *Homo yuppiens*. Granted, serving yuppies was not entirely blissful because they also had baggage to deal with, but they tipped significantly better, which is still the most important factor for servers when deciding where to ply their trade.

Fortunately, **WAITERMAN's** reputation preceded him at the new location and he was regarded as the "new old guy" by the staff. As such, no one gave him any undo grief, and some occasionally marveled at his superhuman abilities to run most of his tables' food, clear most of the plates and glassware from his tables, anticipate the various needs of his customers, and take orders from up to eight people without writing any of it down. But by the end of the second summer, nature had run its course and our silverbacked primate was ready to relinquish control of the troop to the cheeky alpha-males who were nipping at his heels and scoffing at the shear craziness of some of his classic stories. He realized that new stories would continue to be created long after he was gone, but that they would never quite equal what he had participated in or witnessed because of the new politically correct climate that pervaded the restaurant jungle and society as a whole. But after some deliberation, he conceded that maybe that was the best thing for the diverse species residing on this planet. So on the eve of his last shift, **WAITERMAN** refrained from imparting any additional wisdom; instead, he simply handed over his hunting knife and waiter's apron (see Serving Tip #10) and headed back east to complete his program, where he was destined to embark on a new career and experience many new adventures. He didn't forget about his jungle roots and become entirely civilized, though, because he insisted on wearing his tight, forest-patterned Underoos at all times thereafter.

****

SERVING TIP #10: A server's apron is sacred, akin to a medicine man's pouch; therefore, fill it with things that are useful. First, buy a nylon apron (or something similarly slippery and stain resistant) that does up in the back with a plastic closure, not one that is made of cotton/polyester and has long draw strings. Second, use a nylon wallet to store any accrued cash and keep it in its own pocket within the apron. This will prevent you from dropping bills around the restaurant as if you are Daddy Warbucks. Third, always leave some small bills and coinage in your apron as a "float," so that you do not draw the ire of the bartender every shift as you deplete him/her of the entire bar's small change. Fourth, invest in a quality wine opener that has a long corkscrew, a sharp blade, and a stable prop. This will help you not look like the total wine dummy that you are. Fifth, tuck your useless hot cloth into the back of your apron, so the hot cloth police notice it and quit harping to you about the wonderful economic merits of hot cloths. Sixth, carry at least three incredibly garish pens that all dispense the same colored ink. This will hopefully deter customers from walking off with them and ensure you always have a writing instrument on your person. Lastly, carry a small pad of paper and write down every order, because let's face it: you are not a lord of the restaurant jungle.

****

A Cautionary Note...

It's been difficult playing the role of critic thus far, especially in the absence of any notable masterpieces, but if I didn't point out some of the more dangerous pitfalls and health concerns of being a server before I conclude, then some naive wannabes might flock to the restaurant jungle and inadvertently perish while trying to star in their own version of an off Broadway shit show. Needless to say, this shouldn't be contemplated by the majority of vertebrates. This may seem like obvious advice, but even a Batman costume has a warning label that reads, "Caution: cape does not enable user to fly," so common sense is clearly not so common within our jungles.

Aside from waiter's ass, waitering nightmares, kicks to the camel toe, headaches induced by grease weasel incompetence, obscene hangovers from nights of going too hard, and anxiety from chuck and ploying repercussions, serving tables can have pitfalls and health concerns too. Mainly: (1) Alcohol poisoning, which is an omnipresent threat especially if you work nights with a group of alpha-males hell bent on fubars. The real issue isn't actually the poisoning, but rather the asphyxiation that can occur from puking while passed-out in the supine position. (2) If you manage to survive the massive intake of alcohol and its regurgitation, you may not survive the subsequent drive home. Drunk driving is a common scourge that plagues the entire restaurant industry because of the typically late hours, proximity to booze, and mysterious need to take the shit show on the road. And contrary to popular belief, alcohol does not accentuate one's innate ability to operate heavy machinery. (3) Related to the excessive consumption of booze and late night feasts is the inevitability of becoming obese. Every slothful manager and most servers will gain weight and look bloated to some extent. In direct contrast to the *Body for Life* program, late night gluttony combined with no discernible exercise and sleeping until noon will lead to distended guts, swayed backs, and fat "hail damaged" asses. This type of physique wouldn't be such a detriment if we were mountain gorillas, but we don't have the luxury of simply grunting or showing our gleaming red estrus to get laid. (4) Related to getting laid, especially while under the influence, is the increased odds of contracting a sexually transmitted disease while working at a restaurant. Remember, the reason why you can't feel your penis while banging the new hostess is not the ill fitting condom that you avoid at all costs, rather, it's the near fatal level of ethanol in your blood stream that's destroying all the peripheral nerve pathways below your waist. So either wear a prophylactic during your conquests, or learn to masturbate while being ravaged simultaneously by herpes simplex and waiter's ass. And (5) regardless of how wonderful a romantic relationship is outside of the restaurant scene, working alongside high quality T & A and experiencing various emotions with them will either cause infidelity or extreme jealously to flourish sooner or later. So you have the option of inviting your mate into the restaurant's social circle (which could really cramp your style), or becoming a day turd (which is degrading), because if you choose to work nights and abandon your mate at home, you'll be damned if you do and damned if you don't. Therefore, proceed with caution.

The Million-Dollar Question...

So, if I were to magically morph into a teenager again, would I make the same choices regarding entering the restaurant jungle? Yes I would, because if I were in the same socioeconomic position I would have no alternative. The restaurant industry provided me with the opportunity to quell some of the financial angst my Mom continually faced by raising a teenager on her own. It also gave me some financial freedom and taught me the meaning of responsibility, which any job could have done, but it was the flexible evening hours of the restaurant industry that made it possible, especially while I was in grade school. If I would have had unlimited access to parental funds (like some of my friends did), I probably wouldn't have worked a part-time job at all, which would have led to unknown consequences, but certainly far fewer laughs and lesser quality adventures. By being pampered and with additional time on my hands, though, would I have benefited from studying more? No, don't be foolish. Would I have played any different sports? Unlikely, although going to Harvard on a lacrosse scholarship would have been sweet. Would I have gotten into more trouble and been sabotaged by the paradoxical coddling / indifference of an upper middle class upbringing? Possibly, although I certainly would have had more LaCoste shirts and a cooler BMX bike. Would I have ended up where I am today, as a caregiver, a writer, and a first rate smart-ass? Definitely not, because it was the restaurant jungle that helped shape my character, fuel my motivations, and create my dreams. Thus, I wouldn't change a single drunken night or a single sobering morning after from all those years. Thanks then to Trader's Inn, Duke's Place, and all the colorful characters, some vile and some precious, whom I had the pleasure of sharing so many adventures with. But believe me, as a legitimate adult, I'm not pulling a Sean Connery when I say, "I'll never do that shite again."

Some Food For Thought...

So what lessons can be learned from it all? How was I able to escape from the dangerous clutches of the restaurant jungle? Why me and not other worthy individuals? Did I fear underachieving to such an extent that I became a compulsive overachiever instead? Was it this deep-seated fear that saved me from the restaurant jungle's destructive onslaught? Again, I am not a clinical psychologist, but perhaps it was the subconscious creation of **WAITERMAN** that enabled me to survive long enough until I realized what I wanted to accomplish in this life. **WAITERMAN** truly allowed me to make my time within the jungle as a means to an end, which most of my cohorts wanted theirs to be, but few actually accomplished. Consequently, there seems to be a certain amount of tragedy in characters like Zeus, Meat, Nine Fingers, Bobo, General Piggy, Scameron, Missionary Man, Ginger, Medusa, the Rabbit, Big M, Lou and others who remain in the business so many years later. Generally speaking, these are people with tangible talents who probably deserve more respect, job security, and fulfillment than the restaurant jungle could ever provide. So what irrational fears are preventing these people from moving on? Nelson Mandela reminds us our greatest fear is the realization we are powerful beyond measure; perhaps these people need their internal alter egos to manifest themselves to make this point evident and to provide courage so they can transcend the restaurant industry and strive to accomplish many little things with great passion. My hope is that some ponder this over their next grossly over-poured cocktail. Cheers.

THE END

GLOSSARY

cake: a slang term for money earned from gratuities, as in, "Did you make some good cake tonight?" The amount of cake made is often exaggerated by day servers because of their general insecurities regarding their meager station in life. To be distinguished from cake-chute, which can be an exit sphincter for refuse. Generally speaking, waitresses make more cake than waiters, and hostesses make more than bussers. Synonyms include: cash, payola, jack, skins, mother load, coinage, dead Presidents.

camel toe: a visual reference to the much sought after part of the female anatomy that resides in the anterior and inferior aspect of the pelvis. This restricted area can appear bisected if tight enough pants are worn and therefore similar to the two distal toes on the hoof of an Arabian camel. It is assumed, from a male's standpoint, that being kicked in the camel toe would be something of an unpleasant experience. Therefore, a situation that is explained as a kick in the camel toe is a very dire one indeed.

chits: small pieces of computer paper that seem to convey all the vital information within the restaurant. All the food and drink orders come up on chits in the kitchen and the bar, respectively. Chits replace the need to verbally communicate with the bartenders or grease weasels, at least in theory. Chits are decidedly less effective if the bartenders or grease weasels are illiterate. Chits are analogous to winning lottery tickets: if someone loses them, they are S.O.L. (shit outta luck).

chuck and ploy: a child's game that originated in Asia, and played entirely by using a circular hierarchy of hand signs. To people lacking any originality or creativity it is also known as "paper-rock-scissors." Not surprisingly then, the three hand signals resemble a sheet of paper (which can cover a rock), a rock (which can crush a pair of scissors), and a pair of scissors (which can cut paper). Chuck and ploying is the perfect way to determine who must do something undesirable because it can single out a loser quite quickly and there is a powerful code of honor forcing the loser to uphold his/her promise to complete the task in question. Chuck and ploying is typically used to determine the buyer of a round of drinks, the solicitor of a group of attractive females, or the unlucky bastard who must "take one for the team" if said females are not entirely so attractive.

closing the deal: a male sexual expression referring to the moment that complete carnal knowledge is obtained from a member of the opposite sex. See also coital penetration. Often taking much build-up and pre-empted by many failed attempts, closing the deal on someone show-time can lead to lengthy discussions with one's mates involving sordid details. Closing the deal is a feat rarely accomplished by management or grease weasels for obvious reasons. A rampant deal closer might be considered a "player," which is a socially accepted variety of male whore. Synonyms include: dropping the hammer, laying the rails/nuts, shagorama, a good rogering.

cougar: a controversial term for a woman inferring that she is somewhat older, possibly past her physical prime, probably a little too garish in presentation, and pathetically desperate to hook up with a man (or boy) for carnal gratification. The thought of being alone and classified as a cougar will force most women to consider collagen enriched facial creams, full-time bulimia, and laying down the "pregnancy trap" (much to the horror of the slacker whom she has known for only four months). In reality, most men appreciate and even deify cougars because of their tendency to be approachable and have good "game," to omit whining or bitching from the conversation, to actually purchase a few rounds of drinks, and to prioritize selfish, faceless sex. Fair enough we say.

day turd: a wonderfully descriptive term for day servers as it perfectly embodies their tendency to: whine about having to wake up by ten in the morning, bitch about having to work four-hour shifts, complain about getting slammed during the lunch rush, beg night servers to start their shifts early while they are in the middle of their pre-shift dinners, sneak out the door without doing their closing duties, and dream about one day becoming a member of the vaunted night staff. Sadly, most day turds seem to suffer from Chronic Fatigue Syndrome, fibromyalgia, and have grand pianos securely fastened to their asses.

dish pig: a derogatory, although fitting, term applied to all dishwashers. The position of dish pig is virtually the only portal into the realm of the kitchen world. Every grease weasel must withstand its grueling physical demands before they can move onto the position of prep cook. Kitchen managers usually bristle at the term's inhuman connotations, but usually concede that a comparison to swine is not so inaccurate.

expediter: a job that exists within restaurants because its servers are inept at accomplishing their core function: bringing hungry people food. The expediter is a liaison between the line cooks and the servers, who are not permitted to address each other directly. As a result, the expediter is akin to a marriage counselor, albeit at a small fraction of the cost. For the well-trained server, the "expo" is just another obstacle in the way of doing his/her job properly. The expo's paradox is that he/she relies heavily on certain servers to run massive amounts of food, but then expects those same servers to actually tip him/her out for their efforts. This monetary arrangement might strike some observers as sincerely fucked.

features: a distinctly bourgeois term for "food specials," which are erroneously thought to connote a fire sale on week old food. Features are supposed to offer customers new and exciting choices in addition to the tired, old menu. The problem is that the kitchen weasels are not accustomed to preparing or cooking the features, so they invariably get fucked-up. Wise, veteran servers disregard the feature sheet entirely and are content with not winning any feature contests whatsoever.

food runners: existing as two varieties, either designated or undesignated. The designated food runners are not much different from the sherpa guides who must ascend Mt. Everest with six hundred pounds of gear on their backs. These human beasts of burden eventually become the authority on which servers are proficient, and which suck. The undesignated food runners can be anybody in the vicinity of the pass-thru, with the exception of upper management who maintain they are most effective while sipping coffee in a distant booth. Veteran servers stay clear of the pass-thru when not running their own table's food because they have long shed their altruistic tendencies. Inevitably, both types of food runners confuse the customer as to who their real server is, and where the hell they have gotten to.

fubar: a restaurant or military acronym standing for **F**ucked **U**p **B**eyond **A**ll **R**ecognition, which can describe the state of affairs during most nights of going hard. It's unknown whether or not the booze chemically alters one's ability to recognize a situation from before, or if the booze physically changes the faces of those who become drunk which makes them unrecognizable, or if aliens are abducting entire groups of hard drinking servers and creating the perception of a fubar in order to distract them from the fact they are putting titanium instruments up their noses and extracting out pieces of their brain. This latter explanation would account for the mysterious loss of ambition that most restaurant server's eventually experience. However, only those who have access to the "X Files" would definitively know.

gibbon: in keeping with the primatological references, a gibbon is a much sought after species of monkey that occasionally graces the confines of restaurants. Exclusively female in gender and young in body, gibbons can often put cute hostesses and waitresses to shame with their sassy attitude and overt sexiness, which begs comparison to characters named Lolita. Alpha-males can become entranced by gibbons and are often forced to quell their instinctual urges of insemination through frantic, non-consensual copulation. Sadly, gibbons do not usually survive beyond the age of seventeen because of the rampant cannibalization that is practiced within their competitive troop. Synonyms include: tighties, tenders.

going hard: the act of filling oneself with any type of alcoholic derivative at a rate that wouldn't seem tardy to a rugby playing Irish fisherman attending a wake at his favorite pub. It's analogous to chain smoking, and in fact, often goes hand in hand with it. Going hard is a preparatory type of act that is needed to launch oneself into festivities that require diminished judgment, but heightened libido and bravado. A night of going hard is often concluded with a morning of retching hard.

grease weasel: a general term for all prep and line cooks. Regarded as derogatory, especially by managers who become champions of the animal rights movement and endorse the activities of Greenpiece. The origin of the term is unknown, but is most likely related to the fact that kitchen workers are generally greasy and often weasel-like in appearance. From a behavioral point of view, this common species of weasel is nocturnal, has long matted fur, and gives birth to live young.

headbanger: a '70's term of North American origin, referring to the constant head bobbing of heavy metal fanatics. Although modern day headbangers don't bob excessively, they still wear their hair long and greasy with a center part, still wear tight jeans that showcase their skinny legs, and still enjoy a couple of puffs on old "Mary Jane." In fact, they are often heard asking each other, "Dude, do you know Bob Marley?" These characters are often drawn to kitchen employment, which can only be explained in terms of social stratification theories. Synonyms include: metal head, burn out, long hair, freak, loser, and banger.

hot cloths: small black or red cloths about the size of a hand towel meant to shield the server's hands and forearms from plates that make nuclear fission feel like a cool breeze. Unexplainably made of slippery material resembling Teflon, though, which forces servers to discard their hot cloths and use paper napkins instead. This infuriates cost conscious junior managers who view themselves as the "hot cloth police."

in the weeds: slang term inferring that things have gone very, very wrong for a server. While in the weeds, food orders will be forgotten, drinks will be spilled, customers will become extra demanding, and support staff will be AWOL. Being in the weeds can be very dehydrating as much blood, sweat, and tears are usually spilled. Getting slammed by the hostess is the most common cause of finding oneself in the weeds. Generally speaking, good time management skills and nerves of steel allow a server to avoid the weeds. Most common synonyms are: pooched, hooped, fucked, beaten down, and in a free fall.

juicy: a watery, brown substance derived from some domesticated animal source. Juicy is used to splash on prime rib to extend its life under the heat lamps. Not exclusive to Trader's Inn, but limited to restaurants that insist on drowning their meat instead of relying on the meat's natural flavor and tenderness. Known as "au jus" in classier establishments.

mack: derived from "mack daddy," it refers to a waiter with a real way with the ladies. Also one of the three prerequisites to being a restaurant alpha-male (along with being a good athlete and a decent server). To be considered a mack, one must be smooth (bordering on cheesy) and be able to close the deal on the likes of Mother Theresa on a Sunday morning.

mudslide: a derogatory term for a section of customers who resemble the street beggars of Tijuana. This term cannot, in any way, be construed as a positive label. Maddeningly, mud slides don't seem to conform to conventional restaurant etiquette; they might not order any food, they'll randomly pull tables together, they'll pay their tabs with lint covered coinage, they'll smoke hand rolled cigarettes in a non-smoking section, etc. You know that you've served a Mt. St. Helen's quality of mudslide when the busser walks home with more money than you at the end of the night.

one on ones: assumed by junior managers to be on par with a Vulcan mind meld, these meetings between staff and management often prove to be a colossal waste of time. The manager is often too busy leafing through his day-timer, or too distracted by a busty hostess to hear anything of relevance coming from the staffer's mouth. A server could be trying to communicate the "Caramilk Secret," but the manager would be repetitively grunting confirmations as if he was listening to his girlfriend bitch about her secretarial job. In short, one on ones accomplish nothing, but it gives a manager an excuse to sit in a booth and do something other than sip coffee.

patio shirt: a hideous white cotton garment covered with garish pictures of palm trees, parrots, and/or Corona beer (think *Miami Vice*). Last considered cool in the early '80s, a patio shirt is meant to be worn on the patio to promote heavy drinking and general debauchery. Definitely more comfortable than a shirt and tie, but much more tacky. They can be a savior, however, if one is felled in the dish pit area and ruins a dress shirt. Unfortunately, patio shirts are usually sized to snugly fit the forest pygmies of West Africa.

professionalism: in essence, the art of bullshitting. It requires a fairly quick mind, a slightly indignant demeanor, and a stoic poker face to be pulled off successfully. Professionalism is a skill acquired by veteran servers who use it to combat those customers who insist on asking obscure, rhetorical, or stupid questions. It allows servers to appear infallible and all-knowing. Customers usually respond well to the elaborate and enigmatic answers characteristic of professionalism, but sometimes look at their servers like deer caught in a pair of xenon headlights.

promo: a contracted form of the word "promotion," which essentially means for free. Managers have a promo budget, which they wield with much discrimination. Although the common customer will benefit from the occasionally legitimate promo, cute hostesses and waitresses seem to receive disproportionate consideration. Promo items can include drinks, appetizers, entire meals, or entire tabs (especially if the customer is a friend or family member of the hypocritical manager).

regulars: a soon to be endangered species of customer known for its habitual nature. Although regular customers are often treasured by management, their tendency to excessively modify their food orders and to pretend they own the restaurant can draw much scorn from the servers. Regulars often overestimate their value to a restaurant because, in actuality, they are far too finicky and don't tip exceptionally well, which seriously undermines their position when they make hollow threats such as, "You can tell the manager we will consider going elsewhere if chocolate pecan pie is not put back on the menu immediately." A section of tiny violins usually launch into a concerto of, Cry Me A Fucking River, when regulars insist on whining toward deaf ears.

ring outs: the total amount of food, beverage, and merchandise that a server sells during the course of a shift. Ring-outs are used to determine how much a server tips out to the bartenders, hostesses, bussers, expediters, and grease weasels. Ring-outs of over $1,000 were once considered substantial and rewarded with a bottle of wine or a cocktail, but gone are the days of any employee appreciation or incentives. Night servers have consistently higher ring-outs when compared to day servers, which is appropriate because their addictions often cost more.

rye guy: a metamorphosis of mythical proportions, whereas over consumption of rye whiskey terms an otherwise normal male into a stinky, insufferable, raging asshole. Some might argue that these characteristics are merely part of the common male paradigm, but believe me, imagine something much more heinous; perhaps the Incredible Hulk on tainted LSD; yes, this would be the poster child for rye guy.

scamming: any intentional action that costs the restaurant money. Scamming can include giving out free drinks, deleting items already paid for from the computer, claiming bogus promo items, stealing bottles of booze, plates, flatware, tea pots, entire cheesecakes, potted plants, patio umbrellas, salt and pepper shakers, or almost anything not bolted down. Absolutely every restaurant employee scams to some degree or another; it's as common as chaffed butt cheeks on a night waiter. Most servers enjoy scamming well beyond that of the monetary reward; they like to fuck-over the restaurant simply for the sport of it. Scamming eventually begets a game called "cat & mouse," where the managers continually try to figure out and shut down the most current scams. An opportunistic server can scam $10-15 every shift without much difficulty or risk.

shit show: not requiring admission or actual human feces, this type of show sells out to inebriated crowds all over the world and showcases people who are desperate to impress others with their substance fuelled baboonery. Not exhibiting a plot, denouement, or moral, the shit show is a classic exhibition of human digression. Shit shows are usually preceded by the actors going hard, and concluded with the same actors retching hard. A shit show that becomes a runaway hit (on or off Broadway) often morphs into an absolute fubar.

silverback: a title bestowed on the most dominant or respected alpha-male within a restaurant. Although virtually all alpha-males must possess the "ultimate trinity" (being talented overall athletes, proficient at their jobs, and macks with the ladies) to be regarded as such, some are so dominant in certain areas that aspects of the trinity may be overlooked as they ascend to the pinnacle of power. A silverback's responsibilities include: whipping the troop into a partying frenzy as often as possible, settling disputes between lesser alpha-males, approving new food modifications for widespread consumption, providing tutorials on maximization of alcohol intake, and establishing cool restaurant vernacular. In their own way, silverbacks are analogous to captains of pro hockey teams.

slamming: the act of sitting a plethora of tables in a server's section all at once. This might sound economically beneficial, but providing service for as many as thirty people concurrently can be a daunting task. Hostesses are the perpetrators of said slamming because they develop the "see an empty table - seat the table" syndrome. They never quite seem to learn. Slamming a server can put them immediately in the weeds.

snafu: a restaurant or military acronym standing for **S**ituation **N**ormal **A**ll **F**ucked **U**p, which can describe the state of affairs during most lunch hour and weekend night rushes. Snafus can be avoided by placing the more competent servers in the busier sections, by having enough support staff scheduled at all times, by having ample computer terminals around the restaurant, by never training new staff at peak times, and by believing in and preparing for Murphy's Law. But what the hell do I know? Some snafus can be stressful enough to force a manager to sit in a booth with his/her friends and slowly sip coffee.

stiffed: a term referring to a sum-zero tip from a customer, or not getting paid for a staff meal ordered by a grease weasel. Both are intolerable; justification enough to scam the customer or restaurant to compensate for such a slap in the face. Getting stiffed is actually fairly rare, but when it happens smoke will billow out of the server's ears and bile will trickle down his/her chin. Getting stiffed on a big table will put an immediate end to any server's contention that all people are essentially good and decent. Coarse, foul language often erupts in the pass-thru after getting stiffed. Synonyms include: goosed, fucked, sodomized, burned.

T & A: an abbreviation popularized by a variety of entertainers meaning, "Tits and Ass." It infers a general lack of skill or merit, as in "She's straight out of *Flashdance*: all T & A and no classical training whatsoever. What a phony, little bitch." People accused of attaining jobs solely because of their T & A usually do have wonderfully sculpted body parts, but often to the exclusion of much gray matter because they manage to survive quite well without it. While abundant T & A is essential to have at strip clubs, it can prove too distracting at restaurants as junior managers and alpha-male waiters cannot control their rutting behaviors. Unquestionably, T & A will dramatically increase a waitress's gratuities and degree of solicitation.

the wood: the counter top of a bar where many drinks are placed and stories of debauchery told. Also the site of many rejections, shoot downs, crash & burns, put offs, P.F.O.s, rain checks, and emasculations. To be distinguished from the other wood, meaning a stiff penis, which is also a common fixture at the bar.

tip outs: the amount of money a server must pay to the rest of the staff based on his/her total food & beverage sales (i.e. ring-out). Ranging from two to four percent, tip-outs are sometimes justified, but usually not. A tip-out that is begrudgingly given is paid in loose change. This sends a clear message to the dog-fucking recipient. Large tip-outs can pave the way for free drinks, late night sex, and general favoritism. "Accidentally" forgetting to tip-out and hoping the person will overlook it is a very stupid way of trying to save $5-10 because some form of payback or backstabbing is always lurking right around the corner.

up selling: the act of pushing excessive product on a customer in order to test his/her stamina in saying, "No thanks." Also known as "suggestive selling," it represents a fine line between letting the customers know their dining options and obnoxiously assaulting them with a thinly veiled attempt at squeezing more money out of them. This strategy is erroneously thought to increase one's tip because of a higher check. The most commonly up-sold item would be gravy as in, "Gravy with those fries?"

waitering nightmares: a hallucinatory type of dream state that besieges servers if they work too many hours and insist on hitting the sack while filled with chemicals derived from the digestion of deep fried foods and imported beer. In terms of psychological impact, waitering nightmares can range from the mildly annoying to the profoundly disturbing. Night sweats, restlessness, and sudden shrieking are all common signs that one is experiencing a waitering nightmare. The next morning's aftermath may include soiled underwear, sticky legs, greasy matted hair, swollen eyes, or a harrowed facial expression. If caught in time, waitering nightmares can be remedied by regressive hypnosis, a frontal lobotomy, or prodigious levels of scamming.

waiter sandwich: found in restaurants with lascivious waiters as opposed to the local deli, it consists of one hot, moist cut of "grade A" waitress or hostess, sandwiched between two thick slabs of waiter. Usually served without any accompaniments or condiments within a pass-thru, it's sometimes served with a turgid pickle and a mayonnaise-like substance if there is an abundance of breast meat. Waiter sandwiches are a socially accepted way of copping a feel of new hostesses or waitresses.

waiter's ass: a god-awful condition afflicting the inner butt cheeks of most male servers. Deceptively looking like a common rash, it is caused by continual butt cheek friction from many hours of running around a restaurant wearing stifling hot dress pants or denim jeans. It forces heterosexual waiters to consider the application of Vaseline within the cracks of their asses to reduce the friction and resulting pain, which obviously speaks volumes for the desperation of the situation. Waiter's ass hurts, it really fucking hurts, especially when one is in the shower after a long shift and the soap is running down into their anal cleft.

whites: the accoutrements of the grease weasels, consisting of a white chef's coat (with or without an embroidered name depending on one's position in the hierarchy), baggy "rugby pants" (either in gray, black, or a hound's-tooth pattern), and a white chef's hat (either cylindrical and made of paper, or floppy and made of a polyester blend). Always soiled and never ironed, these garments are often left at work overnight, where they sometimes come to life and reenact the final scenes from *Night of the Living Dead*, thus scarring the shit out of the late night cleaners.

APPENDIX

FIVE TIPS FOR BETTER MANAGEMENT:

MANAGERIAL TIP #1: Do not take on the role of ranting asshole as your managerial style. A manager's position in a restaurant is just not that important enough in the grand scheme of things and will most likely end in disgrace or disaster anyway. Therefore, treat your staff with respect, even the young ones, because some of them will become important people in society and otherwise think of you as that ranting, no good asshole. Consequently, these important people will not hire you or befriend you in the future, and in fact, may actually seek revenge against you for all the times you shit on them, which I would strongly encourage them to do if any are reading this.

MANAGERIAL TIP #2: Listen to your staff if they have uncommonly grievous complaints. Granted, there will be many con artists who attempt to bullshit you with faux claims of menstrual distress, ailing relatives, overdo assignments, unfair working conditions, and such, but it is imperative that you see through said bullshit and recognize who has integrity amongst your staff. Those who have some degree of integrity will still wage psychological warfare against you occasionally, but no one expects you to be an expert with the polygraph and have C.I.A. level training in behavioral science. In short, know who to trust for their honesty, and then simply listen to them. Hey, nobody said being a restaurant manager is easy, just that it pays absolute peanuts.

MANAGERIAL TIP #3: Do not be a petty little prick to your staff by busting their balls or crushing their ovaries over comparatively unimportant matters. I call it "crying wolf" because a manager's job is to crack the whip in order to keep things operating smoothly, but if the manager is always bitching and nit-picking people, then the staff will lose all respect for that manager and drown him/her out whenever he/she opens his/her mouth, regardless if it has merit or not. This is counterproductive because everyone needs to hear and internalize constructive criticism to improve. So pick your spots carefully and remember that a pat on the back goes much further than a slap on the wrist. In addition, if someone does need a chastising, do it in private and after work, because otherwise you risk deflating them in front of others and rendering them useless for the duration of their shift.

MANAGERIAL TIP #4: Resist the urge to reinvent the wheel if you have the tremendous fortune of becoming some sort of restaurant manager. There is no need to put your personal stamp on everything by implementing a bunch of new, ill-conceived rules and policies. Keep in mind the restaurant existed and probably thrived long before you became part of the team, therefore, don't throw a wrench into the engine just for the sake of change. If you are struggling with the idea of being labeled a dog fucker, relax, because the servers will respect you more for not pretending to be busier or more important than you actually are. The key to being a successful manager is assembling a hard working, fun loving, cohesive crew, then heading off to the nearest booth to sip coffee and leave well enough alone. And if you're smart, you will consult with the more respected veteran servers about what changes should be made. Finally, remember that a couple pitchers of free beer after a busy shift will make your crew more loyal than a purebred Beagle.

MANAGERIAL TIP #5: When you jump ship to become a manager, put things into the proper perspective. It's been established everyone scams, so don't be a hypocrite by trying to cleanse the restaurant of the "bad element." You were once an eager participant within the bad element, so pull your head out of your tight ass and realize you are not a descendent of J. Edgar Hoover. Your job is to assemble a solid crew and make them happy so they can operate like a well-oiled, low maintenance machine. In order to make them happy and minimize the degree of scamming, show them more respect and pay them more money (either directly per hour or through incentives). In essence, if you can make them feel guilty about scamming such a generous restaurant, they won't scam as much. I call it the "pay now or pay later principle," because if you don't provide for your staff, they will find a way to even the perceived disparity ten fold. Remember the old adage, "An ounce of prevention is worth a pound of cure."

TEN TIPS TO CREATE BETTER SERVERS:

SERVING TIP #1: Yes, it helps if you are a hard working, highly organized, quick witted, master of stress management who has a photographic memory, supermodel looks, and big boobs or pectorals, but these are not essential to become an extraordinary server. In actuality, you should focus on three vital qualities: (1) a sense of urgency - which means you realize when you must bust your ass to get something for a customer, then actually bust your ass to get it. In other words, you must be aware and task oriented. For example, when a customer says he is missing a carving instrument to cut his steak with, you must immediately walk to a cutlery tray and fetch a serrated steak knife for him, or better, steal one off an adjacent table, but not take the long route past the cute hostess to inquire about her plans after work, then pick up your forgotten drinks at the bar, then drop off a butter knife to your hungry customer. No, do not do this. Instead, keep your head in the moment, be able to prioritize, and be prepared to break a sweat; (2) a keen ability to anticipate - which means you can foresee a customer needing something, then actually bring it to him before he has to beg you for it, or remind you a dozen times. For example, if a customer orders some screaming hot chicken wings then you should automatically bring him a finger bowl with lemon and some extra napkins because he will definitely need them. You might also ask him if he needs a glass of water to douse the flames on his tongue. In other words, develop the ability to see a situation from another person's perspective, then act on it; and (3) a capacity for adaptability - which means you can appreciate the social dynamics of a situation and then act accordingly. For example, a table of two love birds who are displaying their mating rituals do not need you doing your stand-up comedy routine for them. Conversely, a table of high school kids wouldn't appreciate your dry wit or white glove service. Therefore, develop a waitering persona that has some range, and leave your own lame identity at home. This is why actors and entertainers often have the potential to be great servers, but usually self-destruct due to their various manias and insecurities.

SERVING TIP #2: If you are a person who has ambitions of becoming something that requires quite a bit of training, studying, and/or productive time spent away from your much needed part-time job, then either avoid the restaurant industry altogether, or make sure you work at a place that has a disproportionate number of people with goals and ambitions similar to yours. This doesn't mean you can't shag the hostess after every shift, eat leftover meat off of customer's plates, commit fraud on credit card slips, experiment with various hallucinogens, drink stolen Coronas until you puke, or drive your beat up Volkswagen into a ditch, but at least there will be an almost imperceptible voice of reason lingering in the air reminding everyone that there are some important things that must be done the next day, and it's OK to do them Or, put another way; make sure your restaurant party train is ambitious and headed for Grand Central Station in New York, not Platform One in Vladivostok.

SERVING TIP #3: If you are a "professional" server who works in a posh restaurant that carries a wine list so extensive that it is bound in hardcover and published in five languages, then by all means spend the time and effort learning about the intricacies of our planet's wine industry because it will pay-off handsomely in the end. But, if you are a server who works in a mainstream establishment that serves a fairly broad spectrum of the population, then save yourself a formidable headache by following these two principles: 1) if the customer actually needs your advice on selecting the color and dryness of the wine, then assume that same customer would not notice if you brought him Welch's grape juice. Consequently, state that the house wine is well above average and would be an excellent choice, and then simply bring him/her the red if they are eating beef, game, or pasta in a tomato based sauce, or the white if they are eating chicken, fish, or pasta in a cream sauce. Keep it basic; and 2) if the customer is well beyond the wine's color and dryness, but is grappling with a type of grape, or a particular region, then clearly you are in over your head if a discussion ensues. Consequently, if a wine connoisseur is looking for guidance, recommend the most expensive Californian Chardonnay if he/she desires white wine, or the most expensive Californian Cabernet Sauvignon if he/she desires red wine, because both types of grapes have met with tremendous success in that region, are quite consistent due to mass production, and are easy to like, but difficult to offend. As such, they are very defensible choices and the price of the wine will inflate the check, which should inflate your tip.

SERVING TIP #4: There will be many occasions during your serving career when you will be forced to choose between two very different styles of response to your customers. Because regardless if whether you must produce an answer to an impossible question, or are pressed to explain why you screwed-up, you can either choose the "apologetic / bend over backwards / brown nosing / pussy" style of response, or the "infallible / pass the buck / indignant / smart-ass" style of response. As long as you take pride in your responses, it doesn't really matter which path you choose, but being **WAITERMAN**, I instinctively chose the smart-ass path. For example, if a customer stated, "Waiter, I asked for fries with my teriyaki chicken and there's a house salad on my plate instead," and revealed my mistake, I replied, "Yes, that's correct sir. Naturally I assumed you would prefer piping hot fries, so I insisted that the kitchen prepare some fresh ones immediately, and I thought you might appreciate our house salad in the mean time. Was I wrong in this assumption?" Invariably, the customer would actually thank me and wait patiently while I sprinted back to the grease weasels in a panic and begged for a side plate of fries. Or if the customer asked, "Waiter, is there any cumin in the guacamole?" and exposed my ignorance, I responded, "In the original recipe, yes. But the kitchen is experimenting with a more authentic Mexican recipe and I'm not sure if they replaced the cumin with fresh cilantro. Allow me to check for you." I would then dash off to the kitchen and frantically check the recipe book.

If you choose this flippant, smart-ass path, you are essentially: (1) never admitting you are at fault (blaming the kitchen works beautifully in this regard), and (2) never admitting that you are not all-knowing. On the off chance a customer calls you on your bullshit, a good back-up line like, "Yes, sorry sir, you're absolutely right. I was just being a silly twit," will most likely rescue your gratuity. Of course one could always go down the path of the pussy, but if the customer doesn't pity your pathetic song and dance routine and leaves you a shitty tip as proof of their displeasure, the resulting kick in the camel toe feels that much more penetrating.

SERVING TIP #5: Do not be an oblivious, repetitive drone who is stuck on automatic pilot while greeting your customers. Obviously, a witty, original greeting for every table is impossible but, depending on the size of the restaurant and the space between the tables, have three greetings in your repertoire so that all the tables in your section do not hear you say exactly the same thing to everybody, thus making you appear like an airline steward/stewardess. The three I used in rotation were: (1) "Good evening, how is everyone tonight?" which is pretty boring, but it was most appropriate for older, more mature tables; (2) "Hi guys, how's it going?" which was most appropriate for younger people within my cohort; and (3) "Well hello there, how are things?" which was most appropriate for regulars, or people who I was familiar with but had not seen in a while. It may be largely subconscious, but your customers will appreciate not being treated like they are on an assembly line, Henry Ford be damned.

SERVING TIP #6: Believe it or not, the way in which you give change influences your tips to a greater extent than does the service you provide. For example, if the check total is $27 and the customer lays down $40, do not bring him/her a ten dollar bill and three ones because you will most likely receive a $3 tip (which is an eleven percent gratuity). A wiser move is to bring back two five dollar bills and three ones, which will probably land you a fiver (which is an eighteen and a half percent gratuity). Related to this, is the art of manipulating the final total of the check to your advantage. In short, wait to add the coffees and the sodas (or any item which is at your discretion to ring in) to the check until the last possible moment because some totals are more desirable than others. For example, since most bank machines exclusively dispense twenty dollar bills, customers will usually pay in increments of twenty if not using their credit card. Therefore, if the check totals $54 and the customer is in a hurry, he/she will most likely leave $60 (which is an eleven percent gratuity), but if you "forget" to add a couple of coffees then the check drops to $52 and the customer will most likely still leave $60 (which is a fifteen percent tip), especially if they notice you've given them two free coffees. Yes, this is scamming, technically, but your ethics are your own problem.

SERVING TIP #7: If you have important plans involving your life outside of the restaurant, book the related shifts off entirely weeks in advance because nothing pisses the other servers off more than having to scramble for an excuse as to why they can't cover your pathetic, whining ass by staying later and working harder. So unless you can produce fresh blood, vomitous, or a psychiatrist's note certifying mental illness, shut your sniveling mouth and work your shift as scheduled. Do you think for a moment that every other server couldn't produce an exhaustive litany of reasons why they should be cut early? In point of fact, every server has other things they would rather be doing, and every server experiences some form of physical discomfort during every shift, so you are not unique. If you do have the audacity to pressure other servers to stay late for you, then you had better offer some serious cash, a tangible asset, or some deviant sexual act as compensation, because the other veteran servers are not compassionate altruists who will accept your bullshit promise of "owing a favor." In short, put up or shut up because your reputation is on the line.

SERVING TIP #8: If one person emerges from a big table as a sugar daddy and wants to pay the entire check with a credit card then that's very fortuitous, but this is typically not the case. A much more common scenario is a wild group of people frantically tabulating what they owe and then waving twenty dollar bills in the air in hopes of depleting you of all your change. To save your self some grief and to ensure a higher gratuity, mentally divide the big table into smaller groupings (based on married couples, families, or seemingly close friends for example) and give them separate checks. Granted, this strategy will require slightly more organizational ability to accomplish, but your overall gratuity will be significantly higher than if you just present one check for everybody to decipher.

SERVING TIP #9: I know it's incredibly tempting and it may actually be the reason you got involved with the restaurant industry, but try to avoid being promiscuous with large numbers of the staff, either concurrently or sequentially. While zoos have signs that read, "Please don't feed the animals," the staff rooms within restaurants should have signs posted that read, "Please don't fuck the staff." The reasons for showing sexual restraint should be obvious, but never underestimate the extent to which the rumor/gossip mill can utterly destroy your reputation. Having various staff members shooting you icy glares and plotting your demise does not create a healthy work environment for you. Masturbation is certainly a viable alternative, and should be practiced more often due to its calming effect and its ability to dissolve a horny disposition. And remember, the good things about masturbation are that you don't have to dress up for it or purchase a lot of strawberry daiquiris. But, if you absolutely must sew your oats with gullible members of the opposite sex on a regular basis, then do so with the customers who are considered groupies. Just remember to practice safe sex because adding a venereal disease to your waiter's ass will render you practically crippled.

SERVING TIP #10: A server's apron is sacred, akin to a medicine man's pouch, therefore, fill it with things that are useful. First, buy a nylon apron (or something similarly slippery and stain resistant) that does up in the back with a plastic closure, not one that is made of cotton/polyester and has long draw strings. Second, use a nylon wallet to store any accrued cash and keep it in its own pocket within the apron. This will prevent you from dropping bills around the restaurant as if you are Daddy Warbucks. Third, always leave some small bills and coinage in your apron as a "float," so you do not draw the ire of the bartender every shift as you deplete him/her of the entire bar's small change. Fourth, invest in a quality wine opener that has a long corkscrew, a sharp blade, and a stable prop. This will help you not look like the total wine dummy that you are. Fifth, tuck your useless hot cloth into the back of your apron so the hot cloth police notice it and quit harping to you about the wonderful economics merits of hot cloths. Sixth, carry at least three incredibly garish pens that all dispense the same colored ink. This will hopefully deter customers from walking off with them and ensure you always have a writing instrument on your person. Lastly, carry a small pad of paper and write down every order, because let's face it; you are not a lord of the restaurant jungle.

ISBN 1553958420-X

Made in the USA